P9-AFK-401

COLERIDGE

THE WORK AND THE RELEVANCE

By the same author

THE USE OF IMAGINATION
Educational Thought and the Literary Mind

A HUMAN IDIOM
Literature and Humanity

COLERIDGE

The Work and the Relevance

WILLIAM WALSH

*Professor of Education
in the University of Leeds*

1967

BARNES & NOBLE, INC. · NEW YORK

Publishers · Booksellers · Founded 1873

Published in Great Britain by
Chatto & Windus Ltd
40 William IV Street
London WC2

*

Published in the United States
in 1967
by Barnes & Noble Inc.
New York, N.Y. 10003

LIBRARY

DEC 1 3 1967

UNIVERSITY OF THE PACIFIC

175684

© William Walsh 1967

Printed in Great Britain

Contents

Preface

THIS book is addressed both to the general reader and the student of literature—not always and not necessarily, surely, different kinds of people. It attempts to sketch the significance of Coleridge's work, in particular of his poetry and his criticism, for the reader today. My concern is with Coleridge not as a figure in a pantheon but as a living presence. I want to treat him as nearly as I can as a contemporary speaking to us now out of an experience that becomes increasingly relevant. Indeed I believe that the degree to which one can do this is a measure of a writer's importance, and that Coleridge by this test alone is a very important writer. My initiating and organising interest is in Coleridge as a *writer*, and everything else is subordinate to this. It is his art and everything which is implied in it that gives him life and makes him relevant, not simply his thought or his principles or his character in isolation. My hope is that this book will be found to be primarily the record of a contemporary reader's response to Coleridge's sensibility.

In writing of Coleridge one is always conscious of the immense debt one owes to critics who have written of him before. What they have written—as I indicate later—is an element in the composition of one's own attitude, Coleridge being one of those permanent facts of literature and thought in relation to which each period has to take up its own posture. But anyone writing today must be particularly conscious of an obligation to the devoted and imaginative scholarship of Earl Leslie Griggs and Kathleen Coburn, the editors of his Letters and his Notebooks. In their work the New World which so much interested Coleridge and towards which he had so liberal an attitude has rendered its own splendid tribute.

In Chapter I I have drawn on my study of Coleridge's letters in *A Human Idiom* (Chatto & Windus, 1964), and in Chapter III on my study of Coleridge's educational ideas in *The Use of Imagination* (Chatto & Windus, 1959).

Chapter I

COLERIDGE HIMSELF

I THE MAN

SAMUEL TAYLOR COLERIDGE was born on October 21st, 1772, at a moment when the nineteenth century was struggling to free itself from the eighteenth. In government, industry, economics, agriculture, engineering, transport, in thought, in religion, in painting, in poetry, in feeling, a new age was labouring to be born. All that was good and bad in the nineteenth century and much of both still with us was beginning—from the emergence of the United States to the accumulation of capital, from the rise of the professional writer to the growth of science and technology, from the development of democracy to the rise of Trade Unions. Coleridge's father, a mild simple man, was both the vicar of the superb cathedral-like church of Ottery St Mary in Devon and the local schoolmaster. He 'had so little of parental ambition in him that he had destined his children to be blacksmiths etc. and had accomplished his intention but for my mother's pride and spirit of aggrandizing her family'.[1] He wanted his youngest son to be a parson and he let him read every book that came his way without distinction (although he once burned *The Arabian Nights* when it gave Coleridge nightmares). Coleridge was not only his father's favourite, he was also his mother's darling, which earned him much tormenting from the other children, especially from his brother Frank, as well as thumps and ill names from Molly the nurse. He was fretful and timorous and a tell-tale—he tells us—he was persecuted by the other boys at school, where he outstripped everybody; he loathed exercise and did nothing but read. 'So I became a *dreamer*, and acquired an indisposition to all bodily activity; and I was fretful, and inordinately passionate, and as I could not play at anything, and was slothful, I was despised and hated by the boys; and because I could read and spell and had, I may truly say, a memory and understanding forced into almost an

[1] Griggs, E. L., *Collected Letters of Samuel Taylor Coleridge*, Oxford, 1956-59, Vol. I, pp. 347-8. Cited henceforth as *Letters*.

unnatural ripeness, I was flattered and wondered at by all the old women. And so I became very vain, and despised most of the boys that were at all near my own age, and before I was eight years old I was a *character*. Sensibility, imagination, vanity, sloth, and feelings of deep and bitter contempt for all who traversed the orbit of my understanding, were even then prominent and manifest.'[1]

His father died suddenly in 1781 and Coleridge became a day boy at the school of his father's successor Parson Warren. He loved to point out to his mother insufficiencies in the parson's knowledge, finding this a sort of oblation to his father's memory. In 1782 he was sent to Christ's Hospital in Hertford, where 'I was very happy, on the whole, for I had plenty to eat and drink, and pudding and vegetables almost every day. I stayed there six weeks, and then was drafted up to the great school at London, where I arrived in September 1782.'[2]

At Christ's Hospital he enjoyed what he called 'an inestimable advantage of a very sensible though at the same time a very severe master', the Rev. James Bowyer[3] who turned him in time into an excellent Latin and Greek scholar and even a tolerable Hebraist. His favourite poetry at the age of seventeen was the sonnets of William Lisle Bowles—and he points out that there is no poet so influential on a young sensibility as a contemporary, whose 'poems themselves assume the properties of flesh and blood'.[4] He read Shakespeare and Milton, from whom he learnt that 'poetry has a logic of its own as severe as that of science, and more difficult, because more subtle, more complex, and dependent on more and more fugitive causes'.[5] And he learnt the very useful negative idea for a critic that poetry is not simply the translation of prose thoughts into poetic language, a false idea which he believed public-school Latin versification tended very strongly to confirm. He was always hard-up, and since he had very few connections in London he spent his leave days in 'friendless wandering', and his great pleasure on such occasions was to fall in with some clergymen who would discuss with him his favourite subjects—the 'preposterous pursuit' he called it—metaphysics and providence, freewill and predestination. Even in his school days it seemed his two great appetites were stirring and biting at one another.

[1] *Letters*, Vol. I, pp. 347-8.   [2] Ibid., Vol. I, p. 388.
[3] *Biographia Literaria*, I, p. 3.   [4] Ibid., I. p. 5.
[5] Ibid., I, p. 3.

Coleridge went up to Jesus College, Cambridge, in October 1791 with a grant from Christ's Hospital, and he was also given a Rustat scholarship in November. He wrote from Cambridge gay and lively letters to his brother George—'the river Cam is a handsome stream of a muddy complexion, somewhat like Miss Yates . . . in Cambridge there are 16 colleges, that look like work-houses, and 14 churches that look like little houses. The Town is very fertile in alleys, and mud, and cats, and dogs, besides men, women, ravens, clergy, proctors, Tutors, Owls, and other two-legged cattle'.[1] He wrote arch ones to Mrs Evans, the widowed mother of a school friend and her daughters, especially to Mary with whom it appears he was in love. There is no doubt both from his own letters and from the account of a contemporary, Samuel Butler, that Coleridge worked hard and had a considerable degree of success at the University. But all his letters are strewn with references to illness— to a 'disagreeable tearing pain in my head; to rheumatism, violent colds, coughs, fevers, abscessed teeth' and so on; and quite casually in a letter to George[2] appears the remark, 'opium never used to have any disagreeable effects on me—but it has upon many'. Opium was already apparently a habitual analgesic. He gives the impression in many of his letters of being cheerfully in want of cash, but there is nothing to prepare one for the lunatic episode of December 2nd, 1793, when he suddenly became so distracted by college debts (which amounted it afterwards appeared to no more than £132, 6s. 2¼d.) that he enlisted in the 15th King's Light Dragoons, 'G' Troop, as Silas Tomkyn Comberbache. And it seems that if he hadn't done this he might have done something even more calamitous: only an accident of 'a very singular kind' had prevented him from 'the dernier resort of misery'[3] he later told his brother. He was, as was to be expected, a hopeless soldier and was left to look after the sick, having to collect his meals from the local poor-house. His brothers bought him out and he returned to college, where his scholarship was continued. His moderate punishment was a reprimand, a month's confinement to college and a quantity of translation from Greek into English. He came down, however, without taking a degree.

Earlier in the year Coleridge had walked over to Oxford, met Southey and with him sketched out the intellectual analogue of

---

[1] *Letters*, Vol. I, p. 31. [2] Ibid., Vol. I, p. 18.
[3] Ibid., Vol. I, p. 68.

the King's Light Dragoons enlistment, namely his scheme for an ideal settlement on the banks of the Susquehanna. It was a blend of Platonic idealism, Godwinian perfectibility and republican organisation. The scheme collapsed when the lady who was chosen to finance it, Southey's aunt, would have none of it, but it left Coleridge engaged to Sara Fricker, the sister of Southey's fiancée, although he was even more seriously in love with Mary Evans than he had been at the time of the Comberbache affair. Southey was engaged to Edith Fricker; Lovell, another Pantisocrat, to another daughter, and Coleridge therefore was to be symmetrically engaged to a third, Sara. He married Sara in Bristol on October 4th and moved to Clevedon. It was a marriage entered into for the sake of principle, which was to founder on the angularity of fact. Cottle had agreed to publish and to pay for anything he might produce. During this Godwinian-Benthamite period he issued a periodical *The Watchman* which ran from March to May for ten numbers. 'I'm in a quickset hedge of embarrassments', he groaned to Cottle, 'and whichever way I turn, a thorn runs into me.'[1] Thomas Poole, his great friend, however, organised a fund which was to bring him forty pounds a year for seven years, and he hoped to earn a corresponding amount by serious writing and by journalism. In the spring of 1797 began his great relationship with Wordsworth, 'the only man to whom and at all times and in all modes of excellence I feel myself inferior'.[2] Part of Wordsworth's great genius was the capacity to feed upon his friends and relations. It is impossible to exaggerate Wordsworth's debt to Coleridge, though it is characteristic of Wordsworth that he not only never acknowledged it but hardly even seemed to be aware of it.

Between 1796 and 1802 three children were born to Coleridge and his wife. He had begun *The Ancient Mariner* and *Christabel* and started his translation of *Wallenstein*. He received an annuity from the Wedgwoods, he paid a visit to Germany in company with the Wordsworths, and stayed on there himself till July 1799, during which time his baby boy Berkeley died of consumption. He learned to speak a fluent but inaccurate German in what he acknowledged himself to be a hideous accent. He gained a considerable knowledge of German literature and philosophy, and projected a study of Lessing which was never completed. It is likely, however, that

[1] *Letters*, Vol. I, p. 185.   [2] Ibid., Vol. I, p. 334.

his knowledge of Kant at this time was no more than what could be gained from an intelligent interest in the general ideas of the time.

When he returned from Germany in July 1799 he made his first walking tour of the Lake District with Wordsworth from October 27th to November 18th. (*The Lyrical Ballads* had been published the year before.) It was at this time that he met and fell in love with Sara Hutchinson, a fair, fat little woman for whom he was to nourish an intense passion for many years. Coleridge himself began to work on the *Morning Post* in London, where his wife joined him but only stayed for two months. Coleridge went on battering out hack work and translating Schiller. He moved with his family to Keswick in 1800. It is clear that things were strained between his wife and himself. He wrote in January to Poole 'Sara being Sara, and I being I, we must live in a town or else close to one, so that she may have neighbours and acquaintances. . . . God knows where we can go; for that situation which suits my wife does not suit me, and what suits me does not suit my wife. However, that which is, is—a truth which always remains equally clear, but not always equally pleasant.'[1]

One cannot help feeling sorry for Mrs Coleridge, a straight-forward unimaginative woman who might have made someone more ordinary than Coleridge a perfectly reasonable wife. But that she did not make one for Coleridge became clearer and clearer. 'If any woman wanted an exact and copious Recipe "How to make a husband compleatly miserable", I could furnish her with one—with a probatum est tacked to it. Ill-tempered Speeches sent after me when I went out of the house, ill-tempered Speeches on my return, my friends received with freezing looks, the least opposition or contradiction occasioning screams of passion, and the sentiments which I held most base, ostentatiously avowed—all this added to the utter negation of all, which a husband expects from a wife—especially, living in retirement—and the consciousness that I was myself growing a worse man. Oh dear sir! no-one can tell what I have suffered. I can say with strict truth that the happiest half-hours I have had, were when all of a sudden, as I have been sitting in my Study I have burst into tears. . . .'[2] Not that he did not still have spurts of affection—or perhaps simply kindness —for her. He wrote to her on December 16th, 1802, when she was

---

[1] Ibid., Vol. I, p. 562.   [2] Ibid., Vol. II, p. 876.

expecting a baby: 'My dear Love, I write with trembling—at what time or in what state my letter may find you, how can I tell? Small need is there for saying, how anxious I am, how full of terrors and prayers! I trust in God, that this letter which I write with a palpitating heart, you will read with a cheerful one—the new baby at your breast—O may God Almighty preserve you! We leave this place in less than an hour. Our route lies thro' . . .'[1] On other occasions, either through sensitivity or simply moral cowardice he seemed hypocritically to be using two voices at the same time, one to Mrs Coleridge and another to his friends.[2]

The years 1800-03 were hard and important ones for Coleridge. He finally threw off the last intellectual categories of the eighteenth century, the psychology of Locke and the theology of Newton, in which 'the mind is a lazy looker-on at an external universe': from now on he was to take his stand at all times on the activity of consciousness. He became a Burkean Tory instead of a Rousseauistic democrat, and an Anglican after the model of the Cambridge Platonists in place of a rationalist after the model of Godwin and Hartley: a far cry from 1797 when he began his letters with the hygienic salutation 'Health and Republicism' and was reported on by a Home Office agent as one of 'a Sett of violent Democrats'. He was appalled by the social injustice which marred society. 'Our enormous riches and accompanying poverty have corrupted the morals of the nation. . . . Property is the bug-bear—it stupefies the heads and hardens the hearts of our Counsellors and Chief men!'[3] And 'the professed democrats who on an occasion of uproar would press forward to be the leaders, are without knowledge, talents, or morals'.[4] He existed in a state of constant bodily misery interspersed with bouts of savage pains, which he tried to keep from being totally intolerable with brandy and laudanum. He was taking as much as a hundred drops of laudanum a day. (He was under the curious illusion that laudanum was less pernicious than tea.[5] Perhaps this last point isn't so odd as it sounds: laudanum and opium were sold like aspirins throughout Lancashire and Yorkshire. A chemist told Coleridge that on market day in the small town of Thorpe, near Doncaster, he would sell two or three pounds of opium and a gallon of laudanum.[6]) By the end of 1801 he was a

---

[1] *Letters*, Vol. II, p. 898.   [2] Cf. *Letters*, Vol. II, p. 1181.
[3] *Letters*, Vol. II, pp. 720-1.   [4] Ibid.
[5] Cf. *Letters*, Vol. II, p. 884.   [6] Cf. *Letters*, Vol. III, p. xl.

confirmed opium narcotic. His affection for Sara Hutchinson grew stronger, his lacerated exasperation with his wife sharper. He suffered horribly from dreams: 'While I am awake and retain possession of my Will and Reason I can continue to keep the Fiend at Arm's length; but Sleep throws wide open all the gates of the beleaguered City—and such an Host of Horrors rush in—that three nights out of four I fall asleep struggling to lie awake, and start up and bless my own loud screams that have awakened me. In the Hope that Change of Scene might relieve me, and that hard Exercise might throw the Disease into *Extremities*, I left my Home on August 15th and made the Tour of Scotland.'[1]

I must take this Scottish opportunity to illustrate one or two characteristics of Coleridge that we often overlook, for example a robust down-to-earth sense of humour not at all unlike Keats's. 'We dined at half past four—just after dinner down came Old Allen—O Christ! Old Nightmair! An ancient Incubus! Every face was saddened, every mouth pursed up! Most solemnly civil, like the Lord of a stately Castle 500 years ago! Doleful and plaintive eke: for I believe that the Devil is twitching him home.'[2] We expect too the great romantic's power to reconstruct a natural scene with the directness of a child's eye seeing it for the first time. But Coleridge also had a sophisticated sense for the feel of a *town*, as well as the ability to convey it in a quick personal shorthand.

What a wonderful City Edinburgh is! What alternation of Height and Depth!—a city looked at in the polished back of a Brobdignag Spoon, held lengthways—so enormously *stretched-up* are the Houses! When I first looked down on it, as the Coach drove in on the higher street, I cannot express what I felt—such a section of wasp's nest, striking you with a sort of bastard sublimity from the enormity and infinity of its littleness—the infinity swelling out the mind, the enormity striking it with wonder. I think I have seen an old Plate of Monserrat, that struck me with the same feeling—and I am sure I have seen huge Quarries of Lime or Free-Stone, in which the Shafts or Strata have stood perpendicularly instead of horizontally, with the same high Thin Slices, and corresponding Interstices![3]

More remarkable still, part of that other neglected Coleridge, is this: during his Scottish tour, this disease-riddled unhappy narcotic walked 263 miles in eight days without any unpleasant

---

[1] *Letters*, Vol. II, p. 1005. [2] Ibid., Vol. II, p. 888.
[3] Ibid., Vol. II, p. 988.

fatigue. Coleridge's body plagued him all his life. But there is no doubt that it also had in it a formidable strain of toughness, just as his temperament for all its trembling sensitivity possessed a real quality of courage. I. A. Richards, himself a mountaineer, pointed out that Coleridge 'anticipated by more than a generation the modern taste for pure mountain adventure indulged for its own sake'.[1] On August 6th, 1802, Coleridge wrote to Sara Hutchinson in Yorkshire from Ambleside. This famous letter, 'The Sca' Fell Letter', magnificently describes Coleridge in action as a climber. Here is the beginning:

> There is one sort of Gambling, to which I am much addicted; and that not of the least criminal kind for a man who has children & a Concern.—It is this. When I find it convenient to descend from a mountain, I am too confident & too indolent to look round about & Wind about 'till I find a track or other symptom of safety; but I wander on, & where it is first *possible* to descend, there I go—relying upon fortune for how far down this possibility will continue. So it was yesterday afternoon. I passed down from Broad-crag, skirted the Precipices, and found myself cut off from a most sublime Crag-summit, that seemed to rival Sca' Fell Man in height, & to outdo it in fierceness. A Ridge of Hill lay low down, & divided this Crag (called Doe-crag) & Broad-crag—even as the Hyphen divides the words broad & crag. I determined to go thither; the first place I came to, that was not direct Rock, I slipped down, & went on for a while with tolerable ease—but now I came (it was midway down) to a smooth perpendicular Rock about 7 feet high—this was nothing —I put my hands on the Ledge, & dropped down / in a few yards came just such another / I *dropped* that too / and yet another, seemed not higher—I would not stand for a trifle / so I dropped that too / but the stretching of the muscle(s) of my hands & arms, & the jolt of the Fall on my Feet, put my whole Limbs in a *Tremble*, and I paused, & looking down, saw that I had little else to encounter but a succession of these little Precipices—it was in truth a Path that in a very hard Rain is, no doubt, the channel of a most splendid Waterfall.—So I began to suspect that I ought not to go on / but then unfortunately tho' I could with ease drop down a smooth Rock 7 feet high, I could not *climb* it / so go on I must / and on I went / the next 3 drops were not half a Foot, at least not a foot more than my own height / but every Drop increased the Palsy of my Limbs—I shook all over, Heaven knows without the least influence of Fear / and now I had only two more to drop down / to return was impossible—but of these two the

[1] Richards, I. A., *The Portable Coleridge*, New York, 1961, p. 14.

first was tremendous / it was twice my own height, & the Ledge at the bottom was (so) exceedingly narrow, that if I dropt down upon it I must of necessity have fallen backwards & of course killed myself. My Limbs were all in a tremble—I lay upon my Back to rest myself, & was beginning according to my Custom to laugh at myself for a Madman, when the sight of the Crags above me on each side, & the impetuous Clouds just over them, posting so luridly & so rapidly northward, overawed me / I lay in a state of almost prophetic Trance & Delight—& blessed God aloud, for the powers of Reason & the Will, which remaining no Danger can overpower us![1]

During the winter of 1803-04 Coleridge became convinced that another English winter would finish him off and that he must find a warmer climate. He set sail for Malta in April, after the usual chaos of mismanagement. He was alarmingly ill during the voyage, which he barely survived. During the next two years there is no mention of drugs in his letters, but this is simply because they became a necessary part of his life. Sir Alexander Ball, an unusual colonial Governor, was most taken with Coleridge and detected in him administrative and diplomatic gifts no one else had perceived. He made him first his private, then his public secretary, though not at the full salary. Coleridge was much involved in complicated Government business, and he performed his duties with efficiency and despatch. Hard as it is to believe, it seems that Coleridge might well have made a career for himself in the foreign service. Supported by the admiring affection of his chief, by the genial climate and by drugs, Coleridge was a comparatively happy man at this time, which he afterwards described in *The Friend* as 'in many respects, the most memorable and instructive period of my life'.[2]

Coleridge returned to England in August 1806 completely dependent upon opium. He tried many times to cut down the quantity of drugs he took, even to give the habit up. But his addiction was now hopelessly nailed to his body. The next ten years were probably the most wretched as they were also the most productive of his life. He was heavily in debt. He lost half his annuity because of the Wedgwoods' business losses, He was constantly ill. He had no settled residence, let alone a home. He became estranged from Wordsworth through gossip passed on by a friend, though that

---

[1] *Letters*, Vol. II, pp. 841-2.
[2] Cf. *The Friend*, The Third Landing-Place, Essays II-VI.

may not have been a total calamity. He was separated both from his wife and from Sara Hutchinson. The reviewers detested him. But he was also during this time an active literary and political journalist, a metaphysician, a poet, a critic, a lecturer, a playwright. *The Friend* began publication on June 1st, 1807, and continued for twenty-seven numbers; in 1818 it was republished in three volumes. He contributed essays to the *Courier*, for the editor of which, Daniel Stuart, Coleridge acted as editorial advisor and political analyst. His play *Remorse* was put on at Drury Lane and it went into more than one edition when published, although its popularity must have tailed off since Coleridge wrote complaining to John Murray in August 1814, 'the *Remorse*, though acted 20 times, rests quietly on the Shelves in the second Edition, with enough copies for 7 years' consumption or 7 times 7'.[1] He published poetry in 1816, including *Christabel* and *Kubla Khan*, his *Lay Sermons* in 1816 and 1817, and *Biographia Literaria* and *Sibylline Leaves* in 1817. And in 1818 he was involved in a plan to edit the *Encyclopaedia Metropolitana*, and his brilliant *Treatise on Method* which was written for this appeared separately in 1818. Between 1808 and 1819 he gave several series of lectures at the Royal Institution, the London Philosophical Society, at Willis's Rooms, at the Surrey Institution, at the White Lion, Bristol, although they did not always turn out to be what the prospectus offered. Fourteen lectures on the History of Philosophy and six on Shakespeare were delivered at the *Crown and Anchor* in the Strand. There is something characteristic of Coleridge's fate in this comic connection, the rubbing of the ideal's nose in the dirt. (He noted ruefully in a letter to Andrew Bell when he was lecturing in Fetter Lane how much the place's exclusive renown for pork and sausages told against him)[2].

This would have been a respectable production for a well man in comfortable circumstances. For Coleridge, undermined by disease, distraught with drugs, ravelled by personal wretchedness and a guilty conscience—after all he *had* a wife and children, and there *was* Sara Hutchinson—harried by creditors, frequently slighted and largely unacknowledged, it is not less than heroic. Nor was he ever the man to achieve a Wordsworthian concentration on himself. He busied himself with the interests of his friends. He gave advice, sympathy, practical help. He spent several months

[1] *Letters*, Vol. III, p. 524. [2] Ibid, Vol. III, p. 349.

in Bristol in 1814 seeking to help a penurious friend, John Morgan, and giving him incidentally quantities of medical advice. He took the most excited and informed interest in the work of Humphrey Davy, going so far in this case as to praise the Royal Institution, which he thought 'in all other things most injudiciously managed— nay perverted', 'because it has assisted, perhaps enabled Davy to do the glorious things he has done, and I trust is doing, and will do —and which assuredly will place him by the side of Bacon and Newton—for his Inventions are Discoveries, and his Discoveries great general principles, fruitful, yea creative'.[1] He took not only an interest but an active part as advisor and propagandist in the public affairs of the day, in the Catholic Question, for example, and in education, of which I will speak elsewhere. He was as sensitive as ever to the rank horrors that disfigured society. It was to Coleridge that Sir Robert Peel, the father of the Prime Minister, turned for help with the Factory Act which he was introducing at the instance of the Lancashire cotton spinners to shorten the factory hours for children. (They were working from 5.30 a.m. to 8.30 p.m.) And though he had doubts about the timing of the Bill and the lack of a due preparation of the public mind,[2] and although he was ill in bed, he responded enthusiastically, and his biting and cogent pamphlet in support of the measure played a part in getting it passed[3].

1816 was a good year for Coleridge. The year before he had written on the advice of Bowles to Byron asking for his help in finding a publisher for a volume of poems. Byron treated him with characteristic generosity and delicacy. He used his influence with the publisher John Murray, he acknowledged what Sir Walter Scott with greater reason had failed to do: namely his indebtedness to Coleridge's *Christabel* (which though long unpublished had circulated freely in the literary world), he wrote to Tom Moore on October 28th, 1815, asking him to review Coleridge favourably in the *Edinburgh Review*: 'Coleridge . . . a man of wonderful talent and in distress . . . he only wants a pioneer and a sparkle or two to explode most gloriously'.[4] Moore's review, however, when it came out in the *Edinburgh Review* of September 1816, was brutal, and

---

[1] Ibid., Vol. III, p. 95.   [2] Cf. *Letters*, Vol. IV, p. 842.
[3] Cf. *The Inquiring Spirit*. Edited by Kathleen Coburn, London, 1951, pp. 12, 351-65.
[4] *Byron Letters and Journals*, Vol. III, pp. 232-3.

when Byron heard from William Sotheby of Coleridge's desperate want of money he immediately sent Coleridge £100 (although he had hardly £150 in the world). They met only once for about half an hour in Byron's house in Piccadilly, just before Byron left England for good on April 25th, 1816; Coleridge was immensely taken with Byron and recited *Kubla Khan* to him. This meeting—happier than several dealings Coleridge had with his contemporaries, although it had a sour footnote in the insult Coleridge received in *Don Juan*[1]—took place just after *the* event of 1816 which was to ensure that henceforth Coleridge would live a more settled and cared-for existence. In a letter to Byron written on April 10th Coleridge revealed his intention 'to pass a month at Highgate, boarding and lodging in the House of a respectable Surgeon and Naturalist for the perfecting of my convalescence mental no less than bodily'.[2] At the same time Dr Joseph Adams was negotiating with James Gillman on behalf of 'a very learned but . . . unfortunate gentleman (who) has for several years been in the habit of taking large quantities of opium'.[3] Coleridge arrived at the Gillmans on Monday evening, April 15th: the 'month' and the convalescence he spoke of to Byron were to last for the rest of his life. Coleridge wrote to the Gillmans a couple of days before he arrived explaining that he would be no trouble to them except in one respect. 'You will never *hear* anything but truth from me— Prior Habits render it out of my power to *tell* a falsehood, but unless watched carefully, I dare not promise that I should not with regard to this detested Poison be capable of acting a Lie—No sixty hours have yet passed without my having taken Laudanum . . . *I must not be permitted* to leave your House, unless I should walk out with you.'[4] The Gillmans did in fact watch over Coleridge with the most attentive and delicate care. They gave him a home as well as a lodging, and affection as well as board; they welcomed his friends and children, accompanied him on his holidays, and

---

[1] Cf. Griggs, E. L., *Letters*, Vol. IV, p. 948.
   Thou shalt believe in Milton, Dryden, Pope;
   Thou shalt not set up Wordsworth, Coleridge, Southey;
   Because the first is crazed beyond hope,
   The second drunk, the third so quaint and mouthy.
Byron believed quite wrongly that Coleridge had joined with Southey in scandalising him.
[2] *Letters*, Vol. IV, p. 628.
[3] Cf. *Letters*, Vol. IV, pp. 628-9.
[4] *Letters*, Vol. IV, p. 630.

made life rather more than what it had been for Coleridge for so long: a barely supportable misery.

His drug habit which in 1816 was at least of fifteen years' standing was never eradicated. In 1832, two years before he died, he was referring to it as 'for more than 30 years the misery of my existence'. And there seems to be no doubt that there were backslidings during his Highgate life when he was using the addict's cunning to get hold of secret supplies.[1] But at least it was kept under some sort of control, and during the next eight years he published *The Statesman's Manual*, finished *Biographia Literaria*, revised *The Friend*, wrote *Aids to Reflection* (1825) and *Church and State* (1830). All these works are flawed, padded, structurally incoherent, and distorted by digression and triviality. They still make up an achievement of tremendous range and profound originality.

But Coleridge's protected retirement was not devoted exclusively to the labours of composition. He kept up his interest in politics and public affairs. He was accessible to his friends and a lively and voluminous correspondent. He read what was being written and did not lose his amateur's interest in science. He was anxiously concerned for his family. Years before, in 1802, Coleridge has spoken to Godwin of his 'heart-withering Conviction—that I could not be happy without my children, and could not but be miserable with the mother of them'.[2] He did in fact preserve a detached goodwill towards Mrs Coleridge and a very present affection for his children. Here is a letter which expresses this rather fussed practical concern and a somewhat harassed father's helpfulness.

My Dear Sara

I cannot write a *letter*, till I have finished a week's work—therefore —briefly, within a week from the date of this you may draw for 50£ at six weeks on R. Fennor, Bookseller, Paternoster Row.—For the rest I can only say that I do not and shall not spend a shilling unnecessarily; & that you or the children will have every shilling beyond my necessities.—Hartley left me on Saturday—he has money enough at present—& I have paid his Bills at Highgate, Boots, Pantaloons, &c together with the money in his pocket some-what about 18£.—I wish to know about my dear Derwent—and whether

[1] Cf. Griggs, E. L., *Coleridge's Letters*, Introduction, Vol. III, p. xl.
[2] *Letters*, Vol. II, p. 432.

you can afford to send him up to me by the first week of November.—
My Health makes it almost necessary for me to be at the Sea side for
6 weeks—as the difference of the expence will not be above 20£, &
the probable advantages in finishing the Christabel much more.—If
you will order him the proper *fit out* that he may want, I will try to
defray great part of it within the six months—. I should, if it be
thought proper, wish him to be at Highgate by the last week of
October.—Do not take this for a Letter—Would to God! I could but
hit on a possibility of seeing my dear Sara—I would work night & day
to bring it about—but unfortunately, we have no bed-room & she
could not sleep out—. My love to all![1]

The money question fretted Coleridge all his life, although he
had some relief in 1824 when the Royal Society of Literature made
him an annual grant of one hundred guineas. His books did not
sell; several of his undertakings—e.g. *The Friend* and some of the
lecture courses—hardly covered expenses. In addition he suffered
an unusual misfortune. His publisher, Rest Fenner, went bankrupt in March 1819. Any professional writer can conceive of
himself going bankrupt: his publisher never: this would be like
cancelling the laws of nature. Coleridge lost money—he estimated
it was £1200—through having to buy back both half-copyrights
formerly held by Fenner and unsold copies of his books; but he
was losing money even before the bankruptcy because Fenner had
been making false returns: the number of copies printed and sold,
says Griggs,[2] greatly exceeded the sales reported to Coleridge. His
stand-by for making money was lecturing. He sometimes had as
many as 150 at his lectures and the fee, according to the prospectus
of the course on Shakespeare in 1811, was two guineas for the
whole course, 'three guineas with the privilege of introducing a
lady'. Coleridge's lectures were frequently not only discourses but
performances. They were not short; it was not unusual for him to
go on for two hours with unhesitating fluency. He had an impressive appearance, a rather corpulent figure, round face, flowing
hair, and large soft eyes, which De Quincey said had a 'peculiar
appearance of haze or dreaminess',[3] and a clear musical voice.
Coleridge himself considered that the purpose of the lecture was
'to keep the audience awake and interested during delivery and

---

[1] *Letters*, Vol. IV, p. 766.   [2] Ibid., Vol. IV, p. 947.
[3] *The Collected Writings of Thomas De Quincey*. Edited by David Masson, London,
1896, Vol. II, p. 150.

to leave a sting behind'.[1] Sometimes he used a sheaf of notes which he frequently pushed aside when a digression took over; sometimes nothing at all; sometimes he didn't even turn up. His lectures were often most applauded when they had been given the least preparation. He had, said Crabb Robinson, an 'infinite ability to riot and run wild on a variety of moral and religious themes. In his sixth lecture he was, by advertisement, to speak on *Romeo and Juliet* and Shakespeare's females; unhappily someone whispered the name of Lancaster in his ear; and we had, in one evening, a talk on the poor Quaker, a defence of boarding-school flogging, a parallel between the ages of Elizabeth and Charles, a defence of what is untruly called unpoetic language, an account of the different languages in Europe, and a vindication of Shakespeare against the implication of grossness!'[2]

These lectures, or monologues, or performances, or 'turns' continued in Coleridge's sitting-room at the Gillmans on Thursday evenings, before an admiring circle, during most of the last ten years of his life. His listeners were entranced by his eloquence, and there is no doubt that on many occasions their fascinated attentiveness was justified. Some people have thought that there was something sickly, something feverish in the almost ecclesiastical rapture of these sessions, and it is true that we do have now some distaste for the guru figure which Coleridge seems to have become in his last years, an aversion which we might with profit carry over into other parts of our intellectual life. On the other hand there seems to be something fitting—perhaps, looking back, one could say it was only decent—that this good, great, ruined man should have had his last years supported by a little more than the kindliness of the Gillmans and the drugs which kept him going. It seems to be right that he should have had something rather more in keeping with his status as a writer and an artist: namely, an audience.

I have just now used the terms guru and religion, not in perhaps the most sympathetic way. But I cannot continue without making one serious point. We are apt to think that Coleridge's religion, in particular his Anglicanism, was simply a formal accompaniment of his development of high-Toryism. But it is quite certain that religion was for Coleridge during the great part of his life much

---

[1] *Letters*, Vol. IV, p. 924.
[2] *Lectures & Notes on Shakespeare.* Edited by T. Ash, London, 1902, p. 24.

more than something which he found philosophically reasonable and politically respectable. It was a profound and personal part of his life. Coleridge was a naturally religious man. Everything he did, however fine or however gross, had a reference to what Henry James called 'an order of goodness and power greater than any this world by itself can show, which we understand as the religious spirit'.[1] I believe that the claim he makes in these words, spoken at the end of his life, is in some deep way, for all his wretchedness and weakness, just and true.

> I am dying, but without expectation of a speedy release. Is it not strange that very recently bygone images, and scenes of early life, have stolen into my mind, like breezes blown from the spice-islands of Youth and Hope—those twin realities of this phantom world! I do not add Love,—for what is love but Youth and Hope embracing, and so seen as *one*? I say *realities*; for reality is a thing of degrees, from the Iliad to a dream; καὶ γάρ τ᾽ ὄναρ ἐκ αἰός ἐστι. Yet, in a strict sense, reality is not predictable at all of aught below Heaven. 'Es enim in *coelis*, Pater noster, qui tu vere *es!*' Hooker wished to live to finish his Ecclesiastical Polity:—so I own I wish life and strength has been spared to me to complete my Philosophy. For, as God hears me, the originating, continuing, and sustaining wish and design in my heart were to exalt the glory of his name; and, which is the same thing in other words, to promote the improvement of mankind. But *visum aliter Deo*, and his will be done.[2]

II THE MIND

The reader of Coleridge comes very quickly to have the sense of a person in the writings. I say *a* person rather than *the* person because the reader is also aware of how difficult it is to define or specify this enigmatic individual. (Which is why, I suppose, I use the word 'person' rather than 'personality', since there are uses of this latter which suggest some abstract constant, capable of being wrapped up, or laid away, in a phrase or a formula.) The positive, personal presence of Coleridge in his work may remind us of a limitation—a kind of classical bias or a preference for anonymity—in Eliot's theory of impersonality in art, or, it may explain, if Eliot's theory is substantially true, the reader's im-

---

[1] Henry James, *Autobiography*. Edited by F. W. Dupee, London, 1959, p. 335.
[2] *Table Talk*.

patient awareness of the structural imperfections of so much of Coleridge's work. Perhaps it does both. Certainly an awareness of Coleridge's always vivid, sometimes intrusive, presence means more than that Coleridge's literary character had a peculiar force of impact, such as we feel, for example, when we read Ben Jonson. Coleridge touches in us the faculty of recognition. We *recognise*, we are familiar with Coleridge as a person, in a way that we are not with Ben Jonson, whose powerful literary character seems to belong to another world altogether. Jonson for all his weight remains strangely remote; but with Coleridge we are on terms of first-hand, family intimacy. And if we ask why this should be so, the answer is that Coleridge represented, and in representing constituted, the first modern consciousness. There is a sense in which Chaucer and Jonson and Pope belonged to the same universe, one informed by the same conceptions of God and order and meaning. This is a world utterly vanished for us—and for Coleridge too, even though he 'believed' in it and wanted to restore it. Ours and his is a world in which the nervous individual consciousness works according to fluid and uncertain categories. Coleridge was the first to speak the language of this world and the first to feel himself obliged to offers answer to questions which had hardly been formulated before. Coleridge's writings, so disturbed and disorganised as works of art, are in their very imperfections, especially in their lack of harmony and finality, analogies of the modern mind.

Clearly there was in Coleridge's nature some profound malformation which, when it came to the business of composing actual works, caused his gigantic intellectual energy to dribble sandily away. He had an anguished sense of possessing simultaneously a plenitude of powers and a disastrous incapacity in action. He speaks despairingly of 'a sense of weakness, a haunting sense that I was an herbaceous plant, as large as a large tree with a trunk of the same girth, and branches as large and shadowing, but with pith within the trunk, not heart of wood—that I had power not strength'.[1] He blamed himself for this contradiction, putting it down to a blocked will and an enfeebled intention, and his opinion fits in with the explanation propagated by Carlyle, and accepted by more than one biographer, that it was all a want of resolution— 'putrescent idleness'. But is it really something so completely under

---

[1] *Letters*, Vol. II, p. 959.

voluntary control? What he did, with all its structural imperfections and chronic disorder, seems an extraordinary achievement, judged simply as a quantity of hard work. And when we think of the conditions in which it was done, and the daunting constant illness from childhood onwards—not to speak of the part that accumulated narcotic debilitation must have played in producing his sense of sapping listlessness—then the legend of drug-drowsed, scruple-clogged lethargy, for which Coleridge himself was as much responsible as Carlyle, seems almost ludicrous. Perhaps Coleridge's facile tendency to blame himself was the more genuine moral fault, not the sheer want of will. Perhaps ultimately his sense of power without strength is to be attributed much less to a moral defect and much more to a deficiency of artistic equipment. Coleridge had a marvellous faculty of creative speculation. But it existed at the highest level of generality. He could dart down in a letter a set of glittering metaphysical categories capable of organising great tracts of intellectual experience. He could also define with exquisite exactness the minutest shreds of natural and psychological existences, as we see in his best poems and in many of his letters. But he lacked a sense of structure of the middle sort, that capacity for a design, in part general, in part particular, which can be sustained throughout a whole work. The two sides of his nature, the philosophical and the poetic, or the general and the particular, because they were not separate and balanced by a third force, a commoner and more prosaic faculty, ground harshly against one another.

One of the most vivid of several descriptions of this self-disabling friction appears in a letter to William Godwin written on March 25th, 1801, from Keswick.

> During my long illness I had compelled into hours of delight many a sleepless painful hour of darkness by chasing down metaphysical game, and since then I have continued the hunt, till I found myself unaware at the root of pure mathematics, and up that tall smooth tree, whose poor branches are all at the very summit, am I climbing by pure adhesive strength of arms and thighs, still slipping down, still renewing my ascent. You would not know me. All sounds of similitude keep at such a distance from each other in my mind, that I have forgotten how to make a rhyme. I look at the mountains (that visible God Almighty that looks in at all my windows)—I look at the mountains only for the curves of their outlines; the stars, as I behold

them, form themselves into triangles; and my hands are scarred with scratches from a cat, whose back I was rubbing in the dark in order to see whether the sparks from it were refrangible by a prism. The Poet is dead in me; my imagination (or rather the Somewhat that had been imaginative) lies like a cold snuff on the circular rim of a brass candle-stick, without even a stink of tallow to remind you that it was once clothed and mitred with flame. That is past by! I was once a volume of gold leaf, rising and riding on every breath of Fancy, but I have beaten myself back into weight and density, and now I sink in quick-silver and remain squat and on the earth amid the hurricane that makes oaks and straws join in one dance, fifty yards high in the element.[1]

This is a highly Coleridgean utterance in which a blend of complex feelings is carried along on an unstoppable fluency, and in which an expressive power of extraordinary clarity conceals, or reveals, a profound ambiguity.

The statement, in spite of its appearing to be so carefully argued, is not an intellectual analysis. It seems to be exposing the anatomy of Coleridge's experience. In fact it is attempting to reconstruct his situation. The tension is between the generalising side of his nature addicted to 'metaphysical game' and aspiring towards 'the root of pure mathematics', and the imaginative or poetic, 'gold leaf, rising and riding on every breath of Fancy'. And the long illness and the sleepless painful darkness—references to which are unavoidable in any piece longer than a few lines from Coleridge's letters—are rather more than the simple occasion which Coleridge seems to be saying they are here. Disease and sleeplessness had such an influence in his life that one feels they are in part the cause as well as the occasion for his chasing of metaphysical game and keeping all sounds of similitude at such a distance from each other in his mind. And the result of the tension, in which Coleridge claims the ethereal abstractions of mathematics have taken him further and further away from poetry 'the hurricane that makes oaks and straws join in one dance' has been, paradoxically, to leave him 'beaten back into weight and density, squat on the earth, the poet . . . dead in me my inspiration . . . like cold snuff on the circular rim of a candle-stick, without even a stink of tallow to remind you that it was once clothed and mitred with flame'. I have no doubt that Coleridge's sense of the opposition within his nature

[1] *Letters*, Vol. II, pp. 713-14.

and his definition of its two elements is accurate, or that his estimate of its effect on him and his hint at its connection with pain and illness are just. But I wonder about his description of the process or activity of this tension. Was it simply that the attractions of generality outdid those of the imagination, that he saw curves instead of mountains or angles instead of stars? Or was it that the two impulses, towards the highest generality and towards the densest detail, continued unreconciled in his nature, crossing and thwarting one another and leaving him suspended in a kind of activity of inanition?

Nor is this the only patch of blankness in the passage. There is the further ambiguity that the poet whose absence Coleridge so movingly laments is on the contrary quite brilliantly present. The electric vitality in the very descriptions of a throttling lethargy, the buoyancy of metaphor, the athletic swerving speed of development make plain that the philosopher has by no means expelled the poet —in fact is grappling with him. The metaphysician's wrists are marked not only by the cat's but also by the poet's scratches.

When I speak of speed, I am referring to a quality everywhere present in Coleridge's work, even in those—frequent—philosophical or theological passages where the reader has the impression of falling about deliriously in a mist of gorgeous nonsense. It is an unfolding, turning, searching quality of the living consciousness which is opposed to nothing but what is finished and sealed off. We can apply to Coleridge's writings words he used himself to describe—of all things—parentheses. 'They are the drama of reason, the thought growing'. This gives exactly the effect Coleridge's writings have of offering the thing as it moves, the idea, the feeling, the dream, the spectacle, before it has been arrested by time or tedium or frozen into convention. And Coleridge conveys the effect of movement, of the volatility of mental action, so unmistakeably because it is the central habit of his mind and so vividly because of the mobility and transparency of a style that is as apt and supple as light.

It was under a figure of this kind that Coleridge chose to describe Pascal, who was at least in one respect very like himself. (His phrase was 'the style is a robe of pure light'.[1]) Pascal, it is true, is a writer of much greater deliberation than Coleridge, for whose peculiar nervy fluency the term 'robe' is rather too stiff. But both

[1] *Letters*, Vol. II, p. 994.

writers have in common a manner with an unusual degree of translucence. Each of them writes in a way which gives the reader a sense of having immediate access to the writer's mind. In Pascal this effect may depend on an extraordinary degree of clarity, in Coleridge on an extraordinary degree of fluency; but in both one has very strikingly the impression of being present at, of looking intently at the operations of the writer's mind. Indeed with Coleridge one feels frequently closer to the subject considering than the object considered. 'The drama of thought': if we take these words to mean the drama—sometimes even the melodrama—of Coleridge's thought, if we interpret thought as thinking, not the results, but the activity, and if in 'thought' we include not simply pure intellectual content but also all its stubborn, wandering roots in feeling, all its flaws of character, all its impurity of motive, then the 'drama of thought' is a far from inaccurate summary of Coleridge's work.

But even if it were it would still, I believe, give us a clue to the understanding of a nature which was in so many ways a nest of paradoxes. Coleridge was one for whom the life of theory really was what Santayana claimed it could be: 'the life of theory is not less human or less emotional than the life of sense: it is more typically human and more keenly emotional'.[1] For Coleridge to be concerned with humanity was to be concerned with human consciousness. 'The aim, the method throughout was, in the first place, to awaken, to cultivate and to mature the truly human in human nature ... or of that in man, which of all known embodied creatures he alone possesses, the pure reason, as designed to regulate the will.'[2] Or as he wrote in Notebook 51 'Consciousness is the problem, the solution of which cannot too variously be reworded, too manifoldly be illustrated. . . . Almost all is yet to be achieved.'[3] And human consciousness whether in its elementary form of perception or in its higher form as imagination is primarily an activity. It is selective, determining, modifying. Perception, he insisted, gathered impressions; it did not simply receive them. It fed on the world and wasn't simply fed by it. 'Mine eye', he wrote to Thomas Poole, 'gluttonizes the sea, the distant island, the opposite coast.'[4] More complex kinds of consciousness, in which

[1] *Three Philosophical Poets*, London, 1940, p. 142.   [2] *The Friend*, II, 10.
[3] *Inquiring Spirit*. Edited by Kathleen Coburn, London, 1951, p. 25.
[4] *Letters*, Vol. I, p. 90.

'things the most remote and diverse in time, place and outward circumstances are brought into mental contiguity and succession, the more striking as the less expected',[1] depend even more directly on the active initiative of the mind. Without 'this staple or starting-post', as Coleridge called it, without an antecedent contribution from the mind itself, human consciousness collapses into delirium. Coleridge's stress on the self-moving energy of consciousness is no doubt conditioned by historical and personal circumstances. In the first place Coleridge, in this as in so much else representing the nineteenth century, struggled all his life to extricate himself and his age from the theology of Newton and the psychology of Locke, systems built on the principle of the passivity of the mind, in which the mind is always 'a lazy looker-on at an external world'[2] and in which thought takes the signature of things. This was the view of 'the party of the Little-ists. . . . Mr Locke was the founder of this sect, himself a perfect Little-ist.'[3] But for Coleridge it was the other way round. In consciousness 'things take the signature of thought'.[4] He rejected a figure of consciousness which pictured the mind as the inactive recipient of impressions. He took a more organic model. 'The initiative thought, the intellectual seed must have its birth-place within, whatever excitement from without may be necessary for its germination.'[5]

Coleridge recognised that the bias of his own temperament favoured an active understanding of consciousness. He saw, too, that the details of his upbringing fell in with this natural bent. In 1797 he wrote a set of letters to Poole which deliberately set out 'to relate the events of his own life with honesty, not disguising the feelings that accompanied them'.[6] These letters blend in the nicest way tolerantly affectionate remembrance with clinically analytic acumen. They don't take us much beyond his schooldays but they do deal with this very point of temperament, upbringing and the activity of consciousness. The reader also gets a glimpse, in this anecdote of his father, of a less familiar side of Coleridge's nature, an untroubled, more homely, rather taking side.

I remember that at eight years old I walked with him one winter evening from a farmer's house, a mile from Ottery, and he told me the names of the stars and how Jupiter was a thousand times larger

[1] *The Friend*, II, 4.
[2] *Letters*, Vol. II, p. 709.
[3] Ibid., Vol. II, p. 709.
[4] *Aids to Reflection*: Introductory Aphorisms, 24.
[5] *The Friend*, II, 11.
[6] *Letters*, Vol. I, p. 302.

than our world, and that the other twinkling stars were suns that had worlds rolling round them; and when I came home he showed me how they rolled round. I heard him with a profound delight and admiration: but without the least mixture of wonder or incredulity. For from my early reading of fairy tales and genii etc., my mind had been habituated *to the Vast*, and I never regarded *my senses* in any way as the criteria of my belief. I regulated all my creeds by my conception, not by my *sight*, even at that age.[1]

For Coleridge, then, the *activity* of mind was the primary characteristic of consciousness. His personal dilemma came both from this general constitution of the mind and its peculiar configuration in himself. There was a kind of eagerness in his nature which carried him everywhere to extremes, so that his own mental activity tended to be turbulent and overbearing, not only modifying but even on occasion dissolving the facts. In the letter I have just quoted he goes on to acknowledge in a general way that activity of consciousness unsanctioned by nature and uncorrected by fact is prone to credulity and superstition. And elsewhere he acknowledges this tendency in himself. 'It was in me the heat, bustle and overflowing of a mind too vehemently pushed on from within to be regardful of the objects upon which it was moving.'[2] 'A wild activity, of thoughts, imaginations, feelings, and impulses of motion, rises up from within me ... my whole Being is filled with waves, as it were, that roll and stumble, one this way, and one that way, like things that have no common master.'[3] Now this impatience, this over-enthusiasm of intellect was accompanied by— or rather, since one excess always balances itself with another, produced—a profound and clogging lethargy of spirit. It was a species of that despairing feeling which comes when a too brilliant, too comprehensive insight contrasts itself with intractability of action and the impossibility of resolution. He could describe it with detachment when it was distanced in somebody else. 'It is a complete *taedium vitae*; nothing pleases long, and novelty itself begins to cease to act like novelty. Life and all its forms move, in his diseased moments, like shadows before him, cold, colourless and unsubstantial.'[4] Or would he cry out himself from one of these 'diseased moments', 'O dear Southey! I am no elm! I am a crumbling wall, undermined at the foundation! Why should the vine with

[1] Ibid., Vol. I, p. 354.   [2] Ibid., Vol. II, p. 959.
[3] Ibid., Vol. II, p. 916.   [4] Ibid., Vol. II, p. 928.

all its clusters be buried in my rubbish.'[1] Knotted into Coleridge's nature was a paradox, a painful contradiction involving what was, as it were, a thyroid condition of the intelligence and a blocked, despairing passivity, this latter something more profound and searing than the mere idleness of the will he is so often accused of. In one of those comic asides which he could throw off in the middle of a serious discussion, he makes this point in a vivid, inverted way. 'As to me, my face, unless animated by immediate eloquence, expresses great sloth, and great, indeed almost idiotic good nature. 'Tis a mere carcass of a face, fat, flabby, and expressive chiefly of inexpression. Yet I am told that my eyes, eyebrows and forehead are physiognomically good; but of this the dependent knoweth not. As to my shape, 'tis a good shape enough if measured, but my gait is awkward, and the whole man indicates *indolence capable of energies*.'[2]

Consciousness to Coleridge was primarily an active agency, but he did not conceive of it as exploding into action without ancestry or preparation. In a letter to Wedgwood about Descartes, Coleridge makes it clear that you cannot separate the mind from its thoughts. The mind is not a muscle, now taking exercise, now not; nor is it a container now filled, now empty. 'In respect of Faculty, the mind *is* its intellectual thoughts',[3] and 'a single thought', he says elsewhere, 'is that which it is from other thoughts, as a wave of the sea takes its form and shape from the waves which precede and follow it'.[4] The mind is not only activity but continuous activity. To Coleridge consciousness became rational as it logically, and aesthetic as it lucidly, realised an initiating, ordering conception. It had to be progressive. The mind possesses not only initiative but also direction, not only energy but flow. So that the activity of the mind is not to be thought of either as a succession of stances adopted in face of a series of external stimuli, nor as a sequence of thoughts, each one simply provoking the next. The ground of the mind's continuousness—and a consciousness of continuousness was to Coleridge a mark of man—is the operation of the whole mind. 'Intelligence involves the notion of order, and it follows necessarily that we can have no notion of desirable Progression (i.e. desirable for the Progressor, as well as for others) but what supposes a growth of consciousness.'[5] The activity of consciousness is a continuous

---

[1] *Letters*, Vol. II, p. 929. [2] Ibid., Vol. I, pp. 259-60.
[3] Ibid., Vol. II, p. 682. [4] *Table Talk*. [5] *Letters*, Vol. II, p. 1196.

development of the implicit, and any particular thought realises some intimation of a complex whole. And that involves as much what we mean by feeling as what we usually mean by thought.

'When I wrote that last sentence,' Coleridge wrote to Southey, 'I had a vivid recollection—indeed an ocular Spectrum—of our room in College Street—a curious instance of association. You remember how incessantly in that room I used to be compounding these half-verbal, half-visual metaphors. It argues I am persuaded a particular state of general feeling—and I hold, that association depends in a much greater degree on the recurrence of resembling states of feeling than on Trains of Ideas, that the recollection of early childhood in latest old age depends on, and is explicable by this. . . . If I were asked, how it is that very old people remember *visually* only the events of early childhood—and remember the intervening spaces either not at all, or only verbally—I should think it a perfectly philosophical answer, that old age remembers childhood by becoming "a second childhood" . . . I almost think, that Ideas *never* recall ideas, as far as they are ideas—any more than leaves in a forest create each other's motion—The Breeze it is that runs thro' them—it is the Soul, the state of Feeling.'[1]

The whole idiom of Coleridge's thought, the bias of his temperament, the focus of his attention, all serve to stress what is intrinsic in consciousness. But it would be misreading him not to see that this is an emphasis on a primacy, not on something absolute and exclusive. The continuousness of consciousness is a system of active connection initiated within the mind but not concluded there. Growth—the image in which Coleridge figured it—requires the collaboration of others. Consciousness is not snapped off at the edge of individual consciousness. 'This state and growth of reflex consciousness . . . is not conceivable without the action of kindred souls on each other, i.e., the modification of each by each, and of each by the whole. A male and female Tyger is neither more or less whether you suppose them existing in their appropriate wilderness, or whether you suppose a thousand Pairs. But man is truly altered by the co-existence of other man; his faculties cannot be developed in himself alone, and only by himself.'[2]

Again we are apt to limit the continuousness, the connection of consciousness, by taking it to be a derivation from the past simply. But there is also, Coleridge claimed, a connection with the future.

[1] *Letters*, Vol. II, p. 961.   [2] Ibid., Vol. II, p. 1197.

The objects of civilisation itself, he held, are 'to bind the present with the past' *and* 'to connect the present with the future'.[1] In the same way the continuity of consciousness is a chain attached not only to the past but to the future. This was why Coleridge distinguished motives—a function of the past—from purposes—a function of the future, and why he said that while motives govern the man, the man makes his own purposes. It explains too why he felt so strongly the necessity for hope, that small, neglected, important virtue. 'At times', he writes, applying a sharp personal turn to his thoughts, 'I would fain be somewhat of a more tangible unity than I am; but so I suppose it is with all of us—one while cheerful, stirring, feeling in resistance nothing but a joy and stimulus; another while drowsy, self-distrusting, prone to rest, loathing our own self-promises, withering our own hopes—our hopes, the vitality and cohesion of our being!'[2]

'The vitality and cohesion of our being.' The phrase contains suggestions of all the three elements in Coleridge's account of consciousness: vitality—activity; cohesion—continuousness; but also assimilation, which I want to turn to now. Consciousness assimilates its objects to itself—'things', as Coleridge puts it again, 'take the signature of thought'. The assimilation is not simply an imposition by the subject upon the object. Consciousness is not an idealistic leech nor are objects the prey of an egotistical consciousness. 'It is not just sticking up little *i by itself*, *i* against the whole alphabet. But one word with meaning in it is worth the whole alphabet.'[3] It is rather that consciousness draws its objects into itself—or what is the same thing—it attracts them into the world of meaning. It constructs, and since its constructions are warranted by the facts, it sets free meanings inarticulately clutched among the brutality of fact. 'So water and flame, the diamond, the charcoal and the mantling champagne, with its ebullient sparkle, are convoked and fraternised by the theory of the chemist. . . . It is a sense of the principle of connection given by the mind and sanctioned by the correspondency of nature.'[4] In the more commonplace forms of consciousness, the degree of assimilation is comparatively external and accidental: facts are recognised and put together according to some elementary or arithmetical classification. In higher forms of consciousness—Coleridge instances poetry,

[1] *Church and State.*   [2] *Letters*, Vol. I, p. 649.
[3] Ibid., Vol. II, p. 709.   [4] *The Friend*, II, 6.

chemistry, philosophy—the assimilation is much deeper: the facts are more thoroughly modified, more radically organised by some principle or feeling donated by consciousness, more profoundly involved in one another in a more intricate geometry of relationships. The former activity Coleridge called an activity of 'aggregation'; the latter one of 'co-adunation'.

It is this gift of 'co-adunation' we see marvellously at work in so much of Coleridge's work. The most various kinds of human experience leap their boundaries, approach, touch and penetrate. No doubt we should expect such range from 'a library cormorant' who loved chemistry and poetry, metaphysics and facts of the mind, and who also aspired to be a farmer and horticulturist. But the range of material makes the compelling, unifying power all the more striking. Politics and psychology, chemistry and theology, literary criticism and pathology, drug-taking and climbing, social analysis and journalism, education and semantics—these are only some of the categories which, under an irresistible mental inititiative, are 'convoked and fraternised'. They fold into one another, separate, melt again, apply the principles and criteria of one to another, and live like elements under so great a pressure that they are all the time transforming themselves into new and fascinating crystals. The variety is endless but the urge towards unity matches it. It is as though Coleridge, having mastered the plurality of knowledge, having developed the special, separate senses necessary to appreciate blossom, leaves, bark and branches, found everything leading back to a more solid and unquestionable unity and finally down to a single powerful root in the imagination, the source of unity.

Coleridge then was not only a theorist of consciousness but also a master of the art of reflection. Or to put it another way, the qualities we see in his best work are of a sort that fit in with or are the ground of his theory of consciousness. In such places—for example in the passage I quoted earlier about the chase of metaphysical game during the sleepless painful hours—we see the assimilative action of consciousness operating easily and powerfully—the self-moved thrust of the mind, the suffusion of feeling, the liquefaction of boundaries between subjects, the mutual modification of different kinds of experience, the appetite for unity. But Coleridge's work also manifests both the deficiency of his theory of consciousness and the weakness of his practice of the art of reflection. As to the theory, so much stress put upon activity of the mind, however valid it may be intrinsically and however relevant to the times when the theory was constructed, does less than justice to that other element of human nature, which Locke, it may be, over-emphasised but which is none the less permanently part of the human consciousness—the element of passivity, of acceptance. The mind may not be simply a *tabula rasa* or 'a lazy looker-on at an external universe'. Nevertheless it still is in part a *tabula*, in part a spectator, and like these it does wait to be *impressed* by an 'external universe'. (That his theory of knowledge neglected this passive character of the mind, that it did not sufficiently allow for inactivity and habit was, of course, the charge Aristotle levelled at Plato.)

Just as Coleridge's theory of consciousness took too little account of the element of passivity, so his practice of the art of reflection was deficient in rhythm, the rhythm that comes when the mind's initiating activity doesn't interfere with that other part of consciousness where things are simply allowed to happen, when one acquiesces without struggling in a mere flow. And this is the gravamen of Keats's famous observation on what Coleridge lacked: 'I mean *Negative Capability*, that is, when a man is capable of being in uncertainties, mysteries, doubts, without any irritable reaching after fact and reason—Coleridge, for instance, would let go by a fine isolated verisimilitude caught from the Penetralium of mystery, from being incapable of remaining content with half-knowledge'.[1]

The bias in Coleridge's nature towards extremes compelled him to try, indeed to strain to try, to saturate every portion of his experience with consciousness. There are times when consciousness contracts, as it were, to a shorter span even to a single point. For example, in the experience of pain consciousness concentrates almost into primitive perception. But not with Coleridge. There was an occasion in October 1801 that he told Thomas Poole about when he ran a thorn deep into his ankle near the Achilles tendon. It broke off inside and the open wound kept suppurating. 'Whether I exaggerate illness or no, remains to be proved; but this I will venture to say for myself, that there is scarcely a *Woman* in the Island that can endure Pain more quietly than I—tho' the Present

---

[1] *The Letters of John Keats*. Edited by Maurice Buxton Forman, London, 3rd edition, 1947, p. 305.

is scarcely an Instance—for I have had such valuable Lights thrown upon me, with regard to the exceedingly interesting & obscure subject of *Pain*, in consequence of this accident, that I am quite in spirits about it. O! how I *watched* myself while the Lancet was at my leg!—*Vivat Metaphysic!*'[1] This instance shows an admirable amount of toughness, and perhaps a remarkable degree of clinical detachment.[2] But it also shows something excessive and distorted in Coleridge's consciousness, a disposition to force it to go on 'knowing' when it should be simply experiencing. There is also in his description of the incident a slightly too self-conscious note, a touch of staginess.

I am reminded at this point of a comment that Santayana used about Rousseau—'His consciousness was an histrionic thing'.[3] I certainly do not wish to apply to Coleridge anything in these words which savours even faintly of hypocrisy. But there was often in Coleridge what I think we see in this instance of the thorn in the leg, a theatrical quality. This idea, one finds without surprise, Coleridge had anticipated himself. In a strange letter to Poole from Germany on May 6th, 1799, written in a mood of morbid and almost desperate wretchedness, Coleridge describes a suicide pact between a Bohemian subaltern Herlt and his mistress Wilhelmine Pfeifer, brought on Coleridge points out—significantly in view of his own situation—by the impossibility of divorce. He remarks at the end of his account, which includes Wilhelmine Pfeifer's romantic melodramatic last message, that 'in all violent states of *Passion* the mind *acts and plays a part*, itself the actor and the spectator at once!'[4] It is true that Coleridge limits this double activity of the consciousness to conditions of stress. Nevertheless, the comment seems to me to have a very pointed application to Coleridge himself. His own consciousness was that of a man of deep feeling. As he himself said, 'My philosophical opinions are blended with or deduced from my feelings, and this, I think, peculiarises my style of writing'.[5] Reflection itself was for Coleridge 'an intense and burning art'.[6] He even had the notion that he could kill

---

[1] *Letters*, Vol. II, p. 772.
[2] Cf. *Table Talk*.
   'Illness never in the smallest degree affects my intellectual powers. I can *think* with all my ordinary vigour in the midst of pain. . . .'
[3] Santayana, George, *The Life of Reason*, London, 1905, Vol. I, p. 156.
[4] *Letters*, Vol. I, p. 493.   [5] Ibid., Vol. I, p. 279.
[6] Cf. *Table Talk*: a phrase Coleridge used of Ben Jonson.

himself by his impassioned thought: 'there are thoughts that seem to give me a power over my own life. I could kill myself by perseverance in the thought. Mem., to describe as accurately as may be the approximating symptoms'.[1] (His very words are an interesting illustration of his mind as at once actor and spectator of itself.)

Describing his symptoms was a great delight to Coleridge. One has the impression that a substantial part of the science of pathology could be illustrated from the detailed descriptions of his symptoms in his letters. (They are often though not always given, it should be remarked, with a caustic good humour which saves them from being just bits of valetudinarian fuss.) His notebooks as well as his letters are packed with meticulously exact descriptions of psychological states. The generation of thought is as interesting to Coleridge as its meaning, its context as fascinating as its sense. In the pursuit of this kind of completeness Coleridge broke up the continuity of argument, and his own work, his own practice of consciousness, is gravely, and often irritatingly, deficient in the continuity of consciousness which he made so much of in his theory of consciousness. Continuity in his arguments is replaced by a series of brilliant moments separated by mist and obscurity. This was the defect of what I have called the double activity of his consciousness as simultaneously actor and spectator. Its advantage was to make him a superb reporter of complicated and ambivalent states of consciousness. This is one reason why he could reconstruct the experiences of childhood so convincingly in his letters. For it is in childhood that such states first begin to be seen, and particularly among intelligent children. The child bruised with injustice is frequently savouring a delicious sense of pity for his injured self. Here is an example from a letter about his childhood in which we see the self-regarding characteristics of Coleridgean reflection.

Dear Poole

From October 1779 to October 1781.—I had asked my mother one evening to cut my cheese *entire*, so that I might toast it: this was no easy matter, it being a *crumbly* cheese—My mother however did it— / went into the garden for some thing or other, and in the mean time my Brother Frank *minced* my cheese, 'to disappoint the favourite'. I returned, saw the exploit, and in an agony of passion flew at Frank —he pretended to have been seriously hurt by my blow, flung him-

[1] *Anima Poetae.*

self on the ground, and there lay with outstretched limbs—I hung over him moaning & in a great fright—he leaped up, & with a horse-laugh gave me a severe blow in the face—I seized a knife, and was running at him, when my Mother came in & took me by the arm—/I expected a flogging—& struggling from her I ran away, to a hill at the bottom of which the Otter flows—about one mile from Ottery. —There I stayed; my rage died away; but my obstinacy vanquished my fears—& taking out a little shilling book which had, at the end, morning & evening prayers, I very devoutly repeated them—thinking *at the same time* with inward & gloomy satisfaction, how miserable my Mother must be!—I distinctly remember my feelings when I saw a Mr Vaughan pass over the Bridge, at about a furlong's distance—and how I watched the Calves in the fields beyond the river. It grew dark—& I fell asleep—it was towards the latter end of October—& it proved a dreadful stormy night— / I felt the cold in my sleep, and dreamt that I was pulling the blanket over me, & actually pulled over me a dry thorn bush, which lay on the hill—in my sleep I had rolled from the top of the hill to within three yards of the River, which flowed by the unfenced edge of the bottom.—I awoke several times, and finding myself wet & stiff, and cold, closed my eyes again that I might forget it.[1]

There were few matters of principle that Coleridge treated of without 'distinctly remembering his own feelings'. For him questions of principle and matters of personal plight flow in and out of one another all the time. This makes him a magnificent analyst of self but an arguer of defective stamina. Not only was continuity in his arguments interrupted on this ground, but it was further weakened by the very strength of each particular thought. An idea had such force with him that it overthrew, as often as it provoked, the next one.

If one thought leads to another, so often does it blot out another. This I find when having lain musing on my sofa, a number of interesting thoughts having suggested themselves, I conquer my bodily indolence, and rise to record them in these books, alas! my only confidants. The first thought leads me on indeed to new ones; but nothing but the faint memory of having had these remains of the other, which had been even more interesting to me. I do not know whether this be an idiosyncrasy, a peculiar disease, of *my* particular memory—but so it is with *me*—my thoughts crowd each other to death.

[1] *Letters*, Vol. I, pp. 209-10.   [2] *Anima Poetae.*

His thoughts crowded each other to death—yes; but on the other side one has to testify to the power of a mind capable of breeding such a concourse of ideas, and one has to acknowledge too that if his thoughts were crowded to death this was because they had once been so living.

I have spoken, following Keats, of Coleridge's anxiety to be at all times 'knowing', of his impatient desire to soak every fraction of his experience in the pool of consciousness. But this is not to say that his own activity of consciousness had not brought home to him the limitations of consciousness. And I do not simply mean by this that he had his views on states or activities where conscience was inappropriate or impossible, as for example when he said 'the more *consciousness* in our Thoughts and Words, and the less in our Impulses and general Actions, the better and more healthful the state both of head and heart'.[1] I mean not so much the functional limitations of consciousness as its structural limitations. Mental activity is not, Coleridge thought, to be identified with consciousness. Coleridge did not draw this idea, as he might have done, from his mastery of the fleeting logic of poetry, but from his capacity to generalise relevantly from a single mental phenomenon. Here is the passage in which there is implied a strong intuitive sense of the other than conscious areas and activities of the mind.

I feel that there is a mystery in the sudden by-act-of-will-unaided, nay, more than that, frustrated, recollection of a Name. I was trying to recollect the name of a Bristol Friend, who had attended me in my Illness at Mr Wade's. I began with the Letters of the Alphabet— ABC &c.— and I know not why, felt convinced that it began with H. I ran thro' all the vowels, a e i o u y, and with all the consonants to each— Hab, Heb, Hib, Hob, Hub and so on—in vain. I then began other Letters—all in vain. Three minutes afterwards, having completely given it up, the name, Daniel, at once stared up, perfectly insulated, without any the dimmest antecedent connection, as far as my consciousness extended. There is no explanation, ὡς ἐμοιγε δοκει, of this fact, but by a full sharp distinction of Mind from Consciousness—the Consciousness being the narrow *Neck* of the Bottle. The name, Daniel, must have been a living *Atom*-thought in my mind, whose uneasy motions were the craving to recollect it— but the very craving led the mind to a reach (?) which each successive disappointment (—a tiny pain) tended to contract the orifice or *outlet* into Consciousness. Well—it is given up—and all is quiet—the

[1] *Aids to Reflection.*

Nerves are asleep, or off their guard—and then the Name pops up, makes its way, and there it is!—not assisted by any association, but the very contrary—by the suspension and *sedation* of all association.[1]

The figure of consciousness as the neck of a bottle sharply evokes the constriction and the thinness of the layer of consciousness (which we silently contrast with the breadth of reality beyond or 'above it'). But it also calls up the 'height' of consciousness, and by implication the depth of the bottle and the mind. And this together with suggestions of sea-green glass, of light thickening down to opaqueness and of mysterious forces 'without any the dimmest antecedent connection' working subterraneously, indicates the complexity and modernity of Coleridge's picture of the mind. Not that we are confined to hints like this for evidence of Coleridge's insight (and foresight) into the organisation of mind and the limitation of consciousness. Elsewhere in the same religious treatise he writes that anyone who has attended sufficiently to the nature and necessary limits of human consciousness will see that 'the lowest depth that the light of our consciousness can visit even with a doubtful Glimmering, is still at an unknown distance from the Ground'.[2]

As a great writer with an unusual power of reflective analysis, Coleridge was bound to be profoundly interested in language itself. And this interest was reinforced by his concern with consciousness which quite naturally would include not only its nature and structure but its use. But to be interested in the use of consciousness is to be concerned with the instruments of consciousness and, for Coleridge above all, with language. Language organises our experience, keeps it in being, makes it continually accessible, ensures that it is useable and transferable, powerfully helps to form the mind of the individual and the style of a society: its assumptions, its motives and purposes, its working images, its beliefs *and* shibboleths. Words, then, for Coleridge are not simply things. Of course they *are* things with origins, morphology, growth and laws. And no one commended more frequently than Coleridge the value of attention to this aspect of language. 'Accustom yourself to reflect on the words you use, hear or read, their truth, derivation and history.'[3] But they are also *more* than things: 'For if words are not things, they are living powers by which things of the most

---

[1] *The Inquiring Spirit.* Edited by Kathleen Coburn, London, 1951, pp. 30-1.
[2] *Aids to Reflection.*   [3] Ibid., Preface.

importance to mankind are activated, combined and humanised'.[1]
Words are the conduits of consciousness, the means by which consciousness flows on to or irrigates man's environment. And even
this figure treats words too much as objects. Words share in the
living quality of the mind. They make things live. They humanise
reality. Not only are words the means by which consciousness
influences reality; they are also the means by which reality is
brought to bear on us: '. . . for words are no passive Tools, but
organised instruments, re-acting on the Power which inspirits
them'.[2] 'All knowledge', said Coleridge, 'rests on the coincidence
of an object with a subject.'[3] Language exists at the point of coincidence. Perhaps it *is* the point of coincidence. It selects, focuses,
strengthens the play of the external world upon us.

I do not know whether you are opticians enough to understand me
when I speak of a Focus formed by converging rays of Light or
Warmth in the *Air*. Enough that it is so—that the Focus exercises a
power altogether different from that of the rays not converged—
and to our sight and feeling acts precisely as if a solid flesh and blood
reality were there. Now exactly such focal entities we are all more or
less in the habit of creating for ourselves in the world of Thought.
For the given point in the Air takes any given *word*, fancy-image, or
remembered emotion. Thought after Thought, Feeling after Feeling,
and at length the sensations of Touch, and the blind Integer of the
numberless number of the Infinitesimals that make up our sense of
existing, converge in it—and there ensues a working on our mind so
utterly unlike what any one of the confluents, separately considered,
would produce, and no less disparate from what any mere Generaliza-
tion of them all, would present to us, that I do not wonder at the unsatisfactoriness of every attempt to undeceive the person by an
analysis, however clear. The focal word has acquired a *feeling* of
reality—it heats and burns, makes itself be felt. If we do not grasp it,
it seems to grasp us, as with a hand of flesh and blood, and completely
counterfeits an immediate presence, an intuitive knowledge. And
who can reason against an intuition?[4]

Who can reason against an intuition? Who indeed? But Coleridge was undoubtedly one who could reason *from* an intuition.
Language as a focus formed by converging rays is a neat parallel

[1] *Aids to Reflection*, Preface.
[2] *The Inquiring Spirit*. Edited by Kathleen Coburn, London, 1951, p. 102.
[3] *Biographia Literaria*, XII .
[4] *The Inquiring Spirit*. Edited by Kathleen Coburn, London, 1951, p. 101.

to consciousness figured as the narrow neck of a bottle. On each side we see how the original intuition conceived as an image becomes easily and naturally a mode of discursive reasoning. Or to use again Coleridge's own terms, the thought moves from the poetically grasped 'shade of its being' to the philosophically generalised 'law of its being'. The originating impulse in a characteristic train of Coleridgean thought is what he calls some 'realising intuition which exists by and in the act that affirms its existence'.[1] Such an intuition depends not on seeing 'the connections of the parts and their local dependencies' but on sensing 'the whole sustained by a living contact'. Coleridge's arguments, more often than not, are the lucid, and more often than he is credited with, the stringent drawing out of elements densely collected in the initial complex image. A realising intuition of this kind was what Coleridge meant by a principle, which he habitually distinguished from a maxim. 'A maxim is a conclusion upon observation of matters of fact, and is merely retrospective: an Idea, or, if you like, a Principle carries knowledge within itself, and is prospective.'[2] It was by reference to this canon, to such an evolving, progressive style of thought, that Coleridge habitually distinguished kinds of minds. 'It is in the order of Providence that the narrative, generative, constitutive mind—the Kepler—should come first; and then the patient and collective mind—the Newton—should follow.[3]' And though *we* may be surprised to find Newton's name in the second category (although to Coleridge it seemed altogether natural) we can appreciate the general distinction he makes in these words, just as we can when he says 'You will find this a good gauge or criterion of Genius—whether it progresses and evolves, or only spins upon itself'.[4]

Everyone, Coleridge once commented, is born either a Platonist or an Aristotelian. It will already be more than clear to the reader that Coleridge was decidedly on the Platonist side, was in fact directly in line with the Cambridge Platonists, although his Platonism was given some bite and contemporaneity by a Kantian anxiety to define and demarcate especially in the field of the theory of knowledge. I do not think myself that anything is to be gained from making claims for Coleridge as a great philosopher, important though he was in the history of the Idealist movement in

---

[1] *Biographia Literaria*, XII.   [2] *Table Talk*.
[3] Ibid.   [4] Ibid.

Britain and America. Coleridge is much more significant as a great writer who *used* philosophic ideas as symbols for his reading of life than as a great philosopher who also happened to be a distinguished writer. Coleridge represented the sensibility of idealism, what in it is permanently valid and correspondent to elements in a substantial human nature. Idealism in this sense stands for what is active and internal in human consciousness, and for the primacy of this over knowledge deduced from without. 'There are three distinct sources from one or other of which we must derive our arguments whatever the position may be that we wish to support or overthrow. . . . These sources are, 1. transcendental, or anterior to experience, as the grounds without which experience itself could not have been. 2. Subjective, or the experience acquirable by self-observation and composed of facts of inward consciousness, which may be appealed to as assumed to have a place in the minds of other(s) but cannot be demonstrated. Each man's experience is a single and insulated Whole. 3. Common and simultaneous Experience, collectively forming *History* in its widest sense, civil and natural.'[1] The Idealist in Coleridge's sense is one who accepts such an order of priority; the non-idealist begins with 3 and goes back to 1. The Idealist and the non-Idealist stare at each other across a gap of incomprehension and hostility. They are divided by assumptions and purposes, by intellectual instincts and procedures, by a whole habit of mind. This is why to Coleridge the non-Idealist—let us call him the Realist—was deficient in 'the sense, the inward organ' of understanding. 'To such a man philosophy is a mere play of words and notions, like a theory of music to the deaf, or like the geometry of light to the blind . . . (but) with me the act of contemplation makes the thing contemplated, as the geometricians contemplating describe lines correspondent; but I am not describing lines, but simply contemplating, the representative forms of things rise up into existence.'[2]

Such 'idealism' is not in conflict, Coleridge goes on, with 'realism', or at least not with the realism of the ordinary man. It is in conflict only with the philosophical realism which offers us an hypothetical explanation of the origin of our perceptions by asserting that there exists something—what or how or where it isn't known—which occasions the objects of perception. But the

[1] *The Inquiring Spirit.* Edited by Kathleen Coburn, London, 1951, p. 124.
[2] *Biographia Literaria*, XII.

realism of the mass of mankind is very different from this. It is the table itself that the man of common sense believes himself to see, not the appearance of a table from which he can argumentatively deduce the reality of a table, which he does not see. The realism of the ordinary man, believing neither more nor less than that the object which he beholds is the real and very object, is very different from a metaphysical system which 'banishes us to a land of shadows, surrounds us with apparitions, and distinguishes truth from illusion only by the majority of those who dream the same dream. "I asserted that the world was mad," exclaimed poor Lee, "and the world said that I was mad, and confound them, they outvoted me." '[1]

I should like to look at this idealist-realist opposition from another point of view and give the abstract distinction a more personal turn. 'The postulate of philosophy and at the same time the test of philosophic capacity', wrote Coleridge, 'is no other than the heaven-descended KNOW THYSELF.'[2] Or to use a less ecstatic idiom, the spring of Coleridge's conception of idealism is the act of reflection: reflection, a term to which Coleridge by explanation and practice gave as full a meaning as anyone in the language. He habitually contrasted *reflection*—refining the consciousness of self—with *observation*—attending to notices furnished by the senses in order to enlarge our knowledge of the world outside the self; and he argues in several places that the latter gets in the way of the former, that observation can thwart reflection. Clearly this is a danger; certainly more of a danger than that reflection should oust observation; and in our world a positive and present danger. But Coleridge's own work hardly endorses the view that there is some natural antagonism between reflection and observation. It would be hard to find any extended passage, even the most reflective, even the most theologico-metaphysical, which does not include some saving sharpness of detail or angularity of observation, like the wrists scarred from the cat's scratching in his letter to Godwin; and much of his writing is exhilaratingly tightened by the hard presences of actual things.

Perhaps, indeed, his view of the discrepancy between reflection and observation is the consequence of undue theorising. Perhaps, in fact, a degree of self-consciousness, even a high degree, is necessary to clarify the world of objects. Perhaps it needs this to scour them

---

[1] Ibid., XII.   [2] Ibid.

from the greasy film of routine. Skill in reflective self-knowledge, in which there is the most intimate coincidence of subject and object, may be the necessary preliminary to expertness in observation, in which subject and object are comparatively separated. And there are occasions when Coleridge seems to be arguing precisely this. 'Spirits may burn unextinguishably in the pure elementary fire of direct knowledge . . . but our faith resembles sublunary fire that needs the fuel of congruous, though perhaps perishable, notions to call it into actuality.'[1] Or again he argues that he wanted 'to make ideas and realities stand side by side, the one as vivid as the other, even as I have seen in a natural well of translucent water the reflections of the lank weeds, that hung down from its sides, standing upright and like substances, among the substantial water-plants, that were growing on the bottom'.[2]

If Coleridge is arguing that reflections must be fed on the fuel of detail, he certainly supported this view by his own practice, especially in his letters; and his observation of 'realities' in these is as various as it is vivid. He had the romantic's peculiarly direct, implacable eye for the natural landscape. 'We drank tea the night before I left Grasmere, on the Island in that lovely lake, our kettle swung over the fire hanging from the branches of a Fir-tree, and I lay and saw the woods and mountains, and lake all trembling, and as it were *idealized* thro' the subtle smoke which rose up from the clear red embers of the fir-apples, . . .'[3] Or again: 'The river is full, and Lodore is full, and silver-fillets come out of clouds and glitter in every ravine of all the mountains; and the hail lies like snow, upon their tops, and the impetuous gusts from Borrowdale snatch the water up high, and continually at the bottom of the lake it is not distinguishable from snow slanting before the wind—and under this seeming snowdrift the sunshine *gleams*, and over all the nether half of the lake it is *bright* and dazzles, a cauldron of melted silver boiling'.[4]

I have referred before to his sophisticated sense for the character of a town, but he also had a marvellously exact vision for other artefacts, as in these notes on painting.

Observe the remarkable difference between Claude and Teniers in their power of painting vacant space. Claude makes his whole landscape a *plenum*: the air is quite as substantial as any other part of the

[1] *Letters*, Vol. II, p. 1194.   [2] Ibid., Vol. II, p. 1000.
[3] Ibid., Vol. II, p. 612.   [4] Ibid., Vol. II, p. 871.

scene. Hence there are no true distances, and everything presses at once and equally upon the eye. There is something close and almost suffocating in the atmosphere of some of Claude's sunsets. Never did any one paint air, the thin air, the absolutely apparent vacancy between object and object, so admirably as Teniers. That picture of the Archers exemplifies this excellence. See the distances between those ugly louts! how perfectly true to the fact![1]

His rapacious eye for detail fell as promptly on humanity as on places. Here are two observations on Wordsworth's strange self-centred nature. 'I saw him more and more benetted in hypochondriacal Fancies, living wholly among *Devotees*—having every the minutest thing, almost his very eating and drinking, done for him by his Sister, or Wife, and I trembled lest a Film should rise and thicken on his moral eye.'[2] 'Of all the men I ever knew, Wordsworth has the least femineity in his mind. He is *all* man. He is a man of whom it might have been said,—"It is good for him to be alone." '[3]

There can be different kinds of observation, depending on where the observer stands on the long line between complete engagement and total detachment. Coleridge could be clinically detached especially when he himself was the object of his observation. The reader will remember how he explained to the Gillmans that he was perfectly capable of acting a lie for the sake of laudanum, or how coolly he examined his festering leg with the lancet in it. But it was more common in him, as it is in most people, for observation to be of a more imaginative, identifying kind. His habitual attitude was that of the engaged, participant observer. There is in most of us an emphatic faculty which causes us to fling ourselves outward into the shape and posture of what we are observing. In Coleridge this faculty was highly developed, as though to keep in check his bias towards intense self-analysis. And it may well be that these two elements in human nature are correlative rather than exclusive. 'One travels along with the lives of a mountain. Years ago I wanted to make Wordsworth sensible of this. How fine is Keswick vale! Would I repose, my soul lies and is quiet upon the broad level vale. Would it act? it darts up into the mountain-top like a Kite, and like a chamois-goat runs along the ridge—or like a boy that makes a sport on the road of running

[1] *Table Talk.*   [2] *Letters*, Vol. II, p. 888.
[3] *The Inquiring Spirit.* Edited by Kathleen Coburn, London, 1951, p. 296.

along a wall or narrow fence!'[1] When distress or injustice was in question, Coleridge was still less the spectator of the scene, still more an actor in the play. His humanity flew to the rescue of another's, even while he tries to be temperate and understanding towards a viewpoint he finds repulsive.

> It is *wrong*, Southey! for a little girl with a half-famished sickly baby in her arms to put her head in at the window of our inn—'Pray give me a bit of bread and meat!' from a party dining on lamb, green peas and salad. Why? Because it is *impertinent* and *obtrusive*. 'I am a gentleman! and wherefore the clamorous voice of woe intrude upon mine ear?' My companion is a man of cultivated though not vigorous understanding; his feelings are all on the side of humanity; yet such are the unfeeling remarks, which the lingering remains of aristocracy occasionally prompt.[2]

There is so much, such extreme, vitality in the movement of Coleridge's mind that it sometimes becomes positively oppressive. It is as though he inherited a more angelic universe, or at least that he breathed a purer oxygen than our lungs can cope with. And yet it still seems to me that when due allowance is made for the special vitality of genius, the action of Coleridge's mind—its general pattern and direction—is much more distinctively human than peculiarly Coleridgean. It belongs to the character of the human mind—not just to Coleridge—to initiate, to modify, to extricate unity from the chaos of experience. This is what we are all doing, most effectively it is true in our most reflective moments, but also, though sluggishly and clumsily, in our long periods of more routine living.

Unity—the necessity for it, the nature of it—was one of Coleridge's consistent concerns. Nor was the importance he gave it simply an intellectual conviction arrived at by 'severe analysis' and expressed in 'naked language'. He spoke of it always in an ardent and feeling way. 'My heart burns to concentrate my free mind to the affinities of the feelings with words and ideas. . . .'[3] And the more disorganised his personal life, the more jumbled his relationships, the more frantic his schemes, the more passionately he urged the necessity of unity. His preoccupation with it clearly had emotional and compensatory motives. This was something which Coleridge understood about himself. I have already quoted

---

[1] *Anima Poetae.*   [2] Ibid., Vol. I, pp. 83-4.
[3] Ibid., Vol. II, p. 671.

his remark, 'My philosophical opinions are blended with or deduced from my feelings, and this, I think, peculiarises my style of writing . . .'.[1] While this characteristic may peculiarise his literary style, the habit of drawing thought from feeling surely brings his human and personal style much closer to that of the general run of human beings, whose ideas are like Coleridge's at least in not being derived from a purely intellectual source, but from the more concrete and inclusive life of feeling. Moreover, Coleridge's appetite for unity, while it is, no doubt, characteristically Coleridgean in being so conscious and intense, is also perhaps no more than a Coleridgean version of a general human hunger. We all strive towards unity. We all struggle for identity, the most intimate kind of unity there is, and we all try, not only for some viable structure of self but also for some degree of coherence in our beliefs. It may only be a vague anxiety in ourselves and in Coleridge an articulate passion, but fundamentally it is the same thing.

When I say that Coleridge's quest for unity had 'compensatory' motives, I hope I shall not be taken as endorsing the notion—which the rather dented psychological term 'compensatory' will be bound to suggest—that there is in any significant way something distorted or pathological in Coleridge's preoccupation. It was natural for Coleridge, integral with the structure of his character, that he should be so concerned. Not only did it issue from a common human source, but it was pressed upon Coleridge by the scale and variety of his gifts, and above all by the conjunction in his nature of philosophical and poetic powers. The desire for unity was a function of the scope of his nature. More limited men face no such problem of mitigating divisive forces; limper energies do not call anything like so imperiously for reconciliation. But for Coleridge with gifts so distinct and powerful, so apt of themselves to break apart, it meant an extreme and sustained effort of reconciliation: an effort of the kind he wrote about—in something of a syntactical flurry—to Godwin. '. . . if the cluster of ideas which contribute our identity, do ever connect and unite themselves with a great whole; if feelings could ever propagate themselves without the servile ministration of undulating air or reflected light—I seem to feel within myself a strength and power of desire that might start a modifying impulse on a whole theatre.'[2] Much of Coleridge's work extending over many years is devoted in a

[1] Ibid., Vol. I, p. 279.   [2] Ibid., Vol. I, p. 624.

wandering and haphazard way to exploring the intimations of these words. And they do indeed hint at many of the significant elements in Coleridge's idea of writing which I have tried to specify. To follow him faithfully would require quotations on a gigantic, impossible scale. It would also mean rehearsing every start, every flight, whether soaring or butterfly-like, every tumble and lurch of his swerving volatile mind; and I am aware that I have had to use a degree of abstract violence to abridge all this dispersed and complicated movement.

I have said more than once—perhaps too often—that the gifts of Coleridge's nature are, for all their intensity and power, the gifts of a substantial human nature. And this is the final impression I take from his work: that his mind was not bizarre or distorted, but in a profound way, fully and generously human—sane as well as brilliant, central as well as extreme. And if it is true, as his letters show all too plainly that it is, that he 'followed the vocation of the ruined man', this surely is a route we all take too, even though ours may not be as savage as Coleridge's. So that when Coleridge claims we can find in his work 'a sketch of the rudiments of self-construction',[1] I believe it is a sketch we can all understand, and a self we are all concerned with. The rudiments of self-construction are these primary human activities of observation and reflection. In his writings we see a great master exercising these human skills. We see them out there in Coleridge but also as a kind of revelation in ourselves. For they show us what Coleridge described to Byron as 'that balance of thought and feeling, of submission and mastery; that one sole unfleeting music which is never of yesterday, but still remaining reproduces *itself*, and powers akin to itself in the minds of other men'.[1]

[1] *Letters*, Vol. IV, p. 767.   [2] Ibid., Vol. IV, pp. 559-60.

Chapter II

COLERIDGE AND CRITICISM

COLERIDGE was a critic wth a poet inside him and a philosopher on his back. He had a wonderfully just, living, inexplicably *right* sense of what went on in a literary work—a fine instinct for the molecular architecture of a poem; he also had a rare power for discerning and formulating relevant principles. What he hadn't got, except on occasion, was anything more than an edgy truce between these two. So that *the* critical problem was almost sharper for Coleridge than for anyone else; and this problem (assuming the critic's primary qualification for the activity—and Coleridge, everyone agrees, was incomparably well qualified) this problem is that of moving from the particular response to the relevant judgment, and back again. In this kind of relationship it is always possible for the abstract either to debilitate or to distort the concrete, and given Coleridge's nature, more than possible that it will be the philosopher who will dumbfound the poet rather than the poet who will throttle the philosopher. Beyond the point of initial equipment, the critical problem is one of passage and transition: a problem of method. Among English critics the greatest master of critical method in this sense was Mathew Arnold; and no one has bettered the decorous and easy grace, the unfought-for balance and control with which he performs the tight-rope walk between response and principle and between principle and response. In Coleridge's writings the position of the critic on the line between literary fact and critical judgment is more tense; and there is always the possibility that he will topple into the disaster of abstraction.

If I use the word 'topple', that is to indicate a certain helplessness, a certain passivity, on Coleridge's part in the transition from response to generalisation and back again; but there has to be a degree of equality (as well as relevance), even a kind of democratic consultation, between the two sides. When one is conscious of something going wrong in Coleridge's criticism it is rarely because of a failure of understanding or sensitivity, but much more often because the generalising side, once it begins to work, assumes too much of an imperious and imperial character. The response then becomes not the source of the generalisation but an illustration of it; the generalisation not the consequence of the response but its governor. The generalisation takes on its own life and begins to breed its own examples. Or it begins to drill and bully the unruly individuals into an abstract order. 'Here the great safeguard,' said Mathew Arnold with just this in mind, 'is never to let oneself become abstract, always to retain an intimate and lively sense of the truth of what one is saying, and the moment this fails us, to be sure that something is wrong.'[1] It is seldom that Coleridge's consciousness, or its expression, fails in liveliness. It is in intimacy that it is apt to falter, in the intimacy, that is, between response and generalisation. The generalisation draws away from the response, moves up to a higher status and, upsetting the law of relative equality or indirect influence, begins to govern directly.

In the following remarks—and they were remarks, spoken comments—on Gibbon, one sees, I think, both kinds of generalisation, the one which is intimate with its source, and the one which is detached from it.

Gibbon's style is detestable, but his style is not the worst thing about him. His history has proved an effectual bar to all real familiarity with the temper and habits of imperial Rome. Few persons read the original authorities, even those which are classical; and certainly no distinct knowledge of the actual state of the empire can be obtained from Gibbon's rhetorical sketches. He takes notice of nothing but what may provide an effect; he skips on from eminence to eminence, without even taking you through the valleys between: in fact, his work is little else but a disguised collection of all the splendid anecdotes which he could find in any book concerning any persons or nations from the Antonines to the capture of Constantinople. When I read a chapter in Gibbon I seem to be looking through a luminous haze or fog; figures come and go, I know not how or why, all larger than life, or distorted or discoloured; nothing is real, vivid, true: all is scenical, and as it were, exhibited by candle-light. And then to call it a History of the Decline and Fall of the Roman Empire! Was there ever a greater misnomer? I protest I do not remember a single philosophical attempt made throughout the work to fathom the ultimate causes of the decline and fall of that empire. How miserably deficient is the narrative of the important reign of Justinian. And that poor scepticism, which Gibbon mistook for Socratic philosophy, has

---

[1] *The Function of Criticism.*

led him to mis-state and mistake the character and influence of Christianity in a way which even an avowed infidel or atheist would not and could not have done. Gibbon was a man of immense reading; but he had no philosophy; and he never fully understood the principle upon which the best of the old historians wrote. He attempted to imitate their artificial construction of the whole work—their dramatic ordonnance of the parts—without seeing that their histories were intended more as documents illustrative of the truths of political philosophy than as mere chronicles of events.[1]

In this passage, casual and incidental as it is, one yet senses— no doubt in a rudimentary and unfinished way—characteristic touches of Coleridge's critical habit. It is a rapid but not unrevealing sketch. There is the primary capacity which all fine critics have of speaking as though from a privileged position inside the text, of being immediately aware of the unique activity going on there. '. . . I seem to be looking through a luminous haze of fog . . . figures come and go, I know not how or why, all larger than life, or distorted or discoloured . . . all is scenical and . . . exhibited by candle-light'. The phrases delineate exactly and nimbly Gibbon's theatrical groupings of marble statuary as well as the mistily rhetorical contexts in which the figures are posed, Gibbon's substitutes for connections and relationships. And then the judgment, its substance implicit in the texture of Gibbon's feeling and sanctioned by the reader's experience, but now drawn out and exposed, its fibres separated but not torn away: 'And that poor scepticism, which Gibbon mistook for Socratic philosophy, has led him to mis-state and mistake the character and influence of Christianity in a way which even an avowed infidel or atheist would not and could not have done'. How apt this is for the self-congratulatory and portentous backing Gibbon supposed himself to have had. Gibbon's certainties melt into plausibilities, his social assurance—a matter of gait and posture, of personality as much as of conviction—puffs into individual pretension, and the admired ironic analysis turns into something more facile and more thrilling, the pleasure and the melodrama of knocking the establishment.

So far, I should have said, so good. But then one finds oneself beginning to bristle a bit at 'I protest I do not remember a single philosophical attempt made throughout the work to fathom the

[1] *Table Talk.*

ultimate causes of the decline or fall of that empire'. *Philosophy, fathom, ultimate* ... perhaps these terms are used to suggest a scale by which we can measure the superficiality and bias of Gibbon's explanations but they carry with them a worrying notion— worrying to the admirer of Coleridge the Critic, that is—of some philosophically pure excavation of some philosophically absolute cause. The statement a moment later, 'Gibbon was a man of immense reading; but he had no philosophy' is at first reassuring: it brings this whole portentous question of philosophy back to the point where it means not bemoaning the lack in Gibbon of some neat, inclusive metaphysical doctrine but, much more modestly, appreciating the inadequacy of Gibbon's intellectual categories for the work he had in hand. He was deficient not in the perfection of absolute theory but in the efficiency, in the scope and point of his analytical ideas. And just here when one is giving Coleridge the benefit of the doubt, just when he seems to be recovering his critical poise, at this point he clashes his discordant cymbals. '... their histories were intended more as documents illustrative of the truths of political philosophy than as mere chronicles of events.' Well, perhaps they were, or some of them, anyway. But it is clear that Coleridge is not simply stating a fact; he is announcing a criterion. That word 'mere' puts events and chronicles in their place which is well below the dignity of principle and 'the truths of political philosophy'.

Nor can Coleridge's contention here be justified on the ground that he is attacking in Gibbon the presence of so many facts unquickened by principle. He is not just objecting, as for example Henry James did in fiction, to detail which has no emblematic function, to 'presence without type'; nor is he claiming like Santayana that the facts of existence are simply facts, no more than 'cacklings of an inexhaustible garrulity' until they become symbols. Both these writers start from the undeniable solidity of fact, whereas for Coleridge in this mood a fact is no more than a derivation from a principle. It is thin and empty and gets all this reality from the principle it illustrates. It does not exist in its own right. It is simply the shadow of a principle or the image of the *a priori*.

But when his critical instinct was not made servile by the bullying of abstractions, Coleridge had a superlative sense of literary fact. He had, even when his own personal predilection was absent, that easy, intimate access to the interior of the work, that special quality of imaginative inwardness which is one of the two great qualities of the finest critics. Because the critic in practising his art performs a double activity. On the one hand, all his resources of perception intensely engaged, all his energies of discernment braced, he attends to the object of criticism with patience and self-restraint: everything in him is bent to respond with purity and relevance. On the other hand, he summons his own apprehension of that body of values called in the past—even by Hume—the Laws of Taste, and by the *Calendar of Modern Letters*—simply—the Standards of Criticism.

The merit of criticism depends then not just on the critic's fineness of tact or the deftness of his analysis but as much on the reality of his possession, the sureness of his grasp, of these standards. 'The strength of applied irony', said Henry James, and the same is true of criticism, 'is surely in the sincerities, the lucidities, the utilities that stand behind it.' 'These postulates, these animating presences' cannot be specified or codified. But if they are not regulations or laboratory gauges, neither are they arbitrary or chaotic. It is true that the accidents of time and circumstance always exert their formidable influence, that personal predilection and the configuration of talent make for individuality and difference. But none of these is determinative, and the surprising thing is not the variety of difference and originality among great critics but the degree of their consent. Particular judgments may be discrepant, although not nearly so often as the devotees of utter relativity in taste would have us believe, but the grounds for these judgments exhibit, in spite of changing idioms, a singular unanimity. In fundamental matters great critics belong to one party.

In distinguishing response and judgment like this I am separating the inseparable since these two flow in and out of one another in an intricate, unflawed unity. They are the one activity at different points in its growth. The response is the ground of the judgment and the judgment prepares for the response. But they *are* distinct emphases in a single act, and it does help on occasion to think of them as being at some distance from one another. Having made this qualification (and having issued this warning to myself) I should like now to adduce some examples of characteristic Coleridgean responses and judgments.

Here, to begin with, is part of Coleridge's reaction to the *Divina Commedia*.

You cannot read Dante without feeling a gush of manliness of thought within you. Dante was very sensible of his own excellence in this particular, and speaks of poets as guardians of the vast armory of language, which is the intermediate something between matter and spirit. Indeed there was a passion and a miracle of words in the twelfth and thirteenth centuries, after the long slumber of language in barbarism, which gave an almost romantic character, a virtuous quality and power, to what was read in a book, independently of the thoughts and images contained in it. This feeling is very often perceptible in Dante. . . . Consider the wonderful profoundness of the whole third canto of the Inferno; and especially of the inscription over Hell Gate: 'Per me si va' etc., which can only be explained by a meditation on the true nature of religion; that is—reason plus the understanding. I say profoundness rather than sublimity; for Dante does not so much elevate your thoughts as send them down deeper. In this canto all the images are distinct, are even vividly distinct; but there is a total impression of infinity; the wholeness is not in vision or conception, but in an inner feeling of totality, and absolute being.[1]

Even in this concentrated report there are flecks and hints of a more wayward Coleridge. There is a touch of the messianic in the 'true nature of religion', and one of Coleridge's great philosophical distinctions, reason versus understanding, is growing quietly in the undergrowth.

In spite of these distracting touches of the natural man, Coleridge still succeeds in registering boldly the deepest impression Dante makes on the unprejudiced reader, namely that extraordinary combination of power and clarity, masculinity and exactness. 'The poet as the guardian of the vast armory of language', the passion and the miracle of words', 'virtuous quality and power': each of these phrases contributes a note to a precise, powerful chord. At the same time Coleridge defines with a kind of loving accuracy the means—Dante's technique of light—by which trains of lucid images lead (not up towards some vague empyrean) but down (and yet not down into any turbid depths) further and further down into a crystalline universe of pure being. Coleridge understands how detail in Dante leads directly to the ultimate, to a world which is hard but mysterious, intense but complete.

[1] *Lectures on Shakespeare*, X.

Similarly he saw (and felt) how the poetry in Shakespeare is structurally, organically dramatic. Poetry was not a pleasing addition to the theatre, nor the drama simply an occasion for the poetry. It was to the living identity of the two that Coleridge responded; just as he responded to the oceanic energy of a mind which realised itself naturally through this form, and which subdued everything it included and everything it touched to its own rhythm. '. . . we find undoubted proof in his mind of imagination, or the power by which one image or feeling is made to modify many others and by a sort of *fusion to force many into one*—that which after shewed itself in such might and energy in *Lear*, where the deep anguish of a father spreads the feeling of ingratitude and cruelty over the very elements of heaven.'[1] Coleridge was, if not the father, at least some relative located among the various rôles of god-, step-, and founding-father to the nineteenth-century tradition of interpreting a Shakespearean play as a set of biographical studies of historical characters: a tradition which made 'character' into the fundamental organising concept in a play and which ended by reading the plays (reading was always conceived of as the one appropriate means of access to Shakespeare) as a kind of fodder for biographical sympathy and detective skill. Coleridge has received his due measure of the rejection, the rather contemptuous rejection, which this nineteenth-century habit has received from modern critics. Not, indeed, that it has not been replaced by something equally abstract and almost as inadequate to Shakespearean complexity. Chains of detached images, common mythical elements, constellations of metaphors—our current truck with these things is not much more than the substitution of one abstraction for another. It may even be that the concept of character has in it a kind of stability and density which makes it less inadequate as a device for measuring the scope of Shakespearean reality than the tenuous, delicate smoke of myth. Certainly critics have some justification for the view that Coleridge's study of *Hamlet* draws more upon Coleridge's psychology than upon Shakespeare's play, although it is only fair to say that after Coleridge has pointed out in Hamlet's character the prevalence of the abstracting and generalising habit over the practical, he jots down in his own copy of Shakespeare the rather rueful observation, 'I have a smack of Hamlet in myself, if I may say so'. Much more than a smack of

[1] *Literary Remains of S. T. Coleridge.* 4 Vols, 1836-39, II, 53-60.

this Hamlet, certainly, would I think be the current opinion. But there is no narcissistic softness in his crisply cogent commentary on the opening of Hamlet. It is a nervously active report, sharp with detail and aware in a nimble, quick-footed way of all that is going on. Words, feeling, action, setting, present themselves to his quick eye. And he is conscious below all the modifying, subtly related detail of the great organism beginning to come to life.

Compare the easy language of common life in which this drama opens, with the wild wayward lyric of the opening of *Macbeth*. The language is familiar: no poetic descriptions of night, no elaborate information conveyed by one speaker to another of what both had before their immediate perceptions (such as the first distich in Addison's *Cato*,[1] which is a translation into poetry of 'Past four o'clock, and a damp morning')—yet nothing bordering on the comic on the one hand, and no striving of the intellect on the other. It is the language of *sensation* among men who feared no charge of effeminacy for feeling what they felt no want of resolution to bear. Yet the armour, the dead silence, the watchfulness that first interrupts it, the welcome relief of guard, the cold, the broken expressions as of a man's compelled attention to bodily feelings allowed no man, —all excellently accord with and prepare for the after gradual rise into a tragedy the interest of which is eminently *ad et apud intra*, as *Macbeth* . . . is *ad extra*.

The preparation *informative* of the audience [is] just as much as was precisely necessary: how gradual first, and with the uncertainty appertaining to a question—

What, has *this thing* appeared *again* to-night.

Even the word 'again' has its *credibilizing* effect. Then the representative of the ignorance of the audience, Horatio (not himself but [quoted by] Marcellus to Bernardo) anticipates the common solution, ''tis but our phantasy'. But Marcellus rises secondly into '[this] dreaded sight'. Then this 'thing' becomes at once an 'apparition', and that too an intelligent spirit that is to be *spoken* to.

Tush, tush! 'twill not appear.

Then the shivery feeling, at such a time, with two eye-witnesses, of sitting down to hear a story of a ghost, and this, too, a ghost that had appeared two nights before [at] about this time. The effort of the narrator to master his own imaginative terrors; the consequent elevation of the style, itself a continuation of this effort; the turning off to an *outward* object, 'yon same star'. O heaven! words are wasted

[1] The dawn is over-cast, the morning lours,
And heavily in clouds brings on the day.

58

to those that feel and to those who do not feel the exquisite judgement of Shakespeare. Hume himself could not but have faith in *this* Ghost dramatically, let his anti-ghostism be as strong as Samson against ghosts less powerfully raised.[1]

This sensitively relevant commentary ratifies for a given scene the philosopher Samuel Alexander's acute observation that Shakespeare did not invent *Hamlet* but discovered it in the language. The idea that the language is both the ground and seed of the play runs throughout the whole piece. It begins in the 'easy language of common life'; it is conducted in 'the language of sensation among men who fear no charge of effeminacy . . .'; the effect of 'the armor, the dead silence, the watchfulness that first interrupts it, the relief of guard, the cold . . .' is established when it becomes articulate in 'the broken expressions as of a man's compelled attention to bodily feelings allowed no man'. It is the activating force of language, Coleridge demonstrates, which is the natural base for a dramatic action in Shakespeare: 'even the word "again" has its *credibilizing* effect'; 'this "thing" becomes an apparition and that too an intelligent spirit that has to be *spoken* to'. Then out of language and action, out of their tension and alliance comes the other thing Coleridge chooses to emphasise, that which is implicit in and sanctioned by language in action, namely the growth of feeling, or rather the delicate adjustments among the many feelings playing with and against one another, balancing one another to compose a characteristic *Hamlet* sensibility.

This is Coleridge's deft and particularised response to a single scene. But he also had a gift for framing the evocative or summoning summary, or the statement which was representative of all his feelings to a body of work. Such a statement is not an abstract digest or a rule of law or thumb, but something distilled and blended by manifold experience. In it one finds selected as though by an infallible instinct the constitutive quality of a writer's work. Who can say more, more shortly, about Swift than 'Swift was *anima Rabelaissii habitans in sicco*—the soul of Rabelais dwelling in a dry place'?[2] Or what hint could be more telling as to the moral impression made by Sterne than this? 'There is a great deal of affectation in Sterne, to be sure; but still the characters of Trim and the two Shandies are most individual and delightful. Sterne's

---

[1] From Coleridge's notes on his copy of Shakespeare.   [2] *Table Talk.*

morals are bad, but I don't think they can do much harm to any one whom they would not find bad enough before. Besides, the oddity and erudite grimaces under which much of his dirt is hidden take away the effect for the most part.'[1] And there were even occasions when one of the great Coleridgean distinctions—in this case the reason-understanding dichotomy—muted, it is true, subordinated to perception and less explicit and thrusting than usual, helped rather than hindered him in refining his exact response to a particular work, as for example when he said of Don Quixote—

> 'Don Quixote is not a man out of his senses, but a man in whom the imagination and the pure reason are so powerful as to make him disregard the evidence of sense when it opposed their conclusions. Sancho is the common sense of the social man-animal, unenlightened and unsanctified by the reason. You see how he reverences his master at the very time he is cheating him.[2]

Coleridge's analysis of Wordsworth—not to speak of his deadly treatment of Wordsworth's heavily unconvincing theory of diction—is probably definitive even though it is cast in a curiously antique eighteenth-century pattern of pro and con, fault and beauty. He speaks of Wordsworth's poetry from the inside with very special authority, almost indeed as a co-creator. But the point I wish to remind the reader of here is Coleridge's capacity for feeling and defining the inward individuality of Wordsworth's poetry. He had the most intimate sense of that strange combination of Wordsworthian qualities which he specified as 'austere purity of language', 'weight and sanity of the thoughts and sentiments', 'sinewy strength and originality', 'meditative pathos', 'and the sympathy . . . of a contemplator'. In particular he had the most intimate sense of the profoundly *natural*, subterranean imagination of Wordsworth working away at the roots of being. In two passages of highly figurative language, one at the beginning, one at the end of his study of Wordsworth in *Biographia Literaria*, in which the images signify a deeply personal response, Coleridge expresses this extraordinarily geological or cosmic quality, this mineral simplicity of Wordsworth's sensibility:

> . . . there is an harshness and acerbity connected and combined with words and images all a-glow, which might recall these products of

---

[1] *Table Talk.*　　　　　　　　　　[2] Ibid.

the vegetable world, where gorgeous blossoms rise out of the hard
and thorny rind and shell, within which the rich fruit was elaborating.[1]

The other passage, which, though Coleridge's comment is not
even in his own words, precedes that peculiarly Coleridgean and,
I think, distinctly inappropriate ambition for Wordsworth—that
he should write the first genuine philosophic poem in the language.

> The following analogy will, I am apprehensive, appear dim and
> fantastic, but in reading Bartram's Travels I could not help trans-
> cribing the following lines as a sort of allegory, or connected simile
> and metaphor of Wordsworth's intellect and genius.—'The soil is a
> deep, rich, dark mould, on a deep stratum of tenacious clay; and that
> on a foundation of rocks, which often break through both strata,
> lifting their back above the surface. The trees which chiefly grow
> here are the gigantic black oak; magnolia magni-floria; fraxinus
> excelsior; platane; and a few stately tulip trees.'[2]

My fear that in distinguishing response and judgment I was
struggling to separate the inseparable has proved only too well
founded. There are shades and shadings of 'judgment', the reader
will have observed, in such of the 'responses' I have cited. Not that
there is anything unexpected in that. A literary response is a total
response, or as near to it as a reader can come. He brings to it all
that he is, not only his immediate apprehension and sensitivity
but also those crucial stabilities and regularities which are the
grounds of his preferences. And preference, or at least a disposition
towards it, whether instinctive or cultivated, is implicit in our
response; it is folded into our appreciation of difference, and the
appreciation of difference is a constituent of our seeing the work of
literature as it is. Seeing the work as it is in its own single existence
means seeing it marked off from other works, or at least, and more
vaguely, as an organisation standing out from the language in
which its roots are bedded. It means seeing its *difference*, 'the
indelible something' which makes its individuality stand out in a
plurality of similar or related things. Difference is the matrix of
judgment. The whole act of response encloses the partial one of
choice. Or to put the emphasis differently, the effect of judgment
issues from the cause of response. We cannot be completely free
and utterly neutral. Just as our most primitive experience, our

---

[1] *Biographia Literaria*, IV.   [2] Ibid., XX; and cf. *Notebooks*, p. 926.

sensations themselves, carries with it the colours of our conceptions and the stain of our past lives, so our response to a literary work is affected, made easier or more awkward, made possible or even impossible, by the cluster of concepts and experiences, the 'animating presences' of Henry James, which control or influence or qualify our lives. A literary response is an alliance, a marriage, a quarrel, a love affair between the 'difference' of the object and the 'difference' of the subject. It is an activity and a construction. It is passive, or more properly disciplined, in the sense that the reader must subdue his own more pronounced quirks and angularity and give the work its chance to turn its influence on him. But it is also creative and originating and subjective. The reader acts and his action is completed or consummated in judgment.

I should like to consider now one of the most sustained and coherent of Coleridge's 'judgments', the famous passage in *Biographia Literaria* in which Coleridge, it will be remembered, undertook to elucidate 'the specific symptoms of poetic power . . . in a critical analysis of Shakespeare's *Venus and Adonis*, and *Lucrece*'. Some might hold this intention to be too generalised a purpose, but in the working out of it Coleridge shows himself to be so exquisitely in touch with the texture and life of the poems that he is never in danger of seeming to use the poetry as a mere occasion for meditation of his own. Nothing, no theoretical membrane, not even the most delicate film of 'philosophy' separates him from the moving life of the poem. And it is this movement which Coleridge, significantly enough, chooses to comment on first. (I shall give as much of the passage as I can, but my space will allow me to quote it only in a fragmentary and interrupted form).

> In the 'Venus and Adonis', the first and most obvious excellence is the perfect sweetness of the versification; its adaptation to the subject; and the power displayed in varying the march of the words without passing into a loftier and more majestic rhythm than was demanded by the thoughts, or permitted by the propriety of preserving a sense of melody predominant. The delight in richness and sweetness of sound; even to a faulty excess, if it be evidently original, and not the result of an easily imitable mechanism, I regard as a highly favourable promise in the compositions of a young man. 'The man that hath not music in his soul' can indeed never be a genuine poet. . . . But the sense of musical delight, with the power of reducing

multitude into unity of effect, and modifying a series of thoughts by some one predominant thought or feeling, may be cultivated and improved, but can never be learned. It is in these that 'poeta nascitur not fit'.[1]

Rhythm is the inmost quality of art and the first signal of life. Poetic rhythm has its biological origins and equivalents: it is the disposition of language which corresponds to man's unfolding, serial existence and to the profound rhythms, circulating, pulsing, breathing, which order his physical life. Rhythm is the one un-fakeable organic thing: others may be worked for or affected, images, ideas, feelings and even Coleridge claims 'their combination and intertexture' in a poem; but the sense of musical delight, with the power of producing it is a gift of imagination . . . [it] may be cultivated and improved, but can never be learned'. Rhythm is, as it were, the way poetry breathes, and one can no more get it up than one can learn to breathe by studying a textbook of physiology. Perhaps for the more acrid modern taste there is a touch too much molasses in Coleridge's terms for this original organic power —'perfect sweetness of the versification', 'richness and sweetness of sound', 'music in the soul', 'the sense of musical delight'. Still, as used by Coleridge, the phrases were free of the accretions and confectionery with which they have been sugared over by so much minor verse and criticism. In any case Coleridge's words certainly formulate the right impression of candid, youthful lyricism given by the verse in *Venus and Adonis*.

In this context, the terms are strictly relevant; and it is this, in fact, the relevance of rhythm in Shakespeare's poems, the fineness of its 'propriety' and 'adaptation' and not simply its buoyant presence that Coleridge is pointing to as proof of Shakespeare's poetic promise. 'Propriety' in *Venus and Adonis* required a comparatively narrow range of effect, with 'a sense of melody predominant' and no 'passing into a loftier and more majestic rhythm than was demanded by the thoughts'. And yet even in this restricted span Shakespeare displays something of that power 'in varying the march of the words' that was to become an endless command of rhythm, a limitless subtlety of movement and stress; even here there are hints and miniature promises of the slipping and flowing, the gliding and tumult of the Shakespearean ocean.

[1] *Biographia Literaria*, XV.

It is the natural power of producing variety and relevance of rhythm that Coleridge offers as the first symptom of a genuine poetic gift. But there is a rhythm of the whole as well as a rhythm of the parts, a rhythm which collects and concentrates the dispersed, fragmentary modulations of each phase into a total rhythm, of *Lear* or *Hamlet* or *The Tempest*. And this is because rhythm, both local and general, is a constituent of meaning, of the inclusive theme of the play and all its particular manifestations. 'His rhythm is so perfect,' Coleridge says elsewhere, 'that you may be almost sure that you do not understand the real force of a line, if it does not run well as you read it.'[1] This is part of that power of 'reducing multitude into unity of effect and modifying a series of thoughts by some one predominant thought or feeling', which also 'may be cultivated and improved but can never be learned'. This also is 'a gift of imagination.'

A second promise of genius [Coleridge goes on], is the choice of subjects very remote from the private interests and circumstances of the writer himself. At least I have found that where the subject is taken immediately from the author's personal sensations and experiences, the excellence of a particular poem is but an equivocal mark, and often a fallacious pledge, of genuine poetic power. . . . In the *Venus and Adonis* this proof of poetic power exists even to excess. It is throughout as if a superior spirit more intuitive, more intimately conscious, even than the characters themselves, not only of every outward look and act, but of the flux and reflux of the mind in all its subtlest thoughts and feelings, were placing the whole before our view; himself meanwhile unparticipating in the passions, and actuated only by that pleasurable excitement, which had resulted from the energetic fervour of his own spirit in so vividly exhibiting, what it had so accurately and profoundly contemplated. I think, I should have conjectured from these poems, that even then the great instinct, which impelled the poet to the drama, was secretly working in him, prompting him by a series and never broken chain of imagery, always vivid, and because unbroken, often minute; by the highest effort of the picturesque in words, of which words are capable, higher perhaps than was ever realized by any other poet, even Dante not excepted; to provide a substitute for that visual language, that constant intervention and running comment by tone, look and gesture, which in his dramatic works he was entitled to expect from the players. His *Venus and Adonis* seem at once the characters them-

[1] *Table Talk.*

selves, and the whole representation of those characters by the most consummate actors. You seem to be told nothing, but to see and hear everything. Hence it is, that from the perpetual activity of attention required on the part of the reader; from the rapid flow, the quick change, and the playful nature of the thoughts and images; and above all from the alienation, and, if I may hazard such an expression, the utter *aloofness* of the poet's own feelings, from those of which he is at once the painter and analyst; . . .[1]

Let me start by adding as a footnote to Coleridge's critique Eliot's statement of a similar notion.

Poetry is not a turning loose of emotion, but an escape from emotion; it is not the expression of personality, but an escape from personality. But, of course, only those who have personality and emotions know what it means to want to escape from these things. . . . There are many people who appreciate the expression of sincere emotion in verse, and there is a smaller number of people who can appreciate technical excellence. But very few know when there is an expression of *significant* emotion, emotion which has its life in the poem and not in the history of the poet. The emotion of art is impersonal. And the poet cannot reach this impersonality without surrendering himself wholly to the work to be done. And he is not likely to know what is to be done unless he lives in what is not merely the present, but the present moment of the past, unless he is conscious, not of what is dead, but of what is already living.[2]

The reader will be struck at once in what are clearly communications of distinguished minds by a radical community of idea and a startling contrast in tone. On the one hand, 'subjects very remote from the private interests and circumstances of the writer himself', goes along with 'Poetry is not a turning loose of emotion but an escape from emotion'; 'alienation and . . . the utter *aloofness* of the poet's own feelings' is balanced by 'the emotion of art is impersonal'. On the other the pacey, enthusiastic confidence of Coleridge stands off against the self-examining anguish of Eliot. And, ironically enough, it is the classically-aspiring Eliot who is so 'personal', who uses the concept of impersonality as a system of emotional therapy, and the romantic idealist Coleridge who is so crisp and objective and self-subduing. Moreover Coleridge's formulation of the common doctrine seems to me superior to Eliot's

[1] *Biographia Literaria*, XV.   [2] *Tradition and the Individual Talent.*

on at least two counts. Eliot, in reacting against a cult of personality and in rightly insisting on impersonal emotion and devotion to
the work, comes to rest in a mandarin, even perhaps in a frigidly
formal position. He might be Boileau speaking here. In pointing
out the importance of the object and of 'significant emotion'
'which has its life in the poem and not in the history of the poet',
he gives the impression, if not of ignoring at least of cutting down
the importance of the subject: of making the whole thing an
arrangement of relationships in an object separated not only from
personality but from subjectivity.

This impression is strengthened by the second oddity in Eliot's
explication, the repeated use of the word escape, the lonely cry
about 'only those who have personality and emotion know what
it means to want to escape from these things' (these *things*!). The
significant phrase 'surrendering himself wholly to the work to be
done'—all this gives me, at least, a suggestion of negative, even
despairing abnegation of self. The impulse of art, Eliot seems to be
saying, lies not only in the attractions of the object but even more
in the terror of the subject. But there is no trace of this self-*denying*
life-avoiding anxiety in Coleridge's account. It is the delight and
activity, the fruition of the self in the life of the object that is his
central premise: 'pleasurable excitement', 'energetic fervour',
'the highest effort of the picturesque in words, of which words are
capable', 'the rapid flow', 'the quick change', 'the playful nature
of the thoughts and images'—and these things calling on 'the
perpetual activity of attention . . . on the part of the reader'. This
is active where Eliot is passive, positive where he is negative and
welcoming where he is evasive. Even the terms which Coleridge
uses for his idea of impersonality, 'alienation',' the utter aloofness
of the poet's own feelings', flicker with nervous life and insist
on the subject's energetic effort. It is characteristic, incidentally, of Coleridge that he should use a term like 'alienation'
which has taken something like one hundred years to get into
currency.

According to Coleridge we see in Shakespeare (and perhaps in
all supremely great art) that 'the utter aloofness of the poet's own
feelings from those to which he is at once the painter and the
analyst' supports and is the condition of an incessant striking of a
penetrating consciousness. The alienation and distancing of the
poet's own feelings set free a rage of constructive skill. I use such

words to indicate that it is not simply a blind creative force—
'energetic fervour'—but rather a storm of consciousness or a greater
and greater intensity of light. Or as Coleridge says it is a matter of
things not only 'profoundly but accurately contemplated'. It has
to do with 'a superior spirit, more intuitive, more intimately
conscious . . . of the flux and reflex of the mind in all its subtlest
thoughts and feelings'. The fullness of consciousness in Shakespeare was even in these narrative and lyrical poems striving towards the more inclusive form of dramatic action. 'You seem to be
told nothing, but to see and hear everything'. The linguistic acting
out of the theme, which Coleridge acutely remarks on in *Venus and
Adonis*, was not just 'to provide a substitute for that visual language,
that constant intervention and running comment, by tone, look
and gesture, which in his dramatic work he was entitled to expect
from the players,—it *was* this but not just this: it was also the
beginning of a development which would be consummated in his
great plays, the harnessing of every possibility of language:
language as performance as well as recital.

In his third note on the topic of 'the specific symptoms of poetic
power' Coleridge concerns himself with imagery, which he has so
far only glanced at obliquely.

> It has been before observed that images, however beautiful, though
> faithfully copied from nature, and as accurately represented in
> words, do not themselves characterize the poet. They become proofs
> of original genius only as far as they are modified by a predominant
> passion; or by associated thoughts or images awakened by that
> passion; or when they have the effect of reducing multitude to unity,
> or succession to an instant; or lastly, when a human and intellectual
> life is transferred to them from the poet's own spirit,
>
>> Which shoots its being through earth, sea and air . . .
>
> As of higher worth, so doubtless still more characteristic of poetic
> genius does the imagery become, when it moulds and colors itself to
> the circumstances, passion, or character, present and foremost in
> the mind. For unrivalled instances of this excellence, the reader's
> own memory will refer him to the LEAR, OTHELLO, in short to
> which not of the '*great, ever living dead man's*' works? . . . Scarcely less
> sure, or if a less valuable, not less indispensable mark . . . will the
> imagery supply, when, with more than the power of the painter, the
> poet gives us the liveliest image of succession with the feeling of
> simultaneousness!

With this, he breaketh from the sweet embrace
Of those fair arms, that held him to her breast,
And homeward through the dark laund runs apace...
Look! how a bright star shooteth from the sky,
So glides he in the night from Venus' eye.[1]

The imagery in *Venus and Adonis* does not give Coleridge much occasion for commenting on its originality. In an earlier note he discriminated among imagery according to provenance rather than novelty. But if the imagery in *Venus and Adonis* is not boldly new, it does not suffer from that immoderate clarity, that almost abstract definition, which he writes in *The Notebooks* tends to debilitate genuine originality. 'Whether or no the too great definiteness of Terms in any language may not consume too much of the vital and idea-creating force in distinct, clear, full made Images and so prevent originality—*original* thought as distinguished from positive thought. . . .'[2] Shakespeare's youthful images at least keep to this negative condition of originality. His mind and the image in which it is expressed do not work by projecting complete thoughts in separate units. At each point the passage melts and fuses into the next. 'Shakespeare goes on creating and evolving *B* out of *A*, and *C* out of *B*, and so on, just as a serpent moves, which makes a fulcrum of its own body, and seems forever twisting and untwisting its own strength.'[3] 'In Shakespeare one sentence begets the next naturally; the meaning is all inwoven. He goes on kindling like a meteor through the dark atmosphere.'[4] Coleridge makes much more of the vivacity of Shakespearean imagery in *Venus and Adonis*: 'the rapid flow, the quick change, the playful nature of the thoughts and images'. Even if the playfulness has something to do with the pleasurable vigour of youth, the nimbleness, the speed of transition signals a mind intensely alive. The speed in Shakespeare is the speed of vitality. Vivacity then but also continuity. The 'never broken chain of imagery, always vivid, and because unbroken, often minute' is the parallel to the self-productive continuity which characterises Shakespeare's thought: 'he always by metaphors and figures' Coleridge says, contrasting Shakespeare with Massinger's Flemish technique of

---

[1] *Biographia Literaria*, XV.
[2] *The Notebooks of Samuel Taylor Coleridge*. Edited by Kathleen Coburn, London, 1957, Vol. I, No. 1016.
[3] *Table Talk*.   [4] Ibid.

clarity and separation, 'involves in the thing considered a universe of past and possible experiences'.[1]

But even these things, lively and connected images, even images, 'beautiful . . . faithfully copied from nature, and as accurately represented in words', are less the proofs of original genius than something else. Images have to be capable of being modified 'by a predominant passion; or by associated thoughts or images awakened by that passion; or when they have the effect of reducing multitude to unity, or succession to an instance; or . . . when a human and intellectual life is transferred to them from the poet's own spirit . . .'. Images are not billiard balls but molecules. They have to be porous to the poet's breath. They are local manifestations, organs of the whole conception.

> The last character I shall mention [Coleridge concludes], which would prove indeed but little, except as taken conjointly with the former; yet without which the former could scarce exist in a high degree, and (even if this were possible) would give promises only of transitory flashes and a meteoric power; is DEPTH and ENERGY of THOUGHT. No man was ever yet a great poet, without being at the same time a profound philosopher. . . . In Shakespeare's *poems* the creative power and the intellectual energy wrestle as in a war embrace. Each in its excess of strength seems to threaten the extinction of the other. At length in the DRAMA they were reconciled, and fought each with its shield before the breast of the other. . . . The Venus and Adonis did not perhaps allow the display of the deeper passions. But the story of Lucretia seems to favor and even demand their intensest workings. And yet we find in *Shakespeare's* management of the tale neither pathos, nor any other *dramatic* quality. There is the same minute and faithful imagery as in the former poem, in the same vivid colours, inspirited by the same impetuous vigour of thought, and diverging and contracting with the same activity of the assimilative and of the modifying faculties; and with a yet larger display, a yet wider range of knowledge and reflection; and lastly, with the same perfect dominion, often *domination*, over the whole world of language. What then shall we say? even this; that Shakespeare, no mere child of nature; no automaton of genius; no passive vehicle of inspiration possessed by the spirit, not possessing it; first studied patiently, meditated deeply, understood minutely, till knowledge, become habitual and intuitive, wedded itself to his habitual feelings, and at length gave birth to that stupendous power by which he stands alone, with no equal or second in his own class. . . .[2]

[1] *Lit. Rem.*, I. 112.   [2] *Biographia Literaria*, XV.

A contemporary reader will undoubtedly want to acknowledge the depth and energy of Shakespeare's thought. He will as certainly get a rough jolt from the invitation to think of Shakespeare as a philosopher. Shakespeare a *philosopher*? Well hardly in any current or technical sense. In justice to Coleridge who was, it is true, temperamentally apt to inflate the literary function of the philosopher, it must be remembered that he is arguing here, as he does more fully elsewhere, against the Voltairean and eighteenth-century view of Shakespeare as *lusus naturae*, a wild sport outside the framework of civilisation. Coleridge will have none of this wild, untutored Phoenix nonsense. Furthermore, by this point in the discussion the context has made clear that Coleridge is not ascribing to Shakespeare any kind of blood-starved intellectualism. Philosopher and philosophy have by now come to have a solid and densely loaded content. Perhaps I can illustrate what Coleridge has in mind here by quoting another entry from *The Notebooks*: 'I do not wish you to act from these truths—no! still and always act from your *feelings*—but only meditate often on these truths, that some time or other they may become your Feelings'.[1] It is truths become feeling or feeling inclusive of truths that Shakespeare powerfully commands: '. . . knowledge, become habitual and intuitive, wedded itself to his habitual feelings, and at length gave birth to that stupendous power, by which he stands alone, with no equal or second in his own class . . .'. Coleridge's figure of the warring wrestlers registers something of the ferocious Shakespearean force, but it also suggests, misleadingly, a fracture in the centre of Shakespeare's genius—'Each in its excess of strength seems to threaten the extinction of the other'. Shakespeare's intellectual energy exists in, is the same as, his creative power, just as both exist in and are the same as what Coleridge rightly calls a 'perfect dominion, often *domination*, over the whole world of language'. Coleridge concedes that Shakespeare's creative power and intellectual energy were 'reconciled' in the drama. But even this concession hints at some radical division. Perhaps I am reading too much into what could be a matter of comparative emphasis or even of careless eloquence, particularly as Coleridge goes on to speak with a fine, figurative cogency of 'the same minute and faithful imagery . . . the same vivid colours, inspired by the same

[1] *The Notebooks of Samuel Taylor Coleridge*. Edited by Kathleen Coburn, London, 1957, Vol. I, No. 989.

impetuous vigour of thought, and diverging and contracting with the same activity of the assimilative and of the modifying faculties . . .': a beautifully Coleridgean evocation of the deep creative unity of Shakespeare's sensibility.

Having set out these samples of Coleridge's discriminated responses and responsive judgments, I want now to turn to the certainties and constancies which sustain and qualify them. What assumptions quicken his critical practice? What intentions point it? What attitudes habitually govern its posture? They seem to me to be certain convictions about the character of criticism, the idea of the organic, the relevance of morality, and the nature of language: I shall comment on each in turn.

The contemporary reader will hardly be disconcerted, and surely not disturbed, if I do *not* begin my remarks on Coleridge's idea of criticism by rehearsing his most famous distinction between Fancy and Imagination and adding yet one more explication of this subject to the existing heap. My purpose throughout is to enquire into the ways in which Coleridge is living now, and into the ways in which he can minister to our necessities as they are in this juncture of time and history. I do not see the contemporary reader being much helped by discussion of 'the primary imagination . . . [as] the living Power and prime Agent of all human Perception, and as a repetition in the finite mind of the eternal act of creation in the infinite I AM' . . . or of 'the secondary Imagination . . . as an echo of the former, co-existing with the conscious will, yet still as identical with the primary in the *Kind* of its agency, and differing only in *degree*, and in the *mode* of its operation'.[1] The contemporary reader, if he is like me, will have the whirling sensation, as he contemplates such constitutive and almost mystical distinctions, that the weight of the world is detaching itself and spinning and spiralling away. Giddiness and lightness loosen one's hold on things. It is preferable, I think, to conceive of this and similar distinctions as summaries and distillations of his experience and not—as Coleridge on occasion was apt to think of them himself—as fixed principles capable of generating their own issue. Coleridge's criticism, that is, is not simply the application of the principles implicit in his various distinctions. It is more than the logical elaboration of abstract truths, which his frequent reference to these distinctions makes it sometimes seem to be. In

[1] *Biographia Literaria*, XIII.

Coleridge's best criticism principles are mostly actively engaged, but as an equal partner in a collaboration or collision with the literary object, and not as prepotent and revelatory general truths. A true critic, he declares, 'can no more be such without placing himself on some central point, from which he may command the whole, that is, some general rule, which founded in reason, or the faculties common to all men, must therefore apply to each... but in the mode of applying it he will estimate genius and judgment according to the felicity with which the imperishable soul of intellect shall have adapted itself to the age, the place, and the existing manners'.[1] It is with 'the age, the place and the existing manners' in mind that I will examine Coleridge's idea of criticism in the hope of reaching at length the 'central point' a 'general rule'. To do it the other way round, which is what one would be doing if one began with Coleridge's distinctions, would be to turn criticism into geometry.

Coleridge saw clearly the historical determinants of his criticism. 'After the Revolution', he remarks, 'the spirit of the nation became more commercial than it had been before; a learned body of clerisy, as such, gradually disappeared and literature began to be addressed to the common miscellaneous public.'[2] In his view there were also revolutions of a different sort more disturbing in their effect than the openly political ones: 'There have been three silent revolutions in England: first when the professions fell off from the Church; secondly when literature fell off from the professions; and thirdly when the press fell off from literature'.[3] His account of his own period uncannily anticipates the state of affairs in ours. 'On the one hand despotism, despotism, despotism, of finance in statistics, of vanity in social converse, of presumption and overweening contempt of the ancient in individuals', on the other, 'government by clubs, committees, societies, reviews and newspapers'. And again 'acquiescence in historic testimony substituted for faith, and yet the true historical feeling, the feeling of being an historical people, generation linked to generation by ancestral reputation, by tradition ... this noble feeling ... openly stormed or perilously undermined.'[4]

In the *Biographia Literaria* he sees the decline of public taste illustrated also by the gradual sinking in the pretensions of authors

---

[1] *Lit Rem.*, II, pp. 65-6.
[2] *The Church and State.*
[3] *Table Talk.*
[4] *The Friend*, 2, 3.

and the change in relationship between them and their readers. Francis Bacon, he notes, took it for granted that it was in the interests of posterity for it to be possessed of his dedications—dedications to Popes and Kings at least implied that 'the honour given was . . . in equipose to the patronage acknowledged'. But then

> Poets and Philosophers, rendered diffident by their very number, addressed themselves to '*learned* readers'; then, aimed to conciliate the graces of 'the *candid* reader'; till, the critic still rising as the author sunk, the amateurs of literature collectively were erected into a municipality of judges, and addressed as THE TOWN. And now finally, all men being supposed able to read and all readers able to judge, the multitudinous PUBLIC, shaped into personal unity by the magic of abstraction, sits nominal on the throne of criticism.[1]

As well as Coleridge's genuine indignation at criticism by numbers, and standards by statistics, there is more than a touch in this comment, and in others which I wish to recall, of that personal rancour which even an indirect reference to critics and reviewers seldom failed to provoke in him. Reviewers—'a kind of Establishment',[2] he called them bleakly—had certainly treated him savagely, and perhaps he felt this gave him the right to fume. In any case it is a flaw, though a small, human one, in his plea for disinterestedness in criticism.

Because it was this quality precisely, disinterestedness, that Coleridge found the criticism of his own time to be the most deficient in. The charge and the terms it is framed in are oddly prophetic of accusations brought first by Arnold and later by Eliot and Leavis against the critics of their own day. Disinterestedness belongs to the nature of the great critic who is so much less mastered by inertia, cramped by his education, addicted to conformity than the rest of us; and no doubt every significant critic, at least since Johnson, found the critical practice and the common reading of his own period abhorrent to him, riddled with what is specious, fashionable, and self-deceiving: 'marked', said Coleridge, 'with the asterisk of spuriousness'. Disinterestedness means being able to base judgments on the highest and most relevant standards and great critics gifted with immediate access to these must seem to themselves to be living in a world concerned with everything

[1] *Biographia Literaria*, III.
[2] *The Notebooks of Samuel Taylor Coleridge*. Edited by Kathleen Coburn, London, 1957, Vol. I, No. 131.

except what they see as essential: purity of response and truth in judgment. '. . . not only individuals, but even whole nations, are sometimes so enslaved to the habits of their education and immediate circumstances, as not to judge disinterestedly even in those subjects, the very pleasure arising from which consists in its disinterestedness, namely, on subjects of taste and polite literature'.[1] The only rule the great critic acknowledges is the pure and lofty one of the best standard. Towards everything else he is fastidiously and fearlessly independent. Coleridge reserved a special contempt for those who would be critics without disinterested courage: like the Wartons, who 'first adventured a timorous attack, the censure so neutralised by compliments and half-retractions, that it might remind one of a wasp staggering out of a Honey Pot, with both wings and sting sheathed in the clammy sweetness'.[2]

When, therefore, Coleridge was specifying 'the causes of false criticism', among which he put such general and permanent ones as 'the great pleasure we feel in being told of the knowledge we possess, rather than of the ignorance we suffer'[3]; our habit of not taking the trouble to *think*; the vague use of terms: it is not surprising that he should add more pointed and local causes. 'The crying sin of modern criticism', he roundly asserts, 'is that it is overloaded with personality', nor that he should buttress this with a still more pertinent and irritable comment. 'This is an age of personality and political gossip, when insects, as in ancient Egypt, are worshipped in proportion to the venom of their stings—when poems and especially satires, are valued according to the number of living names they contain; and where the notes, however, have this comparative excellence, that they are generally more pointed and poetical than the text'.[4] If the observation about the personality-ridden state of criticism might well have been repeated by a modern critic, the same could not be said of the observation which follows it. Coleridge cites as another cause of the falseness of criticism 'the greater purity of morality in the present age, compared even with the last'. By morality here he seems to mean refinement, in the more mincing, squeamish sense of the word. He asks quite seriously what must seem to us a decidedly comic question: 'who now will venture to read a number of the Spectator,

[1] *Lit. Rem.*, II, pp. 65-6.
[2] *The Inquiring Spirit*. Edited by Kathleen Coburn, London, 1951, p. 157.
[3] *Lectures on Shakespeare*, I. [4] Ibid.

or of the Tatler to his wife and daughters, without first examining it to make sure that it contains no word which might, in our day, offend the delicacy of female ears, and shock feminine susceptibility?' One suddenly remembers the slightly shuddering turn of some of his reflections on *Venus and Adonis* and on *Tristram Shandy* which also suggest an over-finicky notion of female delicacy.

But if Coleridge was sufficiently in his age to have some sympathy with its blenching refinement, he was sufficiently out of it to realise its absurdities. He recognised, if one can put it like that, the excesses of primness. 'Even our theatres, the representations at which usually reflect the morals of the period, have taken a sort of domestic turn, and while the performances at them may be said, in some sense, to improve the heart, there is no doubt that they vitiate the taste.'[1] And he did say elsewhere, 'I am pleased to think that when a mere stripling I had formed the opinion that true taste was virtue and that bad writing was bad feeling'.[2]

To be rescued from individual and social quirks, in Coleridge's day, from personality and refinement (or in our day from personality and the opposite of refinement, whatever that is) judgment must be supported, Coleridge insists, 'by reference to fixed canons of criticism, previously established and deduced from the nature of man'.[3] By 'fixed canons' Coleridge does not mean external laws but more permanent and living standards, sanctioned by history, founded in human nature and derived from its finest achievements, and focussed with relevance, '. . . let the dead bury the dead, but do you preserve your human nature, the depth of which was never yet fathomed by a philosophy made up of notions and mere logical entities'.[4] His own account of the first impressions made on him by Wordsworth is a beautiful example of the operation of canons of criticism which are human and appropriate. They are individual and concrete, the product of a complex and purely Coleridgean sensibility, but also informed by principle and alive both to the past and to the crucial present. In such passages we see Coleridge's standards operating together and applied with a singular fineness of tact, and not as they appear elsewhere in his writings, abstract instruments of anatomy and argumentative analysis.

[1] Ibid.   [2] *Anima Poetae.*
[3] *Biographia Literaria,* III.   [4] Ibid., XII.

It was not however the freedom from false truth, whether as to common defects, or to those more properly his own, which made so unusual an impression on my feelings immediately, and subsequently on my judgment. It was the union of deep feeling with profound thought; the fine balance of truth in observing, with the imaginative faculty in modifying the objects observed; and above all the original gift of spreading the tone, the *atmosphere*, and with it the depth and height of the ideal world around forms, incidents, and situations, of which, for the common view, custom had bedimmed all the lustre, had dried up the sparkle and the dew drops.[1]

This is Coleridge at his most telling and appreciative. As a balance I should present an equally effective but severer Coleridge. Let me quote, therefore, not his unfair and period-blinded comments on Dr Johnson, but some remarks on Scott which are as apt and sure as the Wordsworth passage, only negative where they are positive. They have the extra merit of teasing out an imperfection, both moral and artistic, which is general with writers like Scott who will not *decide*, who want to have it both ways: in Scott's case to hold hands at one and the same time with science and superstition. And Coleridge exposes the dilemma by reference to one of the canons of criticism he set most store on—the idea of inward relevance: in the example which follows it can be seen to be an intrinsic congruence between writer and work. It is also a hint at that concept of the organic which, it will be remembered, I undertook to raise next.

Sir W. S., a faithful Cosmolater, is always half and half on the subject of the Supernatural in his Novels. The Ghost-seer and the Appearances are so stated as to be readily solved on the commonest and most obvious principles of Pathology; while the exact coincidence of the Events, and thus as in Guy Mannering, a complexity of Events with two perfectly coincident predictions so far exceeds our general experience, is so unsatisfactorily accounted for by the doctrine of Chance, as to be little less marvellous than the appearance itself would be, supposing it real. Thus by the latter he secures the full effect of Superstition for the Reader, while by the former he preserves the credit of unbelief and philosophic insight for the Writer—i.e. himself. I said falsely, the *full* effect: for that discrepance between the Narrator and the Narrative chills and deadens the Sympathy.[2]

[1] *Biographia Literaria*, IV.
[2] *Inquiring Spirit*. Edited by Kathleen Coburn, London, 1951, p. 190.

'Readers', said Coleridge at the beginning of one of his lectures in 1811, 'may be divided into four classes:

1. Sponges, who absorb all they read, and return it nearly in the same state, only a little dirtied.
2. Sand-glasses, who retain nothing, and are content to get through a book for the sake of getting through the time.
3. Strain-bags, who retain merely the dregs of what they read.
4. Mogul diamonds, equally rare and valuable, who profit by what they read, and enable others to profit by it also.'

When Coleridge writes as he does on Shakespeare or Wordsworth or Scott, he too is a 'Mogul diamond', one of those 'who profit by what they read, and enable others to profit by it also': which is indeed a fine summary of the business of the critic. One of the enabling things the critic has to do is to move, positively to startle, people out of their usual lethargies of thought and attitude. He has to cut through the carapace of habit. The critic, the ideal reader, has to make other readers more naked and more perceptive. Part of the rejection that most good critics receive in their lives is to be attributed to the resentment of reader's at this treatment. They —or perhaps I should say we—have no wish to be emancipated from 'the bedimming influences of custom, and the transforming witchcraft of early associations' which alone prevent us from seeing 'as numerous tribes of fetish-worshippers in the streets of London and Paris, as we hear of on the coasts of Africa'.[1] Coleridge's literary life was spent inviting his contemporaries to reject, and to be justified in rejecting, the whole intellectual constitution of the eighteenth century in which—to quote his vivid specification again—'the mind was a lazy looker-on at an external universe'. In this theory art was the delicate application of established rules, poetry the more and more refined manipulation of existing counters—however inadequate such an explanation might be to the practice of Johnson, Pope and Swift. The passion of Coleridge's life was wholly to dismantle this structure and to replace it by something closer to his own marvellously intimate apprehension of the inward, the *organic* nature of art.

Art begins in the active mind. As I have indicated already, human consciousness, as Coleridge saw it, whether in its elementary or its sophisticated forms, was primarily an activity. Above all

[1] *The Friend*, Essay 14.

F 77

is it true that the act of imagination is self-initiated, self-born. 'One character belongs to all true poets, that they write from a principle within, not originating in anything without. . . .'[1] The activity begins with a stroke of life, an impulse, which is, as Coleridge said in his notes on *Richard II* 'the germ of all after events'. The impulse may be an image or a description or a situation or a question or the glimpse of a character; it can even be a generalisatio or reflection when this is sharpened with the savour of practical experience. Coleridge's Notebooks teem with possibilities and references of this kind. And since the peculiar intensity of Coleridge's criticism comes from its having access to, from immediately drawing on, the creative sources of genius, I want to illustrate these impulses as fully as I can. I can best do this by offering a random selection from the *Notebooks*, but categorised for the convenience of the reader and numbered as they appear in Miss Coburn's Edition.

(Description)
> 'Some wilderness-plot green and fountainous and unviolated by man.' (220.)
> 'October 21, 1800. The dazzling Silver of the Lake in this cloudy, sunny, misty, howling weather!' (833.)
> 'Rabbits hung out to air.' (844.)
> 'A dull kind of Being not yet privileged with life.' (944.)
> 'Friday Evening, November 29. The immoveableness of all Things—thru' which so many men were moving . . . in this dim Light London appeared to me a huge place of Sepulchres thru' which Hosts of Spirits were gliding.' (1592.)

(Situation)
> 'Listening with untir'd eagerness, while the unsnuffed Candle's cone burnt with two points.' (821.)
> 'The half-knit Stocking in the Kitchen-table Drawer.' (955.)
> 'Bright Reflections in the Canals of the blue and green Vitriol Bottles in the druggists' shops in London.—mere plictry-plactry.' (1081.)
> 'Waterfall-tiny-and Leaf- still attracted still repelled.' (1158.)
> 'Poems—Ghost of a mountain—the form seizing my body as I passed, became realities—I, a Ghost, till I had reconquered my Substance.' (1241.)

(Question)
> 'Is not Habit the Desire of a Desire?' (1421.)

[1] *Lit. Rem.*, II, p. 70.

(Glimpse of a Character)
'One of those thoughtful men whose plate of pudding often swims before their eyes while they are eating.' (858.)
'A Man melancholy mad with the Ideal—his contemplation of human faces, all warped, and all detestably ugly.' (1306.)
'Tall thin man stooping and bending in the middle, and there tightly buttoned up, like a cracked Stick, bandaged hard round the Fracture—with Rags or Twine.' (1595.)

In each of these there is some latency, some hint of richness or complexity of structure which contains within itself possibilities of growth. Each of these has a trace of what Coleridge called 'the substance capable of endless modifications'. They manifest again what he described as 'a vitality which grows and evolves itself from within'. The analogy of the force contained in these tiny flecks of life is not the plan or blueprint. That is an external scaffolding; and not what Coleridge meant at all. 'An outline', said Coleridge, 'imprisons the mind of the artist within the first conception'.[1] No, the analogy is much closer to the force contained in a seed, which does indeed 'evolve itself from within'. What corresponds in art to the law of nature implicit in the seed is what Coleridge, speaking of Shakespeare, describes as 'the law of unity which has its foundations not in the factitious necessity of custom, but in nature itself, the unity of feeling which is everywhere and at all times observed by Shakespeare in his plays'.[2]

The development of the impulse necessarily involves modification and increasing complexity. But this is not the effect of the imposition of external rules. It is not the imitation or the copying of some model outside itself. Clearly there is a logic, there are laws. But these are determined by a force from within. 'Could a rule be given from *without*, poetry would cease to be poetry and sink into a mechanical art . . . the rules of Imagination are themselves the very power of growth and production.'[3] Genius is not opposed to rules. 'The spirit of poetry like all other living powers, must of necessity circumscribe itself by rules, were it only to unite power with beauty. It must embody in order to reveal itself; but a living body is of necessity an organized one; and what is organization but the connexion of parts in and for a whole, so that each part is at once end and means?'[4] So that the exterior appearance

---

[1] *Notebooks*, Vol. I, 1312.   [2] *Lit. Rem.*, II, p. 75.
[3] *Biographia Literaria*, XVIII.   [4] *Lit. Rem.*, II, p. 66.

of art, its actual bodily or verbal form, is the consequence of intrinsic pressure. It is not a copy of something outside itself which would simply make it an example of mechanical regularity. It is the product of an organic form. 'The form is mechanic, when on any given material we impress a pre-determined form, not necessarily arising out of the properties of the material—as when to a mass of wet clay we give whatever shape we wish it to retain when hardened. The organic form, on the other hand, is innate; it shapes, as it develops, itself from within, and the fulness of its development is one and the same with the perfection of its outward form. Such as the life is, such is the form.'[1]

These remarks all bear on Shakespeare, and Coleridge brings them to a point by taking Shakespeare to be the artistic equivalent of nature itself. Each is 'inexhaustible in diverse powers, . . . equally inexhaustible in forms'; in Shakespeare as in nature, 'each exterior is the physiognomy of the being within, its true image reflected and thrown out from the concave mirror'; as with the effect so with the cause which supports it: there is a correspondence between the creative force of nature and Shakespeare's genius, 'understanding directing . . . a power and an implicit wisdom deeper even than our own consciousness'.[2]

Coleridge's criticism, in assumption and practice, was modelled upon, was indeed 'the physiognomy of the being within', his own creative activity—which itself affected and was affected by his interpretation of the creative activity of other writers, and supremely of Shakespeare. When he speaks, therefore, of 'an implicit wisdom deeper than our consciousness', as one of the profound sources of Shakespeare's creativity, he is making reference to something within himself as a critic as well as pointing to something there in Shakespeare. He is making not only a statement about Shakespeare but a revelation about himself. This is not only one of the sources of literary creation but one of the essential canons of criticism. 'An implicit wisdom', is a phrase carrying with it suggestions of rhythms 'deeper than our consciousness', of something like a tribal disinterestedness or a more than personal sagacity, and of a radical inclusive common sense. It brings with it the idea of a fundamental human morality: not the superior morality which Coleridge speaks of, a trifle complacently, as an achievement of the nineteenth century, but something more permanent

[1] *Lit. Rem.*, II, p. 68. [2] Ibid.

and significant, more like a central, instinctive human tradition. Coleridge has in mind here that moral life, or moral being as he called it, which even more than man's intellectual powers distinguished him from the animals and made him truly human. It is a feeling, as Coleridge explained when writing about women in Shakespeare of all 'that *continuates* society, as sense of ancestry and of sex, with a purity unassailable by sophistry, because it rests not in the analytic processes, but in that same equipoise of the faculties, during which the feelings are representative of all past experience . . .'. As it disclosed itself in Shakespeare this was a positive and tremendous *ordinariness*, a centrality of experience and judgment which was itself never twisted by aberration whatever aberration it was turned upon.

> Keeping at all times in the high road of life, Shakespeare has no innocent adulteries, no interesting incests, no virtuous vice . . . Shakespeare's fathers are roused by ingratitude, his husbands stung by unfaithfulness; in him, in short, the affections are wounded in those points in which all may, nay, must, feel. . . . He neither excites, nor flatters, passion, in order to degrade the subject of it; he does not use the faulty thing for a faulty purpose, nor carries on warfare against virtue, by causing wickedness to appear as no wickedness, through the medium of a morbid sympathy with the unfortunate. In Shakespeare vice never walks as in twilight: nothing is purposely out of its place; . . . he does not make every magistrate a drunkard or glutton, nor every poor man meek, humane, and temperate; he has no benevolent butchers, nor any sentimental rat-catchers.[1]

There is a sentence in *Biographia Literaria* which offers a neat transition to the last of the conceptions I specified as lying at the back of Coleridge's criticism, namely his idea of language. '. . . in all societies there exists an instinct of growth, a certain collective unconscious good sense working progressively to de-synonymise those words originally of the same meaning . . .'[2]. Coleridge's thought on language is in resonance with his thought on the mind. The mind constructs and refines relationships, language constructs and refines meanings. Each has a collective and unconscious base, an individual and conscious crown. Neither is simply a mirror reflecting an object nor a garment clothing a form: '. . . to know is in its very essence a verb active',[3] he affirms, and '. . . words are not

---

[1] *Ibid.*, II, p. 80.
[2] *Biographia Literaria*, IV.   [3] Ibid., II.

things, they are living powers . . .'.[1] It was a particular anxiety of Coleridge to show the connection between language and human experience as something closer and subtler than it was commonly taken to be in Locke or Hobbes or Horne Tooke. Language was neither an 'invalid surrogate' for experience nor a veil floating deceptively across and around our ideas. He questioned whether language is no more than an arbitrary attachment of words to thoughts and things, which Collingwood argued would amount to saying that language was a set of technical terms.[2] Of course language is arbitrary in the sense that it is artificial and various, but it is not arbitrary in the same way as a new technical term is arbitrary, or the words in a nonsense language, or the rules of a new game. Or as he wrote to William Godwin:

> Is *thinking* impossible without arbitrary signs? And how far is the word 'arbitrary' a misnomer? Are not words etc. parts and germinations of the Plant? And where is the law of their growth?—In something of this order I would endeavour to destroy the old antithesis of *Words and Things*, elevating, as it were, words into Things, and living Things too.

'Growth' is a figure which condenses into itself a whole variety of notions—of naturalness as opposed to arbitrariness, of an intrinsic initiative, of the burgeoning of life according to an implicit pattern and of a completion of it which cannot be totally forecast, of an elaborate complexity of structure. Coleridge realised as well as any modern linguistician how many more than merely verbal elements go into language. 'I include in the meaning of a word not only its correspondent object; but likewise all the association it recalls. For language is framed to convey not the object alone, but likewise the character, mood and intentions of the person who is representing it'[4]. Language constructs meaning and this gives our experience its peculiarly human note; at the same time it makes meaning relatively permanent, preserving in experience a kind of force and density which otherwise might simply evaporate. Language to some degree and literature, the most intense form of language, to a much higher degree, 'preserved' he points out, 'a

[1] *Aids to Reflection.* Preface.
[2] Cf. Collingwood, R., *Philosophical Method*, London, 1933, p. 203.
[3] *Letters*, Vol. I, pp. 625-6.
[4] *Biographia Literaria*, XXII.

purity of meaning to many terms of natural objects. Without this holdfast, our vitiated imaginations would refine away language to mere abstractions.'[1] Coleridge wished not only to insist on the part of language in making experiences permanent, but on the intimacy the unity even, between language and human experience itself. 'For if words are not things, they are living powers, by which things of most importance to mankind are activated, combined, and humanized.'[2] He rejected the tradition, still current today, which took the use of language to be the fixing of passive labels to completed experiences. He wished, instead, to abolish the distance between language and thought. Language was not only an instrument but a source of thought, not only an agency but an initiator. And the more language was this, the more was it significantly human. '. . . the best part of human language, properly so called, is derived from reflection on the acts of the mind itself.'[3] And what is true of language in a general and loose way is true of literature in the most particular and intense way, and true above all of the language of poetry. Shakespeare's language, for example, 'was not drawn from any set fashion, but from the profoundest depth of his moral being'.[4]

All language constructs and continues meaning, all language organises and humanises things. The language of poetry adds not only a special harmony or a particular attractiveness of pattern, although it does add these. The special function of art, 'the figured language of thought', is 'to partake of the reality which it renders intelligible'. The language of poetry adds performance to memory, it is revealing as well as commemorative. Coleridge distinguished the translation of abstract notions into a picture language from poetry in which language itself is a symbol 'characterised by a translucence of the special in the individual, or of the general in the special, or of the universal in the general'.[5] *Translucence*, an actual shining through: the language of poetry does not merely refer outside itself to objects and thoughts and feelings. It performs what it hints at and it undertakes what it promises. If this is the nature of the language of poetry, its condition, its health, is to stand in a relationship with life which is direct but also detached. Not the direct, naively realist relationship that Wordsworth

[1] *Table Talk.*   [2] *Aids to Reflection.* Preface.
[3] *Biographia Literaria*, XVII.   [4] *Lit. Rem.*, II, p. 94.
[5] *The Statesman's Manual.*

argued for, not the active adoption of the very language of life or of any particular set or class, and certainly not a selection of the language of mountaineers and peasants. (*Peasants*, Coleridge seems to sigh.) No, the language of poetry must be intimately connected with life. It must draw on real rhythms and vital uses. Coleridge wholly rejected any remote or mandarin diction. He wrote to Thomas Wedgwood, 'I should think your judgment on the sentiment, the imagery, the flow of a Poem decisive . . . but in point of poetic Diction I am not so well s[atisf]ied that you do not require a certain aloofness from [the la]nguage of real Life, which I think deadly to Poetry'.[1] Neither aloofness, therefore, nor identification, but rather a language involved with life, quickened by imagination and disciplined by reflection. Such a language in Coleridge's generous interpretation could occupy a point on a great range stretching all the way from Milton to Massinger.

> The style of Massinger's plays and the *Samson Agonistes* are the two extremes of the arc within which the diction of dramatic poetry may oscillate. Shakespeare in his great plays is the midpoint. In the *Samson Agonistes*, colloquial language is kept at the greatest distance, yet something of it is preserved, to render the dialogue probable: in Massinger the style is differenced, but differenced in the smallest degree possible, from animated conversation by the vein of poetry.[2]

Assumptions of the sort I have sketched—on the character of criticism itself, the organic in art, the relevance of morality, the nature of language—are present and vivifying throughout Coleridge's critical writing. They bring solidity to a criticism apt to float away into a thin, and to modern nostrils distasteful, philosophic air. They correct, or at least check, Coleridge's inveterate bias towards metaphysics. They are rebarbative and awkward and they refuse to fit into a habit of thought which often gives the impression that it would like to make criticism a system of adamantine deduction from philosophic principles. In so far as he tries to do this, and in so far as he tries to turn literary criticism into a form of spiritual exercise and metaphysical speculation, Coleridge's criticism is not relevant or acceptable or even comprehensible to the contemporary reader. But his criticism as often as not, more often perhaps, reposes on quite other foundations and was impelled by quite other expectations than religious or philosophic ones. And

---

[1] *Letters*, Vol. II, pp. 876-7.   [2] *Table Talk*.

to the extent that it was so, to the extent that it drew on concrete perception, on concrete skill in analysis and generalisation and distinction lived through and felt within, then Coleridge's criticism has point, more point than any other critic's, I believe, for the contemporary reader.

It is the athletic not the mystical Coleridge who helps the modern reader to profit by what he has read, the man with marvellously quick reflexes in response and a corresponding mobility of thought and expression in discussion. Coleridge reacted against a social code which in its decline imposed routine expression on the writer and conventional evaluation on the critic. Sometimes this reaction took the form of replacing Augustan assumptions with Idealistic presuppositions, and of dissolving criticism into applied philosophy. And certainly a new current of ideas was about due in the stale English atmosphere. But the truths of philosophy have this in common with those they supplant, that they will follow them into disrepute and oblivion. As a theoretical system Coleridge's Idealism is less influential today than the philosophy of the eighteenth century. But what matters in Coleridge's criticism is not really this. It is its fiercely individual and personal bite. His criticism counts because it is the creation of a sensibility of genius. It gains its authority from the insight of an individual, not from the theory of a school.

The contemporary reader wants to be brought closer and closer to the text, to be given access through the writer's words to the humanity he shares with the writer. He does not get the required assistance from a Coleridge swinging, sometimes deliriously swinging, aloft on a trapeze of abstractions. Or as Coleridge put it himself, though hardly with himself in mind, in a statement which perfectly exposes the weakness of his own criticism:

> We call, for we see and feel, the swan and the dove both transcendently beautiful. As absurd as it would be to institute a comparison between their separate claims to beauty from any abstract rule common to both, without reference to the life and being of the animals themselves—say rather if, having first seen the dove, we abstracted its outlines, gave them a false generalization, called them principle or ideal of bird-beauty and then proceeded to criticize the swan or the eagle—not less absurd is it to pass judgement on the works of a poet on the mere ground that they have been called by the same class-name with the works of other poets of other times and

circumstances, or any ground indeed save that of their inappropriate-
ness to their own end and being, their want of significance, as symbol
and physiognomy.[1]

But there is another Coleridge who profits by his own reading
and enables us to profit by it too. It is this Coleridge who is intent
upon the poem as symbol and physiognomy and who is concerned
in it at the presence or absence of appropriateness to its own end
or being; and this Coleridge whose 'understanding' is of so much
more significance than his 'reason', if I may give these terms a
current, non-Coleridgean sense. His counsel is highly practical,
his critical advice most pointed. It is not, for example, 'the poem
we have *read*, but that to which we *return*'[2] which matters. Or again,
'What ever lines can be translated into other words of the same
language, without diminution of their significance, either in sense
or association, or in any worthy feeling, are so far vicious in their
diction'.[3] Not only is his advice practical, it is also inward, an
immediate and sensitive clue to the work as 'symbol and physiognomy', like his comment on Schiller: 'Schiller's blank verse is bad.
He moves in it as a fly in a glue bottle. His thoughts had their
connection and variety, it is true, but there is no sufficiently corresponding movement in the verse. How different from Shakespeare's endless rhythm.'[4] Practical, then, inward but also extensive: Coleridge's criticism ranged over a variety of writers from
Shakespeare to Schiller, from Dante to Scott, Massinger to Wordsworth, Chaucer to Milton. His treatment of Shakespeare,
Wordsworth and certain general issues apart, it takes the form of
aphorism and aperçu, of hints and clues and suggestive reflections.
This irregular and sketchy manner irritates those who see what a
more disciplined use of his superb gifts might have produced. All
promise, they are inclined to say, little performance. But a Coleridgean hint is infinitely more translucent than a volume by a more
commonplace critic, a clue from him more provocative and clari-
fying than a course of lectures from anyone else.

I have tried by a variety of examples to give the reader the
opportunity to decide for himself whether or not he agrees with

---

[1] *Coleridge's Shakespearean Criticism.* Edited by Thomas Middleton Raysor, Cambridge, 1936, Vol. I, p. 196.
[2] *Biographia Literaria*, I. [3] Ibid. [4] *Table Talk.*

this view. If he does, it will be for several reasons. First, there is Coleridge's faculty for being present, for being actually there, at what strikes the reader as the inmost workings of the nature of whatever it is he is addressing himself to. He could always, or nearly always, find and time the individual pulse of a particular work, and it was rare indeed for any strangeness, any difference of time or belief or feeling, any lack of sympathy, to make his touch clumsy or fumbling. Hardly anything was impermeable to the flow of his curiously liquid sensibility: liquid, I mean, in its purity and 'neutrality' and in its uncontainable onward movement. At its best Coleridge's initial reflection is what he called 'that intuition of things which arises when we possess ourselves as one with the whole. . . . Here there is neither that which affirms, nor that which is affirmed; but the identity and living copula of both.'[1] It was his genius for forming an 'identity and living copula' with so many and such different works of literature that made his commentary on them no ordinary hints or tips but a suggestion about essence—which he defined as the inmost principle of the possibility of anything—or what he called 'the self-unravelling clue'.

Secondly, Coleridge's criticism is so impressive because it always, even at its lightest and most glancing, connects with convictions which have a fine human inclusiveness. His convictions do not depend, do not simply derive, either from his idealistic philosophy or his Anglican theological beliefs, or from both. They are 'a total act of the soul . . . the whole state of the mind'.[2] They exist, they work, at a level below that of abstraction at that great depth where differences vanish, and where a person is simply himself alone, and so, that much closer to other human beings. '. . . all the subtler parts of one's nature must be solitary—man exists herein to himself and to God alone—yea in how much only to God—how much lies *below* his own Consciousness'.[3] Coleridge's convictions had a deep root in his own nature and instincts. They were more solid and more personal than any purely theoretical inferences or philosophical conclusions could have been. It is true, as Keats thought, that Coleridge was excessively possessed by the importance of consciousness. He was almost feverishly anxious to

[1] *The Friend*, II, 11.
[2] *The Friend*, I, 15.
[3] *Notebooks*, 1554.

be explicit. He wanted to force every ground of every judgment into the open. Nevertheless his judgments are developments of his instincts. They are as much articulations of his character as expressions of his theory. There is an unbroken line joining his highest flights to the depths of his nature. Coleridge's criticism, that is, exhibits a great human range, not just the addition of an angelic intelligence to a grosser humanity.

Perhaps I could put the same point differently. Coleridge took literature with immense seriousness (but not solemnity). It nourished the individual mind and was a measure of the quality of social life. Not that his attitude is bleakly Puritan or didactic. His seriousness as a critic was always liable to be interrupted—or since that suggests something alien—to be luminously served by and realised in his wit. Literature itself, he never forgot, was created to be enjoyed. Whatever else it appealed to or succeeded in fostering, it had to be productive of pleasure. 'Their tragic scenes,' he says of the great dramatists of England and France, 'were meant to affect us indeed, but within the bounds of pleasure, and in union with the activity both of our understanding and imagination.'[1] And on the other hand in the comedy of Shakespeare and Molière, which by definition is designed for pleasure, 'the more accurate my knowledge, and the more profoundly I think, the greater is the satisfaction that mingles with my laughter. For though the qualities which these writers portray are ludicrous indeed, either from the kind or the excess, and exquisitely ludicrous, yet are they the natural growth of the human mind. . . .'[2] So that the pleasure of which literature is productive involves the intense exercise of our highest capacities and our concern with the natural growth of the human mind. The criticism which corresponds to this idea of literature both deploys and addresses itself to 'the whole soul of man': its attention too is directed to the growth of the human mind and its concern is with the human happiness achieved by the exercise of imagination and understanding. Not only imagination, Coleridge always believed, but also understanding, because of the fundamental rationality of literature.

So that the reading encouraged by Coleridge's criticism could never be even distantly related to that drowsed, narcotic habit

---

[1] *Satyrane's Letters:* letter II.
[2] Ibid.

many of us are given to now. This was the reading, 'the pass-time or rather kill-time', which Coleridge said was able to reconcile two contrary propensities of human nature, 'indulgence of sloth and hatred of vacancy', and which he tartly classed with 'gaming; swinging or swaying on a chair or gate; spitting over a bridge; smoking; snuff-taking; tête-à-tête quarrels after dinner between husband and wife; conning word by word all the advertisements of the *Daily Advertiser* in a public house on a rainy day'.[1] His own criticism has a tonic effect on the reader. It braces and concentrates attention and, given only half a chance, trains the reader not in the results of knowledge but in the activity of knowing. All that it asks from the reader is a portion of the same effort the writer puts into it. We have 'to think with the author, or the author will have thought in vain for us'. It has been remarked by the celebrated Haller, Coleridge drily points out in the same context, 'that we are deaf while we are yawning'. The same act of drowsiness that stretches open our mouths, closes our ears. It is much the same in acts of the understanding. 'A lazy half-attention amounts to a mental yawn'.[2] Not that there is much danger of mental yawning and deafness for the reader of Coleridge's criticism, even for the half-sympathetic one. Its effect is to freshen our attention and to charge our lethargy with something of the energy manifested in the rapidity of his thought and in the mobility of his expression, as well as in the clean movement of his eager sensibility.

It comes, I think, to this: the effect of Coleridge's criticism on us is to add to our most significantly human powers. It increases intelligence and refines feeling. 'Poetry is a free and vital power', and the criticism which serves it must be free and vital. It must pass no Acts of Uniformity against poets, we remember. 'Criticism which would bind it down to any one Model and bid it grow in a mould is a mere Despotism of False Taste, a usurpation of empty Rules over Life and Substance.'[3] The whole of Coleridge's criticism in intention, the best part of it in effect, that is the genuine criticism and not the applied metaphysics, ministers to the free and vital power of imagination. It stands for life and substance, against despotism and empty rules. Coleridge's critical idiom brings into play at every point the most fundamental and creative

---

[1] *Biographia Literaria*, III, footnote.
[2] *Essays On His Own Times*, III.
[3] *The Inquiring Spirit*. Edited by Kathleen Coburn, London, 1951, p. 151.

of Coleridge's distinctions, the one indeed of which all the others, Imagination and Fancy, Reason and Understanding, Culture and Civilisation, are but translations and applications.

Remember that there is a difference between form as proceeding, and shape as superinduced; the latter is either the death or the imprisonment of the thing; the former is its self-witnessing and self-effected sphere of agency.[1]

[1] *On Poesy or Art.*

Chapter III

COLERIDGE AND POETRY

FROM Milton by way of Cowper to Coleridge: or from *Paradise Lost* (although one should, perhaps, in deference to a great genius, say, from *Paradise Regained*), from *Paradise Regained* via *Divine Chit-chat* to *The Milk of Paradise*—this is the route of Coleridge the poet. His early verse exhibited all the cleverness and imitativeness of the brilliant young man who, in Eliot's sharp distinction, wants to be a poet rather than to write poems. Coleridge latched on to the current routines of movement and diction and managed them with the precocious but hollow skill of a prodigy. Everything is technique and manner, hardly anything significance and substance. His early poems include Miltonic approximations, handfuls of couplets which are meant to balance like Pope's but which keep only a lurching equilibrium, melancholy pieces in a descriptive minor eighteenth-century mood, some stretches of Cowperian-Christian wambling, imitations of Anacreon, Spencer and Ossian, translations of Catullus, and comic efforts in which the humour depends on the discrepancy between a swelling portentous manner and an almost idiotically trifling subject, as in *Monody on a Tea-Kettle*. They are, in fact, all the conventional five-finger exercises of a poetic novice of the period. Here are some characteristic examples.

LINES

To a beautiful Spring in a Village

Once more! sweet Stream! with slow foot wandering near,
I bless thy milky waters cold and clear,
Escap'd the flashing of the noontide hours,
With one fresh garland of Pierian flowers
(Ere from thy zephyr-haunted brink I turn)
My languid hand shall wreath thy mossy urn.

HONOUR

The fervid Sun had more than halv'd the day,
When gloomy on his couch Philedon lay;

His feeble frame consumptive as his purse,
His aching head did wine and woman curse;
His fortune ruin'd and his wealth decay'd,
Clamorous his duns, his gaming debts unpaid,
The youth indignant seiz'd his tailor's bill,
And on its back thus wrote with moral quill:
'Various as colours in the rainbow shown,
Or similar in emptiness alone,
How false, how vain are Man's pursuits below!
Wealth, Honour, Pleasure—what can ye bestow?
Yet see, how high and low, and young and old
Pursue the all-delusive power of Gold. . . .'

ON RECEIVING AN ACCOUNT THAT HIS ONLY SISTER'S DEATH WAS INEVITABLE

The tear which mourn'd a brother's fate scarce dry—
Pain after pain, and woe succeeding woe—
Is my heart destin'd for another blow?
O my sweet sister! and must thou too die?
Ah! how has Disappointment pour'd the tear
O'er infant Hope destroy'd by early frost!
How are ye gone, whom most my soul held dear!
Scarce had I lov'd you ere I mourn'd you lost;

MELANCHOLY

A Fragment

Stretch'd on a moulder'd Abbey's broadest wall,
  Where ruining ivies propp'd the ruins steep—
Her folded arms wrapping her tatter'd pall,
  Had Melancholy mus'd herself to sleep.

The fern was press'd beneath her hair,
  The dark green Adder's Tongue was there;
And still as pass'd the flagging sea-gale weak,
  The long lank leaf bow'd fluttering o'er her cheek.

RELIGIOUS MUSINGS

A Desultory Poem, written on the Christmas Eve of 1794

This is the time, when most divine to hear,
The voice of Adoration rouses me,
As with a Cherub's trump: and high upborne,

Yea, mingling with the Choir, I seem to view
The vision of the heavenly multitude,
Who hymned the song of Peace o'er Bethlehem's fields!
Yet thou more bright than all the Angel-blaze,
That harbingered thy birth, Thou Man of Woes!
Despiséd Galilaean! For the Great
Invisible (by symbols only seen)
With a peculiar and surpassing light
Shines from the visage of the oppressed good man,
When heedless of himself the scourgéd saint
Mourns for the oppressor. . . .

As we should expect, it is Coleridge himself who has made the
appropriate comments on this early verse, as his editor Ernest
Hartley Coleridge realised when he included them as footnotes in
his edition of the poems.[1] One of them, Coleridge said in a letter
to his brother George, belonged to the 'namby-pamby genus'[2];
by another he was reminded of 'old Jemmy Bowyer, the *plagose
Orbilius* of Christ's Hospital, but an admirable educer no less than
Educator of the Intellect, [who] bade me leave out as many epithets
as would turn the whole into eight-syllable lines, and then ask myself
if the exercise would not be greatly improved. How often have I
thought of the proposal since then, and how many thousand
bloated and puffing lines have I read, that, by this process, would
have tripped over the tongue excellently. Likewise, I remember
that he told me on the same occasion—"Coleridge! the connections of a Declamation are not the transitions of Poetry—bad,
however, as they are, they are better than 'Apostrophes' and 'O
thou's', for at the worst they are something like common sense.
The others are the grimaces of Lunacy." '[3] Namby-pamby, the
connections of a Declamation, even perhaps bloated and puffing,
although Coleridge hardly intended these epithets to be applied
directly to himself—these harsh phrases have their justice. But the
most significant of Coleridge's judgments on his early poems is that
in which he says that while 'such Verses as *strivings* of mind and
struggles after the Intense and Vivid are a fair promise of better
things', they still are no more than 'a *Putting of Thought into Verse*'.[4]
Coleridge's early verse, like that of any other beginner, is cracked

---

[1] *The Poems of Samuel Taylor Coleridge.* Edited by Ernest Hartley Coleridge,
London, 1927.
[2] *Letters*, Vol. I, pp. 57-8.
[3] *The Poems of Samuel Taylor Coleridge*, p. 3.   [4] Ibid., p. 2.

by a gap. 'Putting of thought into verse' implies both the duality of the elements out of which the verse is made, the thought and the language, *and* the discrepancy, the gap, which remains when one is put into the other as into a container. As the poet grows, the gap closes. The thought is *in* the language and the language is *of* the thought.

Even in the verses of his earliest period, however, there are hints of a closure of the gap and touches which promise a more truly Coleridgean presence. For example, in the first colourless piece of those I have quoted, *To a beautiful Spring in a Village*, the line

> I bless thy milky waters cold and clear,

has a faint something in it of that characteristic Coleridgean rhythm in which part melts into part and the whole moves with an unbroken streaming fluidity; at the same time there is a point of sharpness, an emphasis, which does not interrupt the flow: the phrase 'milky waters' indents but doesn't slow up the line and it has the force that comes when an epithet almost contests the term it illuminates. Or take another example like the following, which was sent in a letter to Southey on July 6th, 1794. 'Description of Heat from a Poem I am manufacturing—the Title "Perspiration, a Travelling Eclogue".'

> The Dust flies smothering, as on clatt'ring Wheels
> Loath'd Aristocracy careers along.
> The distant Track quick vibrates to the Eye,
> And white and dazzling undulates with heat.
> Where scorching to th' unwary Traveller's touch
> The stone-fence flings its narrow Slip of Shade,
> Or where the worn sides of the chalky Road
> Yield their scant excavations (sultry Grots!)
> Emblem of languid Patience, we behold
> The fleecy Files faint-ruminating lie.—[1]

This odd little snatch of verse was written out of a haze of Pantisocratic, Republican sentiment and genuine indignation against 'the lingering Remains of Aristocracy'—all of which is taken up in the careering, and at this point not too congruous, chariot of 'loath'd

---

[1] *Letters*, Vol. I, p. 84.

Aristocracy'. The letter also includes one of those sharp little descriptive notes preparatory to a poem, of the kind that Dorothy Wordsworth used to provide for William's poems. 'Our Journeying has been intolerably fatiguing from the heat and whiteness of the Roads—and the *unhedged* country presents nothing but *stone*-fences dreary to the Eye and scorching to the touch.'[1] In spite of the curious combination of a romantic propaganda and a quantity of tired Augustan cement (sultry Grots, languid Patience, fleecy Files) the middle lines do render more completely the experience of the prose note, and do so with that mobile and active clarity which was to distinguish Coleridge's writing as it developed. 'The stone-fence flings its narrow Slip of Shade' has the precise and bodily quality in it of grasped sense experience, all the more striking amid the shadows of eighteenth-century diction and nineteenth-century cliché.

The set of political and social sonnets written during 1794-95, although some of them have been favourably spoken of, seem to me to be all shadow, cliché and diction, with only the most shrunken bodily quality. Poetry as political or religious or social propaganda was not the distasteful thing it seems to us, in an age which had less reason than we for believing only in the validity of private experience as the matter of art. But the sonnet form so traditional and *given*, is yawningly inappropriate to themes intended to be contemporary and even revolutionary. The form in these poems affects me like an ancient piece of fur round a young body. At any rate the relation between words and feeling, expression and thought, in these poems, is almost exactly the opposite of what Coleridge explicitly recommended when he wrote— 'The *heart* should have *fed* upon the *truth*, as insects on a leaf, till it be tinged with the colour, and show its food in every the minutest fibre'.[2] Contrast this advice with the declamatory and abstract sonnet *To Earl Stanhope*, hardly more than noble intentions and a vague wash of feeling.

> NOT, STANHOPE! with the Patriot's doubtful name
> I mock thy worth—Friend of the Human Race!
> Since scorning Faction's low and partial aim
> Aloof thou wendest in thy stately pace,

---

[1] *Letters*, Vol. I, p. 83.
[2] Ibid., Vol. I, p. 115.

Thyself redeeming from that leprous stain,
Nobility: and aye unterrify'd
Pourest thine Abdiel warnings on the train
That sit complotting with rebellious pride

'Gainst *Her* who from the Almighty's bosom leapt
With whirlwind arm, fierce Minister of Love!
Wherefore, ere Virtue o'er thy tomb hath wept,
Angels shall lead thee to the Throne above:

And thou from forth its clouds shalt hear the voice,
Champion of Freedom and her God! rejoice!

One can understand why Coleridge should have written as he did at the end of an immense letter to John Thelwall 'I love Sonnets; but *upon my honor* I do not love *my* Sonnets'. And an unfeeling person, after reading several of Coleridge's sonnets which are both Godwinian and religiose in equally repulsive proportions, might well want to apply to Coleridge himself the words which precede this conclusion: 'he is a man of fluent Eloquence and general knowledge, gentle in his manners, warm in his affections; but unfortunately he has received a few rays of supernatural Light thro' a crack in his upper storey'.

How different is the billowy outline of the Stanhope sonnet, and the Pitt, Burke, Southey and Godwin ones too, from the more stripped and wiry appearance of the kind of poetry Coleridge was beginning to compose during 1795. It was a poetry that could be called, clumsily but fairly, reflective-descriptive and reflective-conversational. Examples are the Somerset poems, *Lines composed while climbing the Left Ascent of Brockley Coomb*, and *The Eolian Harp*. It is more personal, less apt to float away on piety and generality, its rhythm more broken, its stress more distributed. In *Lines composed while climbing the Left Ascent of Brockley Coomb*, for instance, the cool discipline of climbing, which Coleridge loved, clears away much hazy generality and gives scope for his sense of movement, in this case physical movement; one feels the upward thrust of the climber, the foot scraping the stone, the sharply registered sense impressions which cluster round the central experience and crowd the climber's consciousness.

With many a pause and oft reverted eye
I climb the Coomb's ascent: sweet songsters near

Warble in shade their wild-wood melody:
Far off the unvarying Cuckoo soothes my ear.
Up scour the startling stragglers of the flock
That on green plots o'er precipices browze:
From the deep fissures of the naked rock
The Yew-tree bursts! Beneath its dark green boughs
(Mid which the May-thorn blends its blossoms white)
Where broad smooth stones jut out in mossy seats,
I rest:

The Eolian Harp, on the other hand, is controlled by Coleridge's sense of mental movement. The mobility of his own mind was something he was acutely conscious of, and he was beginning now to produce a corresponding movement in his verse. 'The heaven-descended Know Thyself' was Coleridge's great motto; but in fact knowing thyself means knowing thyself knowing, and *that* means knowing thyself knowing an object. *The Eolian Harp* is a poem on the action or conduct of consciousness. There is a passage in *Biographia Literaria* in which Coleridge speaks of precisely this:

> Most of my readers will have observed a small water-insect on the surface of rivulets, which throws a cinque-spotted shadow fringed with prismatic colours on the sunny bottom of the brook; and will have noticed, how the little animal *wins* its way up against the stream, by alternate pulses of active and passive motion, now resisting the current, and now yielding to it in order to gather strength and a momentary *fulcrum* for a further propulsion. This is no unapt emblem of the mind's self-experience in the act of thinking.[1]

Self-experience in the act of thinking (as long as we make 'thinking' as inclusive a term as we can and as long as we remember that 'thinking' means thinking of something) is the experience illuminated in *The Eolian Harp*. Nor is the Harp itself,

'that simplest Lute,
Placed lengthways in the clasping casement'

an unapt emblem of the mind's conscious action, winning its way forward 'by alternate pulses of active and passive motion'. The Harp, like the mind, is passive as it yields to the influences playing upon it, and active as it organises and directs them. The conversational informality of the poem, composed of several kinds of

[1] *Biographia Literaria*, VII.

mental performance, of direct address, of reflection, of generalisation, of the exact and delighted registration of sense-impression, is a model of the movement of consciousness as it slips and glides from point to point, or gathers itself to balance here or to leap on there or to swerve back again. The movements and pauses of the mind are not formal or legislated. They begin and end according to an intrinsic logic. The casual gait and the undressed-up attitude is one of the remarkable achievements of this new verse. It is the manner least constrained by anything outside itself, and the rhythm most accommodated to the mind's discursive, flowing action. The sense of movement in so concentrated an activity as poetry depends greatly upon the appreciation of stillness, and the mastery of movement Coleridge shows in this conversational verse is connected with skill in managing what I can only call the variety of stillness. Look at the different modes of movement and suspended movement in this first verse paragraph:

> My pensive Sara! thy soft cheek reclined
> Thus on mine arm, most soothing sweet it is
> To sit beside our Cot, our Cot o'ergrown
> With white-flower'd Jasmin, and the broad-leav'd
> Myrtle,
> (Meet emblems they of Innocence and Love!)
> And watch the clouds, that late were rich with light,
> Slow saddening round, and mark the star of eve
> Serenely brilliant (such should Wisdom be)
> Shine opposite! How exquisite the scents
> Snatch'd from yon bean-field! and the world *so*
> hush'd!
> The stilly murmur of the distant Sea
> Tells us of silence.

The movement at first is quiet, almost passive, with a relaxed drifting motion appropriate to a mood of simple, unimpassioned intimacy.

> My pensive Sara! thy soft cheek reclined
> Thus on mine arm, most soothing sweet it is . . .

But it tightens into a slightly more clipped and regular pace at:

> To sit beside our Cot, our Cot o'ergrown
> With white-flower'd Jasmin, and the broad-leav'd
> Myrtle, . . .

which presents a physical object—our Cot—with its decorative
defining additions. The pace changes to accommodate the vaguer
beat of the gently reflective generalisation

(Meet emblems they of Innocence and Love!)

Immediately it sharpens for the more positive physical action of
'And watch the clouds' (a phrase which is in balance with 'To sit
beside our Cot', three lines before), so that our attention is braced
and our hearing prepared for the organ-like sound and the grandly
solemn pace of:

> . . . that late were rich with light,
> Slow saddening round, and mark the star of eve
> Serenely brilliant . . .,

a movement which is reined in by a second but different kind of
generalisation '(such should Wisdom be)'. The difference lies in
the stronger more normative spring of this statement as against
the level sighing monotone of the first generalisation. And yet it *is*
comparatively withdrawn and contemplative: the observer (and
the reader) at this point seems to have retreated from the scene,
so that what follows, the summoning and orienting sharpness of
the dramatically placed phrase 'Shine opposite', comes with an
even more startling effect of actuality and presence. The crown of
this subtlety of combined and contrasting movement and stillness
comes in the marvellous lines which follow:

> . . . How exquisite the scents
> Snatch'd from yon bean-field! and the world *so* hush'd!
> The stilly murmur of the distant Sea
> Tells us of silence.

They begin with a delighted exclamation which is not allowed, as
an exclamation generally is, to lose itself in the air, but which is
given, on the contrary, a bodily force in the strongly physical
metaphor of *snatch'd*, a word carrying with it intimations both of
the intensity of the scents as they rise from a particular bean-field
('yon' is an active directing word here) *and* the gathering action of
the eager nostrils. The certainty and closeness of an exquisite
sense-experience refine themselves, by an odd but acceptable
human logic, into something as sure and precise, but also much

more remote and piercing, in which movement and stillness are unified and the terms themselves transferable. There is a passage from the height of the scent to the deep murmur of the sea and its identification of movement and stillness, sound and silence.

Sense-experience is significant and structural in *The Eolian Harp*. The first paragraph is organised round a set of sense-experiences, each one delicately evolving into the next, first touch, next sight, then scent and sound. The modulation of one form of sense-experience into another was a psychological phenomenon Coleridge was particularly sensitive to '. . . the sense of vision itself', he said about the beginnings of sense experience in children, 'is only acquired by a continued recollection of touch'.[1] The melting and modification of one form of sense experience into another —the activity which is implicit in this first verse paragraph and of which the Eolian Harp itself, turning the movement of air into the movement of music, is a kind of model—this is the idea or intuition which is generalised at two points later on in the poem. First at:

> O! the one Life within us and abroad,
> Which meets all motion and becomes its soul,
> A light in sound, a sound-like power in light,
> Rhythm in all thought, and joyance every where . . .

which is some distance in the direction of explicit philosophical abstraction from the actual and concrete experience of:

> The stilly murmur of the distant Sea
> Tells us of silence.

And yet the poem is not simply the illustration of an abstract thesis. Some degree of abstraction is even appropriate in a situation in which the poet's mind is held in a passive, ungoverning posture, concerned more to register than to organise whatever notions or phantasies float across it:

> As wild and various as the random gales
> That swell and flutter on this subject Lute!

[1] *The Philosophical Lectures of S. T. Coleridge.* Edited by Kathleen Coburn, London , 1949, p. 115.

So that the second generalisation has been prepared for and its vaguely patheistic inclination rendered less ineffable, especially by the highly indicative and toning phrase 'swell and flutter'.

> And what if all of animated nature
> Be but organic Harps diversely fram'd,
> That tremble into thought, as o'er them sweeps
> Plastic and vast, one intellectual breeze,
> At once the Soul of each, and God of all?

Not only has this swelling and fluttering utterance been prepared for and then put into its place by the interrogative, which gives it only a hypothetical status, but it also includes a phrase—'tremble into thought', which shows us that it is meant to be as much a psychological description as an ontological statement. It is the poet's sense of, it may even be more a yearning for, the harmonious and organic in the universe which trembles into thought in these lines. So that a passage which in itself seems dangerously ready to float away off the ground altogether, becomes in the context attached and justified. It is its origin in the poet's consciousness which counts in the poem, not its validity as a metaphysical doctrine.

The Eolian Harp draws to its end with a rather perfunctory patch of sermonising of a kind to be found in several poems written during these years, for example *Reflections on having left a Place of Retirement* (1795), *To a Young Friend on his proposing to domesticate with the Author* (1796), *To a Friend* (1796), *To the Rev. George Coleridge* (1797). Although these poems contain passages of natural description of a quite unveiled immediacy their significance lies less in their intrinsic merits than in their being the means or discipline by which Coleridge worked himself loose from the obese-declamatory of *The Destiny of Nations* and the orotund-religiose of *Religious Musings* and developed an idiom and a rhythm of casual and supple virtuosity.

To put it like this is perhaps to suggest too directly and with insufficient justification something like a temporal succession. And in fact *Religious Musings* was written during 1794-96 and much of *The Destiny of Nations* during 1796. But even if there wasn't a neat working out of a new style, there is no doubt that Coleridge was separating out the public-declamatory kind of poetry from a poetry of private experience, and that he was opting finally for the latter.

As Humphry House pointed out in his learned and subtle essay,[1] the Romantics and Coleridge particularly inherited from Milton and tried to renovate a tradition of poetry which combined political, philosophical and religious themes. This poetry of public propaganda is almost unreadable today. It is vague, pompous, unorganised and fatigued by ugly abstractions. Here is a characteristic piece from *Religious Musings*:

> There is one Mind, one omnipresent Mind,
> Omnific. His most holy name is Love.
> Truth of subliming import! with the which
> Who feeds and saturates his constant soul,
> He from his small particular orbit flies
> With blest outstarting!

Contrast this 'Truth of subliming import' with some lines from *Reflections on having left a place of Retirement*:

> *Here* the bleak mount,
> The bare bleak mountain speckled thin with sheep;
> Grey clouds, that shadowing spot the sunny fields;
> And river, now with bushy rocks o'er-brow'd,
> Now winding bright and full, with naked banks....

Or with this from *To a Young Friend*

> O then 'twere loveliest sympathy, to mark
> The berries of the half-uprooted ash
> Dripping and bright;

In these lines we see the verse medium cleared of any blurring generality and we feel the rhythm of a natural movement instead of the bustle of ideas pushed along by an external force like the will to convince. We are aware too that these qualities are at the service of a descriptive faculty able at once to suggest both an appearance and the object which projects it. We sense the twisted wood under 'the berries . . . dripping and bright', and we have a feeling of the harsh country beneath 'the bare bleak mountain speckled thin with sheep'. Coleridge's power to delineate the natural world with such exact, individual rightness is matched by his capacity to reproduce with comparable sureness not simply

---

[1] *Coleridge: The Clark Lectures 1951-52*, by Humphry House, London, 1962, pp. 63-7.

the general energy of the mind but the precise activity of his own consciousness. In *This Lime-Tree Bower My Prison*, the poem I wish to turn to now, each of these abilities has the fullest scope; at the same time the shape of the poem as a composition—as a pattern of movement and repose—is established by the passage, intricate and smooth, from one to the other. The preparatory prose note defines the ground and makes it possible for the poem to take off immediately.

> In the June of 1797 some long-expected friends paid a visit to the author's cottage; and on the morning of their arrival, he met with an accident, which disabled him from walking during the whole time of their stay. One evening, when they had left him for a few hours, he composed the following lines in the garden-bower.

(It was in fact on the seventh of July that Charles Lamb arrived and on the fourth of July that 'dear Sara accidentally emptied a skillet of boiling milk' on his foot.[1]) Coleridge's throw-away opening exhibits that special brand of casual daring found in the work of a master in any art who has perfected a style. It is evidence of a sovereign confidence in himself and in the development of his subject, together with complete control of his idiom and rhythm.

> Well, they are gone, and here must I remain,
> This lime-tree bower my prison! I have lost
> Beauties and feelings, such as would have been
> Most sweet to my remembrance even when age
> Had dimm'd mine eyes to blindness!

What seems like simple spontaneity is really carefully organised round a triple contrast between *they* and *I*, *are* and *must*, *gone* and *remain*. The contrast is enforced by the sharp break dividing movement and focus in the first line, which sets up at once a duality of place and person and condition, and it is reinforced by the shift in the position of the subject on either side of the division: *they are* is open and unimpeded but *must I* carries a burden of compulsion. One runs on, the other is trapped. It is, however, trapped in a very special prison, *this lime-tree-bower*, an exquisitely fresh and scented jail. So that from the beginning the principal theme is broken out and signals—it may be no more than guarded ones—are despatched

[1] Cf. *Letters*, p. 334.

about the procedure the poet will adopt. The poem is to be concerned with those deep, primary, human experiences of presence and absence, while the conduct or development of the poem turns upon the movement from one to the other: the themes of presence and absence run through the poem intertwining, separating, balancing and turning from one to the other.

It is absence, the negative element in his Lime Tree Bower which affects the poet first. He is imprisoned by injury, and his mind flicks forward from weakness to blindness and age, in a progression as natural in the context as the quiver of self-pity which trembles through the lines. Absence equals loss and the feeling of the poet at this point is a passive, unfocused sense of loss. It cannot be detailed since what he has lost are plangent and generalised possibilities, hypothetical memories, 'Beauties and feelings . . . most sweet to my remembrance . . .'. How this generalised melancholy contrasts with the grip and energy of what follows!

> They, meanwhile,
> Friends, whom I never more may meet again,
> On springy heath, along the hill-top edge,
> Wander in gladness, and wind down, perchance,
> To that still roaring dell, of which I told;
> The roaring dell, o'erwooded, narrow, deep,
> And only speckled by the mid-day sun;
> Where its slim trunk the ash from rock to rock
> Flings arching like a bridge;—that branchless ash,
> Unsunn'd and damp, whose few poor yellow leaves
> Ne'er tremble in the gale, yet tremble still,
> Fann'd by the water-fall! and there my friends
> Behold the dark green file of long lank weeds,
> That all at once (a most fantastic sight!)
> Still nod and drip beneath the dripping edge
> Of the blue clay-stone.

The first words, 'They, meanwhile, / Friends, whom I never more may meet again', with their depressed sense of contingency and loss, connect with the mood of the lime-tree prison, but they also open out into a powerful, joyous celebration of *presence*. I have spoken before of Coleridge's remarkable empathic faculty—'One travels along on the lines of a mountain . . .'[1]—and it is the buoyant

---

[1] *Anima Poetae.*

support of this which makes it possible for him to leap from his cell
to be with, or within, his friends as they

> On springy heath, along the hill-top edge,
> Wander in gladness, and wind down, perchance,
> To that still roaring dell. . . .

Presence is a vibrant, humming state, or an activity rather than a
state, the images of which are intensely alive and charged with
energy—springy heath, his friends winding down, the roaring
dell, the ash trunk arching. Being with, in this sense, is an activity
or dance of being, in which even poor yellow leaves, unsunn'd
and damp, that the gale cannot reach, still tremble. The first
expression of this active state, as close to it as sight is to intelligence,
is a peculiarly creative kind of observation in which the onlooker
is taken up into, and takes up into himself, the life of the observed.
There are two places in this part of the poem at which the reader
is particularly aware of the mutual invasion of observed and
observer, or of what Coleridge called the coincidence of subject
and object. The first is at 'The roaring dell, o'erwooded, narrow,
deep', where the violence of sound, being enclosed, is still more
intense and possessing; the second is at the end of the paragraph:

> and there my friends
> Behold the dark green file of long lank weeds,
> That all at once (a most fantastic sight!)
> Still nod and drip beneath the dripping edge
> Of the blue clay-stone.

where the bruising force of the detail is heightened by the contrast
with the interpolated, oddly colloquial reflection, 'a most fantastic
sight', and driven home by the repeated *drip*, and by the sharply
edged, stonily heavy quality of the short words and the clipped
rhythm. The first part of the poem ends, then, on a note of density
and concentration. The second part starts on a more open and
aerial one, appropriate to 'the wide wide Heaven' and 'the many-
steepled tract' on which his friends emerge. Its aerial and luminous
quality comes through, for example, in:

> sails light up
> The slip of smooth clear blue betwixt two Isles
> Of purple shadow!

And again in:

> Shine in the slant beams of the sinking orb,
> Ye purple heath-flowers! richlier burn, ye clouds!
> Live in the yellow light, ye distant groves!
> And kindle, thou blue Ocean!

The almost painterly sense of the depths and colours of light flowing across the brilliant landscape is beautifully in keeping with the tonic and reviving effect of the natural world, its capacity to renovate in man his powers of joy, the idea which Coleridge brings into prominence at this point. Coleridge's empathic faculty in the passage takes in not only the physical world but the psychological one. Charles Lamb is his surrogate here, and Charles Lamb's response is Coleridge's.

> So my friend
> Struck with deep joy may stand, as I have stood,
> Silent with swimming sense; yea, gazing round
> On the wide landscape, gaze till all doth seem
> Less gross than bodily;

The whole solidity of the natural world is seen aspiring to the quality of light. In the same way the density of physical experience when it becomes this positive, human presence climbs to a level of fineness and intensity which Coleridge rightly takes to be spiritual.

To be present, then, as Coleridge felt it, is with every bodily sense and mental faculty alert to meet in a most intense unison the life and forms of the natural world; to experience in that meeting a mutual communication of life so that, as he says, for example, in *Fears in Solitude*:

> that huge amphi-theatre of rich
> And elmy fields seems like society—
> Conversing with the mind, and giving it
> A livelier impulse and a dance of thought . . . ;[1]

and with the self at once tethered in actuality and transformed by otherness to be possessed by a great depth and fineness of feeling along the whole scale of man's impulses. In the second part of this

[1] Nether Stowey, April 20th, 1798.

poem Coleridge has this experience as it were at a distance, through his analogue Charles Lamb, outside his lime-tree prison. In the last part of the poem his revived spirit and freshened senses turn back to the place he is in. There is undoubtedly some reference here to the Romantic consolatory function of nature, the kind mother soothing the fevered child. But there is a great deal much more intense and immediate in Coleridge's conception of the relationship than anything that is fully described as consolation, which implies certainly a close but also a definite duality, as well as a passivity on the part of the recipient. Nature for Coleridge is very much more the infuser of life than the provider of comfort. And it is with this new access of life that 'a delight / comes sudden on my heart . . .'. His absence from there becomes his presence here. But it is a present that is the immediate state of the past, not something torn off from it. Coleridge uses an awakened memory as well as sharpened senses. And he begins with one of the double negatives that he and Wordsworth were so fond of and generally employed so clumsily. But in this instance it has the effect of a net thrown into the past as it slips by, which draws expertly out fragments on the point of oblivion.

> Nor in this bower,
> This little lime-tree bower, have I not mark'd
> Much that has sooth'd me. Pale beneath the blaze
> Hung the transparent foliage; and I watch'd
> Some broad and sunny leaf, and lov'd to see
> The shadow of the leaf and stem above
> Dappling its sunshine! And that walnut-tree
> Was richly ting'd, and a deep radiance lay
> Full on the ancient ivy, which usurps
> Those fronting elms, and now, with blackest mass
> Makes their dark branches gleam a lighter hue
> Through the late twilight: and though now the bat
> Wheels silent by, and not a swallow twitters,
> Yet still the solitary humble-bee
> Sings in the bean-flower!

As the lines proceed the just gone turns into the immediate moment. One has a sense of time gliding forward. The whole stay in the lime-tree bower has been saved and each impression caught with the crispest accuracy. Presence, as it is reconstructed in this poem, is not exhausted by any abstract *now*. It takes in, indeed it is

creative of, the past and it has, as the conclusion of the poem
shows, its significance for the future: both its personal significance,

> Henceforth I shall know . . .
> No plot so narrow, be but Nature there,
> No waste so vacant, but may well employ
> Each faculty of sense, and keep the heart
> Awake . . .

and its larger one

> 'No sound is dissonant which tells of Life'.

I turn now to a set of poems, totally different in style and sensibility, *Christabel, Kubla Khan, The Rime of the Ancient Mariner,* which
have been paid such a volume of attention that they have been the
occasion of a severe distortion in Coleridge's poetic reputation. It
is as the author of *Christabel, Kubla Khan, The Rime of the Ancient
Mariner,* that Coleridge is a household word, not as the author of
The Eolian Harp, This Lime-Tree Bower my Prison, and *Frost at Midnight,* although these are poems in which one is aware of an
individual poet speaking in a contemporary voice of his private
experience, something which represented a truly original and
independent achievement and which introduced a new art into
a new world. In these poems it is the poet's private experience which
is the massive focal thing—any themes and subjects are implicated
in this and the poet comes to them in exploring the intimations
of his personal life. In the poems of magic, on the other hand, if I
may use this formula tentatively for a moment, it is the impersonal
thing or theme treated which is important, and one comes to the
personal life by following the implications and the vibrations of
the theme; and this was a traditional habit and a traditional poetry.
The date of *Christabel* is probably 1800-01, that of *Kubla Khan*
probably 1798, and *The Rime of the Ancient Mariner* 1797-98, but I
want to treat them in the order in which I list them since this is also
I think the order of their ascending worth.

Christabel displays an effective sense of the macabre and a
characteristically Coleridgean skill in *involving* the natural world
in the feeling of the poem:

Is the night chilly and dark?
The night is chilly, but not dark.
The thin gray cloud is spread on high,
It covers but not hides the sky.
The moon is behind, and at the full;
And yet she looks both small and dull.
The night is chill, the cloud is gray:
Tis a month before the month of May,
And the Spring comes slowly up this way.

The diction throughout the poem is as pure and simple as this, the rhythm, 'being founded on a new principle: namely, that of counting in each line the accents, not the syllables' (as Coleridge said in his introduction) is, precisely because of this 'new principle', traditional and thoroughly English in gait. But while Coleridge shows throughout a great virtuosity and sophistication in the use of his deceptively simple rhythmical line, he is not able to preserve the same restraint in the treatment of the macabre effect. He is apt on occasion to pant and huff; he is quite explicit in telling the reader to get ready to be terrified—

Hush, beating heart of Christabel!
Jesu, Maria, shield her well!
She folded her arms beneath her cloak,
And stole to the other side of the oak.
What sees she there?

Coleridge, as he showed in his drama *Remorse*, shared the romantic poets' incapacity for creating a convincing human figure; at the same time he has not been content to let Christabel, Geraldine and the Baron stay remote figures in a tapestry or a window. He wants them to have a thrilling, personal effect on the reader, and they end up by seeming to have neither content nor effect. The staging of the poem is disfigured by a good deal of historical costume cliché, and by the peculiar romantic feebleness in dealing with anything remotely sexual in tone. One is left with an unexplained sense of something enigmatically nasty in the relationship of the trembling Christabel and the ambiguous Geraldine but it is all in the air, unjustified and undetailed. Hazlitt wasn't simply being brutally wrong-headed when he wrote, 'there is something disgusting at the bottom of his subject, which is but ill glossed over by a veil of

Della Cruscan sentiment and fine writing . . .'[1] This general air of inexplicability may be partly due to the world in which *Christabel* is set. I believe that A. H. Nethercot[2] made a perfectly valid point when he applied the well-known theological distinction preternatural-supernatural to *Christabel* on the one hand and *The Rime of the Ancient Mariner* on the other. The supernatural is a world of God and order, sin, guilt, grace and of rational balance— the world of the Ancient Mariner; the preternatural a sub-divine, extra-human one which is murky and vague and irrational. It is occupied by malevolent beings and there lurks in it everywhere and at all times a kind of meaningless menace.

But even more responsible for the arbitrary quality of *Christabel* is its deficiency in composition. What *Christabel* as a narrative needed most was organisation, which is what it conspicuously lacks. The poem was written in two gulps in 1797 and 1800, with a journey to Germany[3] intervening, and never finished. Encouraged by Byron who thought it a 'wild, singularly original and beautiful poem', Coleridge tried, or persuaded himself that he tried, several times to go on with it. But though the poem has a certain thematic complexity, which one would have thought had within it the possibilities of development, Coleridge was quite incapable—and it wasn't the *will* that was missing—of drawing out the tangle into anything like lucidity and completeness. *Christabel* has at its best a romantic brilliance and wildness (Byron's term is a good one); but it also has a Victorian namby-pambyness (as I have found in teaching it to the young) which is at least faintly repellent today.

Christabel has the arbitrariness of the imperfect; *Kubla Khan* the perfection of the inexplicable. There it stands as certain and solid as an object while it is also as evanescent and ungraspable as a dream. The great question about *Kubla Khan* for the reader is whether its visionary brilliance can be said to include a rational structure. Lowes'[4] great feat of literary forensic science has exposed every fragment of its anatomy and every element in its genesis. But it is much less clearly helpful about the life of the poem. He has shown, that is, that there is a rational structure outside the poem. But is there one implicit in it? Extreme views on this matter are put

---

[1] *Examiner*, June 2nd, 1860.
[2] *The Road to Tryermaine*, Chicago, 1929, pp. 200-1.
[3] Cf. *Letters*, Vol. IV, p. 601.
[4] Lowes, *The Road to Xanadu*, London, 1931.

on the one side by Hazlitt, who thought it proved that Coleridge was one of the best writers of nonsense poems in English, a view which is not so outrageous if we take nonsense to be non-sense in the current philosophical usage; and on the other by Humphry House who asks—'If Coleridge had never published his Preface, who would have thought of "Kubla Khan" as a fragment? Who would have guessed at a dream? Who, without the confession, would have supposed that "in consequence of a slight indisposition, an anodyne had been prescribed?" Who would have thought it nothing but a "psychological curiosity?" Who, later, would have dared to talk of its "patchwork brilliance?" '[1] Well, Eliot for one. '. . . the imagery of that fragment, certainly, whatever its origin in Coleridge's reading,' he writes, 'sank to the depth of Coleridge's feeling, was saturated, transformed there—"those are pearls that were his eyes"—and brought up into daylight again. But it is not *used*: the poem has not been written. . . .'[2] Eliot is responding to something really present in *Kubla Khan*, an oddly static quality. And I do not mean a lack of movement, so much as a lack of development. *Kubla Khan* is an ecstatic spasm, a pure spurt of romantic inspiration. It was a composition, 'if that indeed can be called composition in which all the images rose up before him as *things*, without any sensation or conscious effort', dominated by images and it is as a set of images that Eliot and Coleridge himself think of the poem. The images have that unnatural clarity which we are told drug-taking confers upon the objects of sense: and not only of sense, we must believe, but also of memory; and it is true, as Eliot tartly points out, 'As we have learnt from Dr Lowes's *Road to Xanadu* (if we did not know it already) [that] memory plays a very great part in imagination, and of course a much larger part than can be proved by that book; Professor Lowes had only literary reminiscences to deal with, and they are the only kind of reminiscence which can be fully traced and identified: but how much more of memory enters into creation than only our reading!'[3] But while the separate images have this burning intensity of definition, each modulates into the next with the shadowy transition of a dream. 'We understand it', as Coleridge wrote about children 'as we all understand our dreams while we are dreaming,

---

[1] *Coleridge: The Clark Lectures, 1951-52*, by Humphry House, London, 1962, p. 114.
[2] T. S. Eliot, *The Use of Poetry and the Use of Criticism*, London, 1933, p. 146.
[3] Ibid., p. 69.

each shape and incident or group of shapes and incidents by itself —unconscious of, and therefore unoffended at, the absence of the logical copula or the absurdity of the transitions.'[1]

Kubla Khan is less a poem about the act of poetic imagination, as Humphry House maintains, than a suggestion about the energy of imagination as a force which finds its release in images. It is a sketch—although that is too deliberate a term—an impression of 'that shadowy half being...just on the vestibule of consciousness'.[2] The state of trance, the hypnotic beat, the almost total absence of any discursive content, the atmosphere at once sexual and sacred, the images crystalline in their clarity and yet melting into one another, the dreamy balances: sunless sea—fertile ground, sacred river—lifeless ocean, pleasure dome—caves of ice, ancestral voices —damsel with a dulcimer, honey-dew—milk of paradise, these are the elements of a poem which present the imaginative act as an uncaused and numinous event. It is the distillation of the purest romanticism. But—and it is important to insist on this—this is only a small part of Coleridge's genius as a poet.

In *The Rime of the Ancient Mariner* the romanticism is submitted much more deeply to arrangement and composition. Wordsworth, as he remembered it, first suggested a possible scheme for the poem on November 13th, 1797, while walking with Dorothy and Coleridge. 'I had been reading in Shelvocke's *Voyages*, a day or two before, that, while doubling Cape Horn, they frequently saw albatrosses in that latitude, the largest sort of sea-fowl, some extending their wings twelve or thirteen feet. "Suppose," said I, "you represent him as having killed one of these birds on entering the South Sea, and that the tutelary spirits of these regions take upon them to avenge the crime?" This incident was thought fit for the purpose and adopted according.' The poem took months to compose and years to revise. Wordsworth's hint, filled out with Coleridge's own reading in the literature of voyages and of conversion, and touched by the influence of Percy and a medieval religious pattern, offered Coleridge a character, a situation, a drama, a geography and context, a machinery wholly fitted to encourage that combination of management and acceptance necessary in art. The world of *The Ancient Mariner*, so inclusive and so dramatic, powerfully attracted the poet's profoundest experi-

---

[1] *Inquiring Spirit.* Edited by Kathleen Coburn, p. 204.
[2] *Letters*, Vol. II, p. 814.

ence: it strongly encouraged that essential flow of unconscious forces of which Coleridge said, 'In every work of art there is a reconcilement of the external and the internal, the conscious is so impressed on the unconscious as to appear in it. . . . He who combines the two is the man of genius; and for that reason he must partake of both. Hence there is in genius itself an unconscious activity: nay, that is the genius in the man of genius.' But Coleridge was not only a genius. He was also very emphatically a great artist, the supreme discriminator. And the world—and the medium—of *The Ancient Mariner*—is most delicately sensitive and responsive to any control the poet exercises in the interests of his vision.

I stress the *medium* because discussions of *The Rime of the Ancient Mariner* habitually ignore this vital element of the poem. They concern themselves with the poem's origins and antecedents, with its references, symbols, its scaffolding of myth. Even the best of such discussions, Robert Penn Warren's,[1] an argument as temperate as it is understanding, refers to everything but the qualities of the medium itself. The rhythm has the minimum of conditions. It is mobile and unclogged. The simple ballad line, an alternation of four and three beats, disposed into two phrasal units, is admirably suited in its economy and speed to drive the narrative forward:

> The fair breeze blew, the white foam flew,
> The furrow followed free;
> We were the first that ever burst
> Into that silent sea.

Its spareness fits it for action:

> With throats unslaked, with black lips baked,
> We could nor laugh nor wail;
> Through utter drought all dumb we stood!
> I bit my arm, I sucked the blood,
> And cried, A sail! a sail!

The rhythm, even at the most intense moments of the poem, is never far from the movement of speech and falls into actual speech with perfect naturalness:

[1] *The Rime of the Ancient Mariner*, with an essay by Robert Penn Warren, New York, 1946.

'God save thee, ancient Mariner!
From the fiends, that plague thee thus!—
Why look'st thou so?'—With my cross-bow
I shot the ALBATROSS.

And when the context requires it the rapid pulse of the rhythm
can be held back and delayed, as for example in the last line of this
stanza where the turmoil of activity becomes a state or condition
of colour.

About, about, in reel and rout
The death-fires danced at night;
The water, like a witch's oils,
Burnt green, and blue and white.

As this last example shows, the formal similes are direct and explicit.
They have an almost medieval brilliance and innocence beautifully
in keeping with the moral and physical universe implicit in the
poem. But though they are intense and decorative and in a curious
way *miniature*, like illuminated illustrations, they are used in the
service of a sophisticated intention. They are, that is, for all their
apparent 'separatism' as decorative workings at any given point,
closely incorporated into the texture of the poem and charged
with the significance of the developing theme. Contrast, for example the following two stanzas:

Then like a pawing horse let go,
She made a sudden bound:
It flung the blood into my head,
And I fell down in a swound . . .

which comes from part V just where 'the lonesome Spirit from the
south-pole carries on the ship', and this stanza from part VI where
'the ancient mariner beholdeth his native country'.

The harbour-bay was clear as glass,
So smoothly it was strewn!
And on the bay the moonlight lay,
And the shadow of the Moon.

The movement of the ship in the first of these stanzas is not
the consequence of smoothly co-ordinated, responsible action
directed from within; it is as irrational as the wild shying of the

nervous horse suddenly 'let go'; and this swerving agitation prepares the reader's mind for the 'inexplicable' intervention of the
Polar Spirit's fellow daemons, 'the invisible inhabitants of the
elements' and their inquisitorial, moral dialogue. It is the half-
fearful violence of the horse which registers the mood here; it is
the homeliness and clarity of the glass which carries it in the second
stanza: homeliness because the Ancient Mariner is on the edge of
rediscovering his own country and of being welcomed into the
human community signalled by the light-house and the kirk, and
clarity because the transparency of the glass figures the grace and
light which now transfigures the density and guilt of the Ancient
Mariner's world. Perhaps I may quote one more of these similes, a
very famous one, to make again the point that this seemingly
straightforward usage had a distinctly complex function. The
ship, it will be remembered, was becalmed, fastened in a thick,
unmoving medium and watched by a small sinister bloody sun
from a copper sky.

> Day after day, day after day,
> We stuck, nor breath nor motion;
> As idle as a painted ship
> Upon a painted ocean.

We observe at once the propriety of that *painted* in a scene saturated
with colour, and we note how the effect is twisted tighter by the
imposition of *painted* upon *painted*. Unreality is laid upon unreality,
a mere illusion of a ship is placed upon an artificial sea. The word
idle placed exactly where it can do most work serves to extract the
vitality from an episode which would in the normal state of affairs
be full of life and force. At the same time the repetition of *day after
day*, and then of *painted*, monotonous and echoing and unprogres-
sive, makes heavier the sense not only of the absence, but of the
futility, of action. We should perhaps notice that repetition, a
characteristic feature of the poem and one in keeping with the
'primitive' character of the ballad, is with Coleridge not simply an
accepted but an active device. He uses it, as in the example I have
just given, to give an added dimension of depth and sonorousness
to language which might seem too childlike and treble, and a
further complication to a rhythm of which the base is a decidedly
simple pattern: simple, that is, for the profundity of the theme he
is working with. What we are to make of this theme and how we

are to take it have been matters of dissension almost from the time it was written. Wordsworth, with a characteristic lack of generosity, thought its presence had turned readers away from *Lyrical Ballads* and that its grave defects included a 'principal character [who] has no distinct character . . . [who] does not act but is continually acted upon . . . events having no necessary connexion [which] do not produce each other . . . [and] imagery . . . somewhat too laboriously accumulated'.[1] 'Mrs Barbauld once told me,' says Coleridge, 'that she admired the Ancient Mariner very much but that there were two faults in it,—it was improbable and had no moral', as though Coleridge had been guilty of writing an insufficiently persuasive tract for the R.S.P.C.A. Coleridge, perhaps with his tongue slightly in his cheek, replied that he thought the chief fault of the poem was 'the obtrusion of the moral sentiment so openly on the reader . . .'.[2] The main difference of opinion lies between those who attend more to the origins of the poem and those who attend more to its life. Among the 'geneticists' are that literary positivist J. M. Roberts who, throwing the *Ancient Mariner* together in a heap with *Kubla Khan* and *Christabel*, finds them all 'an abnormal product of an abnormal nature under abnormal conditions . . . the special quality of this felicitous work is to be attributed to its being *all* concerned and composed under the influence of opium in the first stages of the indulgence'.[3] Walter Pater is another impressed by the narcotic influence,[4] and Kenneth Burke adds the guilt of Coleridge's marital troubles to drugs as a predisposing cause.[5] David Beres treats the poem as immediate clinical evidence for investigating the disorders of Coleridge's psyche,[6] in particular those rooted in his 'intensely ambivalent' attitude to his mother. The most controlled and delicate analysis on these lines is by D. W. Harding.[7] 'The human experience,' he writes, 'on which Coleridge centres the poem is the depression and the sense of isolation and worthlessness which the Mariner describes in Part IV. The suffering he conveys is of a kind which is perhaps not found except in slightly pathological

[1] *Lyrical Ballads*, Vol. I, 1800.　　　　　　　　[2] *Table Talk*.

[3] *New Essays towards a Critical Method*, London, 1897, p. 187.

[4] *Appreciations*.

[5] *The Philosophy of Literary Form*, New York, 1941.

[6] *A Dream, A Vision, A Poem*. Year Book of Psychoanalysis, VIII, New York, 1952; cf. D. W. Harding, *Experience into Words*.

[7] *Scrutiny*, IX, 334-42, and *Experience into Words*, London, 1963, pp. 53-71.

conditions, but which, pathological or not, has been felt by a great many people. . . . The essence of the poem is a private sense of guilt, intense out of all proportion to public rational standards. The supernatural machinery of the poem allowed Coleridge to convey something of this—for the small impulsive act which presses the supernatural trigger does form an effective parallel to the hidden impulse which has such a devastating meaning for one's irrational, and partly unconscious, private standards.'

On the other side are those unconcerned, or less concerned, with the origins of the poem and more intent on the structure of meaning *in* the poem (although D. W. Harding who is at pains to appeal to the text of the poem to justify his reading might with justice be put here too). Of these interpretations, which depend on taking the poem not as an expression of personality but an object existing in its own right, the two most notable are those by John Livingston Lowes and Robert Penn Warren, and the second of these is a refinement of the first. Neither finds anything 'abnormal' in the sources of the poem or 'pathological' in its feeling. Each indeed emphasises the sanity and centrality of the poem's theme. Livingston Lowes makes the essence of the poem 'one of the immemorial, traditional convictions of the race . . . the train of cause and consequence. . . . You do a foolish or an evil deed, and its results come home to you. You repent, and a load is lifted from your soul. But you have not thereby escaped your deed. You attain forgiveness but cause and effect work on unmoved. . . .'[1] Robert Penn Warren's statement (or the first half of it since the other half is an unconvincing effort to thread back into this theme Coleridge's later, developed theory of the imagination) is a theological version of this classical doctrine of man's limitation. 'The bolt whizzes from the crossbow and the bird falls and all comment that the Mariner has no proper dramatic motive or is the child of necessity or is innocent of everything except a little wantonness is completely irrelevant, for we are confronting the mystery of the corruption of the will, the mystery which is the beginning of "the moral history of Man". The fact that the act is unmotivated in any practical sense, that it appears merely perverse, has offended literalists and Historians alike, and for that matter Wordsworth. . . . The lack of motivation, the perversity, which flies in the face of the Aristotelian doctrine of *hamartia*, is exactly the significant thing about the

---

[1] *The Road to Xanadu*, London, 1930, pp. 296-8.

Mariner's act. The act symbolises the Fall, and the Fall has the qualities important here: it is a condition of will, as Coleridge says, "out of time", and it is the result of no single human motive.'[1]

If the shooting of the Albatross is an act without a motive, without an antecedent cause, it is certainly not one—to use a distinction Coleridge was fond of—not one without a purpose: which is to assert the primacy of the individual self against an impersonal, beneficent order. If it is an act without a past, it is not one without a future, since its effects go on vibrating through every level of existence. The shooting of the Albatross is an expression of the state of a soul; it is not a conscious decision deliberately calculated against its consequences. It is not brought about, it happens.

> 'God save thee, ancient Mariner!
> From the fiends, that plague thee thus!—
> Why look'st thou so?'—With my crossbow
> I shot the ALBATROSS.

At a second critical juncture in the poem, at the point when the redemption of the Ancient Mariner begins, the same condition of unmoved immediacy is present. The return of life is not wages appropriate to the Ancient Mariner's penitential work. It is a gift. The unmotivated fall, that is, is balanced by the unmerited grace. The same objective things are now seen with a redeemed perception. After the fall,

> The very deep did rot: O Christ!
> That ever this should be!
> Yea, slimy things did crawl with legs
> Upon the slimy sea.

But the world, as well as the Ancient Mariner, is transfigured by this grace.

> Beyond the shadow of the ship,
> I watched the water-snakes:
> They moved in tracks of shining white,
> And when they reared, the elfish light
> Fell off in hoary flakes.

[1] *The Rime of the Ancient Mariner*, New York, 1941, pp. 81-2.

Within the shadow of the ship
I watched their rich attire:
Blue, glossy green, and velvet black,
They coiled and swam; and every track
Was a flash of golden fire.

O happy living things! no tongue
Their beauty might declare:
A spring of love gushed from my heart,
And I blessed them unaware:
Sure my kind saint took pity on me,
And I blessed them unaware.

The self-same moment I could pray;
And from my neck so free
The Albatross fell off, and sank,
Like lead into the sea.

The Ancient Mariner is a poem about the imperfection in man
which makes it possible for him for no reason to spoil or destroy
life, and about that other capacity which enables him to *receive*
from life itself rescue and revival. It has to do equally with man's
capacity for failure and with that which makes available to him
resources for recovery. This is a tremendous theme, the subject of
the profoundest religious experience as well as of the greatest art—
the last plays of Shakespeare, for example. I cannot conceive that
any critic would want to claim this status for *The Ancient Mariner*, a
poem with its own perfection and its own limitations. Here the
great classical theme is assimilated to, can exist only at the level
of, the medium. One notices how the ballad-form itself with its
attendant simplicities of rhythm and imagery, its primary colours,
its brilliant, child-like perception, its highly personal sense of
causality, its neo-platonic cosmology, its apparatus of spirits and
demons, all seem to domesticate the tragic theme in the wild and
singular parish of fantasy.

Not that the poem is simply fantastic, it is deeply serious, profoundly human. But a theme can exist with different degrees of
presence in a work of art. It can be the burning centre consuming
everything that approaches it or the dominant form which imposes
itself at every point on the poem. But it can also be present in a
quieter way, operating at a greater distance from the centre. It

can exist, as in *The Ancient Mariner*, as a deeply implicit structure, circumscribing and defining, establishing premises and pointing directions, and showing itself explicitly on the surface only at critical places, as in the stanzas I quoted just now. The defect of interpretations, like Robert Penn Warren's for example, is to assume an equal distribution of theme throughout the fable, and an even correspondence of meaning and story. In the same way his treatment twists the shape of the poem from its proper coherence by setting up a lucid series of abstract equations, a symbol on one side, a point of meaning on the other. So sensitive a critic could not but be aware of this, and Robert Penn Warren is distressed on occasion at the reluctance of the symbols to fit the scheme: the way, for instance, the moonlight can be both a beneficent influence and then only ambiguously good, or the way in which the sunlight can be both a sinister symbol but also a gay and life-giving one. The truth is that the logic of poetry is not stretched out in a straight line as this critic's interpretation supposes. It bends. It is much more accommodating. The foreground of *The Ancient Mariner* is occupied by the fable and the nature of any particular image, as of any turn of rhythm, depends upon the necessities of the fable at any given moment. It is only at intense and dramatic phases in the story that the images attain the more inclusive life of symbol. The moonlight, that is, is sometimes the light of grace and goodness, and at other times just the moon's light.

The value of *The Ancient Mariner* to Coleridge's progress as a poet was that it provided an 'objective' fable, including a nucleus of assumption, a dramatic situation, a *persona*, if not a character, a line of direction, an organisation into which Coleridge could pour the whole of his self. Even the ballad-form itself, if it was to be adequate to the requirements of the theme, called on all Coleridge's rhythmical virtuosity—real virtuosity here, not the trivial kind displayed in his 'translations' of classical metre into English which are all manner, no content. The whole undertaking of *The Ancient Mariner* challenged Coleridge's power and made use even of his personal deficiencies. It was 'a total act of the soul'. While it may be wrong to make Coleridge's personal tensions, his marital anxieties, or his guilt at his drug addiction either the initiating impulse or the centre of importance in the poem, there is no doubt that these elements of his life have a positive if partial

effect on it. The Ancient Mariner's isolation has a very personal
quaver, his depression and guilt have an inward autobiographical
quality.

> I looked to heaven, and tried to pray;
> But or ever a prayer had gusht,
> A wicked whisper came, and made
> My heart as dry as dust.

The rotting sea, the things with legs upon the slimy sea, the copper
sky, the bloody sun, the baked black lips, the dead men's stony
eyes, the frightful fiend that treads close behind—these things
heave with the horror of a narcotic's vision. There are passages
wryly reminiscent of Coleridge's disease-riddled life. For example,
the Ancient Mariner's admission to the guest is an ironic inversion
of Coleridge's personal history of action blocked by pain.

> Forthwith this frame of mine was wrenched
> With a woeful agony,
> Which forced me to begin my tale;
> And then it left me free.

> Since then, at an uncertain hour,
> That agony returns:
> And till my ghastly tale is told,
> This heart within me burns.

And elsewhere there is an image which conveys something of
Coleridge's psychological insight, particularly his discernment
into the psychology of extremes, of pain for instance, in which one
gets the phenomenon of the displacement or dislocation of one
kind of sense experience by another.

> I closed my lids, and kept them close,
> And the balls like pulses beat;

Finally the great constitutive idea in the poem, the concept of the
fall and of man's damaged nature, was one of the ultimate facts of
faith for Coleridge, which all his active life coloured his sensibility
and governed his judgment. In March 1798 he wrote to his brother
George, 'But I believe most steadfastly in original Sin; that from
our mothers' wombs our understandings are darkened; and even
were our understandings in the Light, that our organisation is

depraved…'[1]. And at the end of his life he said 'A Fall of some sort or other—the creation, as it were, of the non-absolute—is the fundamental postulate of the moral history of man. Without this hypothesis, Man is unintelligible; with it every phenomenon is explicable. The mystery itself is too profound for human insight.'[2]

Although *The Rime of the Ancient Mariner* is saturated with subjectivity, the final effect it makes on the reader is outgoing and objective. It trembles in tune with Coleridge's life but it also 'tells of life' in a wider sense. Such a pattern fits in with the division of responsibility for *Lyrical Ballads* Coleridge described in *Biographia Literaria*. Wordsworth was 'to give the charm of novelty to things every day by waking the mind's attention from the lethargy of custom'; Coleridge himself was to direct his endeavours towards 'persons and characters supernatural, or at least romantic yet so as to transfer from our inward nature a human interest and a semblance of truth sufficient to procure for these shadows of imagination that willing suspension of disbelief for the moment which constitutes poetic faith . . .'[3]. *The Ancient Mariner* certainly succeeds in transferring a human interest from our inward nature and giving it a semblance of truth sufficient to constitute poetic faith. *The Ancient Mariner*, although it is fed in every fibre by private experience, belongs to the poetry of the public world. But the best of the rest of Coleridge's poetry is the poetry of private experience. And in saying this I do have in mind that other public poem, *France: An Ode*. It seems to me quite undeserving of the praise it has received. It is an interesting historical document explaining Coleridge's change of attitude towards the French Revolution but as a poem it is soft, lacking any hardness or concreteness of achieved art. The idiom is stuffed with the higher Romantic cliché, the movement loosely declamatory, the tone vacantly moralising, the imagery that of political rhetoric, the feeling—'the patriot emotion', as he calls it—swollen. However commendable politically, it is poetically dull. Coleridge also wrote in 1798 some boneless Wordsworthian pieces like *The Old Man of the Alps* and *To a Young Lady* which offer natural piety and arch domesticity. But the characteristic, the best of Coleridge's poetry, written after *The Ancient Mariner*, is one in which descriptive and introspective skills collaborate in the exploration of private experience and an art of scrupulous personal examination.

[1] *Letters*, Vol. I, p. 396.　　[2] *Table Talk*.　　[3] *Biographia Literaria*, XIV.

Even in *Fears in Solitude,* which straddles the public and private worlds, the patriotism is of a passionately personal kind, and the poem gets its force and edge from the contrast between the ghastliness of public action, of which war is the extreme example, and the integrity of private experience; or between the public place;

> . . . at home,
> All individual dignity and power
> Engulfed in Courts, Committees, Institutions,
> Associations and Societies,
> A vain, speech-mouthing, speech-reporting Guild,
> One Benefit-Club for mutual flattery . . .

and that other private place:

> A green and silent spot, amid the hills,
> A small and silent dell! O'er stiller place
> No singing sky-lark ever poised himself.
> The hills are heathy, save that swelling slope,
> Which hath a gay and gorgeous covering on,
> All golden with the never-bloomless furze,
> Which now blooms most profusely: but the dell,
> Bathed by the mist, is fresh and delicate
> As vernal corn-field, or the unripe flax,
> When, through its half-transparent stalks, at eve,
> The level sunshine glimmers with green light.

As these lines suggest, place as the setting and extension of the individual is important in these poems. I am thinking not just of the superb *Frost at Midnight* and *Dejection* but of such poems as *The Nightingale, The Keepsake, The Picture, Inscription for a Fountain on a Heath.* The habit of these poems is to open with a tender and exact evocation of the place the poet is in. *The Nightingale* begins

> No cloud, no relique of the sunken day
> Distinguishes the West, no long thin slip
> Of sullen light, no obscure trembling hues. . . .

The Keepsake
> The tedded hay, the first fruits of the soil,
> The tedded hay and corn-sheaves in one field,
> Show summer gone, ere come. The foxglove tall
> Sheds its loose purple bells, or in the gust,
> Or when it bends beneath the up-springing lark,
> Or mountain-finch alighting. . . .

The Picture

> Through weeds and thorns, and matted underwood
> I forced my way; now climb, and now descend
> O'er rocks, or bare or mossy, with wild foot
> Crushing the purple whorts. . . .

These poems issue from sources in the poet which have not suffered repression or pollution. They leave with the reader an impression of spontaneous candour unaffected by any exterior framework, the kind of simplicity only a great artist is capable of achieving. It is a character contributed to by the liquid motion of the lines and the purity and coolness of the language, as we see, for example, in the beginning of *Inscription for a Fountain on a Heath*:

> This Sycamore, oft musical with bees,—
> Such tents the Patriarchs loved! O long unharmed
> May all its aged boughs o'er-canopy
> The small round basin, which this jutting stone
> Keeps pure from falling leaves! ...

All these features, purity of language, mobility of rhythm, inwardness of experience, are displayed—if displayed is not too ostentatious a term for so organically controlled a presence—in Coleridge's marvellous *Frost at Midnight*. The language is pure not only in being 'natural language, neither bookish, nor vulgar, neither redolent of the lamp, nor of the kennel',[1] but also in possessing an unclouded transparency, sensitive to every fleck of meaning, every shift in movement of the poetic idea. The mobile rhythm is in consonance with that deep sense of the flux, the oceanic slide and lapse of reality, which was part of the structure of Coleridge's sensibility. It was the absence of living movement in man's context, all the hard oppression of fixity, which Coleridge faced in cities with a kind of horror. 'The immoveableness of all things through which so many men were moving—a harsh contrast compared with the universal motion, the harmonious system of motions in the country, and everywhere in Nature. In the dim light London appeared to be a huge place of sepulchres through which hosts of spirits were gliding.'[2]

In *Frost at Midnight* a profound awareness of life as a system of harmonious motion supports an intent self-scrutiny. It checks any

---

[1] *Biographia Literaria*, I.   [2] *Notebooks*, Vol. I, No. 1592.

touch of the narcissistic fever Romantic self-analysis was so liable
to. And it makes the subjectivity disinterested, part of a more
inclusive, on-going universe. The ground of the poem is the poet's
feeling—both a vision and a conviction—for 'the universal
motion of life'; which sustains the rest of the development throughout. But what is prominent, what works in the foreground, is a
simultaneous summoning and cancellation of movement which at
once establishes and dismisses the exterior world so that at the
end of the first part of the poem one is brought completely into a
concentrated present, aware only of a single point of consciousness,
a single flicker of immediate movement.

> The Frost performs its secret ministry,
> Unhelped by any wind. The owlet's cry
> Came loud—and hark, again! loud as before.
> The inmates of my cottage, all at rest,
> Have left me to that solitude, which suits
> Abstruser musings: save that at my side
> My cradled infant slumbers peacefully.
> 'Tis calm indeed! so calm, that it disturbs
> And vexes meditation with its strange
> And extreme silentness. Sea, hill, and wood,
> This populous village! Sea, and hill, and wood,
> With all the numberless goings-on of life,
> Inaudible as dreams! the thin blue flame
> Lies on my low-burnt fire, and quivers not;
> Only that film, which fluttered on the grate,
> Still flutters there, the sole unquiet thing.
> Methinks, its motion in this hush of nature
> Gives it dim sympathies with me who live,
> Making it a companionable form,
> Whose puny flaps and freaks the idling Spirit
> By its own moods interprets, every where
> Echo or mirror seeking of itself,
> And makes a toy of Thought.

How thriftily the trilled r's in the opening line depict the frost's
meticulous working, and how effectively these few words model
the technique of the whole first part of the poem. 'The Frost
performs': it is in continuous motion but its ministry is secret and
silent, 'unhelped by any wind' and startled by the young owl's loud
cries (that it was an *owlet's* double cry which 'came loud' makes

the effect of the silence still stronger). The cottage, the sleeping family, the infant in the cradle, pick up the note of tranced stillness but (the poet at once turns back on himself and inverts the contrast he has been making) the quality of stillness is so intense and active that it is itself a kind of motion: 'it disturbs / and vexes meditation with its strange / and extreme silentness'. The device of simultaneous reconstruction and abolition is used with strong and confident tact in the next lines:

> . . . Sea, hill, and wood,
> This populous village! Sea, and hill, and wood,
> With all the numberless goings-on of life,
> Inaudible as dreams!

The slight alteration in the repeated phrase, one of Coleridge's subtlest uses of a favourite technique, 'sea, *and* hill, and wood', hints at the incessant modulations of life, just as the populous village and the numberless goings-on of life sparely and vigorously declare the endless movement of reality; and yet they are also, 'inaudible as dreams', fixed in an unmoving trance. Even the thin blue flame, whose very life is to be agitated, lies quiescent. The one thing moving in a vacant universe is the dusty film fluttering on the bars of the grate, energy at its feeblest and most pointless. And yet this very character makes it significant, 'a companionable form' for the shiver of the poet's vague self-awareness. For, Coleridge goes on clinically and ironically to observe, consciousness is ineradicably self-interested: at its dimmest it is never so passive as not to interpret existence, even when this is brought down to the barest moment, in its own mood and image.

Having successfully cancelled every external element of the experience, having brought the poem to a single fine point of consciousness, Coleridge begins to burrow into the one existing instant in search of the past which is buried in it and the future which is enclosed in it waiting to be born. There is an intrinsic logic in the sequence. So strong an insistence on the present leads irresistibly to exploring its intimations, the other dimensions of time. And there are connections, more homely and direct. The 'toy of thought' on one level and the fluttering film in the grate, the *stranger*,[1] on another, lead on to his boyhood: to Ottery St Mary's and:

---

[1] 'In all parts of the Kingdom these films are called *strangers* and supposed to portend the arrival of some distant friend.' *Poetical Register*, 1802.

> the old church-tower,
> Whose bells, the poor man's only music, rang
> From morn to evening, all the hot Fair-day . . .

to Christ's Hospital and the loneliness of school—

> Awed by the stern preceptor's face, mine eye
> Fixed with mock study on my swimming book. . . .

The past promises the future, his childhood turns him naturally towards the infant sleeping beside him. At the same time as his self-concentration widens to take in the child, the intense physical confinement of the first part of the poem opens out into the broad natural world again. For himself it had been the great city 'pent 'mid cloisters dim', for the boy it is to be a life spent:

> By lakes and sandy shores, beneath the crags
> Of ancient mountains, and beneath the clouds,
> Which image in their bulk both lakes and shores
> And mountain crags: so shalt thou see and hear
> The lovely shapes and sounds intelligible. . . .

There is a discernible slackening of tension in the next five lines in which the unregenerate metaphysician seems to be catching up with the poetic Coleridge. A mixture of religious and paternal feelings, and the occasion of 'The lovely shapes and sounds intelligible' lead Coleridge away into declamation on the divine nature. It may be these lines have a certain relevance in being addressed by a father to his child out of a real conviction. One cannot but feel, however, that at any moment poetic discipline may give way to evangelical fervour.

> Of that eternal language, which thy God
> Utters, who from eternity doth teach
> Himself in all, and all things in himself.
> Great universal Teacher! he shall mould
> Thy spirit, and by giving make it ask.

Whatever the weakness, of abstraction or preaching, there may be in these lines, it is more than made up for in the exquisite valediction which promises the child joy in the physical conditions of life and by implication joy in life itself. It is concrete in a characteristically Coleridgean way, dense in detail and yet supple and free in articulation. On the one hand is the firm definition of 'the tufts of snow on the bare branch', on the other a lucid, running syntactical structure, 'Whether . . . or . . . whether. . . . Or if . . .', which, seeming to cover every logical possibility and to take in every season and weather, gives the prophecy an air of certainty and inevitability. The strong clear colours, green, red, white, are Chaucerian in their freshness and belong to the world of youth towards which the baby is growing. The deep-sprung yet tranquil rhythm suggests that the nervous movements of human conscious-ness have been replaced by the steadiness of organic growth. The bodily element in physical growth is made visible and palpable. The thatch *smokes* in the sun-thaw, the frost *hangs up* the icicles. And the poem ends where it began with the delicate, decisive ministry of the frost, an unbroken line enclosing the whole area of the poem and perfectly defining its sensibility.

> Therefore all seasons shall be sweet to thee,
> Whether the summer clothe the general earth
> With greenness, or the redbreast sit and sing
> Betwixt the tufts of snow on the bare branch
> Of mossy apple-tree, while the nigh thatch
> Smokes in the sun-thaw; whether the eave-drops fall
> Heard only in the trances of the blast,
> Or if the secret ministry of frost
> Shall hang them up in silent icicles,
> Quietly shining to the quiet moon.

In these lines we see the glimmering of that fine creative emotion Coleridge called joy. It was a feeling which corresponded in the spiritual realm to health in the physical, and for Coleridge it was as rare. Or it was the emotional tone of heightened subjecti-vity and exercised imagination. 'It was the union of deep feeling with profound thought; the fine balance of truth in observing, with the imaginative faculty in modifying the objects observed; and above all the original gift of spreading the tone, the *atmosphere*, and with it the depth and height of the ideal world around forms, incidents, and situations, of which, for the common view custom had bedimmed all the lustre, had dried up the sparkle and the dew drops'.[1] It involved a perfect wholeness of self and an utterly just disposition of all one's forces. It is the lost, longed-for Paradise which Coleridge (like everyone, surely) remembered from child-

[1] *Biographia Literaria*, IV.

hood or which he saw in the play of his own children or experienced piercingly and pleadingly in some moment of poetic creation. Joy had for Coleridge the powerful significance it was bound to have for a man with a genius for awareness, with a faculty of consciousness so acute that he became what he observed and with such a depth of emotion that he was what he felt. 'With me the act of contemplation makes the thing contemplated, as the geometricians contemplating describe lines correspondent; but I do not describe lines, but simply contemplating, the representative forms of things rise up into existence.'[1] Coleridge's letters demonstrate that he was a man of heavenly gaiety and bewitching wit but his life, saturated with pain and littered with frustration, was only not 'a long disease' but the grimmest warfare. In a few lines, written probably in 1803, he describes the nightmare he so often lived in. The dream here is an image of his waking life:

> I know 'tis but a dream, yet feel more anguish
> Than if 'twere truth. It has been often so:
> Must I die under it? Is no one near?
> Will no one hear these stifled groans and wake me?

A life emptied of joy was cold, isolated, stifling and terrifying, and in a famous entry in *The Notebooks*, also written in 1803, Coleridge offers an anatomy of his wretchedness.

The general Fast Day—and all hearts anxious concerning the Invasion.—A grey Day, windy—the vale, like a place in Faery, with the autumnal Colours, the orange, the red-brown, the crimson, the light yellow, the yet lingering Green, Beeches & Birches, as they were blossoming Fire & Gold!—& the Sun in slanting pillars, or illuminated small parcels of mist, or single spots of softest greyish Light, now racing, now slowly gliding, now stationary—the mountains cloudy—the Lake has been a mirror so very clear, that the water became almost invisible—& now it rolls in white Breakers, like a Sea; & the wind snatches up the water, & drifts it like Snow—and now the Rain Storm pelts against my Study Window!—ο Σαρα Σαρα why am I not happy! why have I not an unencumbered Heart! these beloved Books still before me, this noble Room, the very centre to which a whole world of beauty converges, the deep reservoir into which all these streams & currents of lovely Forms flows—my own mind so populous, so active, so full of noble schemes, so capable of

[1] *Biographia Literaria*, XII.

realizing them this heart so loving, so filled with noble affections—
o Aσρα! wherefore am I not happy! why for years have I not enjoyed
one pure & sincere pleasure!—one full Joy!—one genuine Delight,
that rings sharp to the Beat of the Finger!—*all cracked, & dull with
base Alloy!—Di Boni! mihi vim et virtutem vel tu, . . ., eheu! perdite
amatio!

* But still have said to the poetic Feeling when it has awak'd in the Heart
—Go!—come tomorrow.—[1]

There is a true Coleridgean discrepancy between the manner of
this note and the burden of its message. On the one side extreme
vitality, on the other nervous exhaustion; on the one side nimbleness of expression and lucidity of diagnosis, on the other the
materials of despair. No doubt this is yet another manifestation of
that deep wound in Coleridge's nature I referred to earlier as a
self-disabling friction. Coleridge used this condition as a poetic
theme more than once. In *Psyche*, written in 1808, he represented
the two sides of the unfruitful dialectic as the butterfly and the
reptile:

> The butterfly the ancient Grecians made
> The soul's fair emblem, and its only name—
> But of the soul, escaped the slavish trade
> Of mortal life!—For in this earthly frame
> Ours is the reptile's lot, much toil, much blame,
> Manifold motions making little speed,
> And to deform and kill the things whereon we feed.

Coleridge saw his soul's part as the reptile's—'manifold motions
making little speed'—just as he saw in *Dejection* reality itself as a
dark dream. But there continued in his consciousness the memory
of joy and the image of the butterfly as the lost Paradise, positive
and creative, against which he measured the cold and brutal
negation experience had become. There is a kind of nostalgic
droop and backwardness in the relationship highly likely to
encourage Coleridge's standing temptation to self-pity. But there
were occasions—too rare for the admirer of Coleridge's poetry—
in which the lost Paradise and the present horror, the butterfly
and the reptile, as it were, achieved a simultaneous existence
and the result was something tense and current: in the terse

[1] *The Notebooks*, No. 1577.

effective poem *Work Without Hope*, for example, which was composed in 1825.

> All Nature seems at work. Slugs leave their lair—
> The bees are stirring—birds are on the wing—
> And Winter slumbering in the open air,
> Wears on his smiling face a dream of Spring!
> And I the while, the sole unbusy thing,
> Nor honey make, nor pair, nor build, nor sing.
>
> Yet well I ken the banks where amaranths blow,
> Have traced the fount whence streams of nectar flow.
> Bloom, O ye amaranths! bloom for whom ye may,
> For me ye bloom not! Glide, rich streams, away!
> With lips unbrightened, wreathless brow, I stroll:
> And would you learn the spells that drowse my soul?
> Work without Hope draws nectar in a sieve,
> And Hope without an object cannot live.

'Nor honey make, nor pair, nor build, nor sing': the singing accuracy of these short precise words bears no trace of self-pity. They raise a mood to the level of a state of affairs by basing it on a set of objective operations, and it becomes not an indulgence in unattached subjectivity but a disciplined statement of 'facts of the mind'. Coleridge, that is, is observing not hugging himself. Even the amaranths bloom without sickliness, and the concluding generalisations confer on the experience in the poem a more than individual validity. They constitute—to use a pair of opposites Coleridge was fond of—the 'law' of the experience, whose 'being' he has established with such finesse.

But 'Work Without Hope', however impressively focused, is still a miniature. An immensely fuller and more powerful treatment of the theme of the damaged self comes in *Dejection: An Ode*, one of the finest of all Romantic poems. Its first draft was in a verse letter to Sarah Hutchinson written on Sunday evening, April 4th, 1802,[1] which is more than twice as long as the received text. There are those, for example Humphry House,[2] who prefer the more exposed and fluent letter to the formal ode and it may be that there is more of the naked nerve in the letter. In my own response I see

---

[1] Cf. de Selincourt, Ernest, *Essays and Studies*, XXI, 2, 1937. It is reprinted in an appendix to *The Clark Lectures* by Humphry House, 1951-52.

[2] House, Humphry, op. cit.

a decided preference for the ode. The formality and regularity of the ode, the manifold and complex rhymes, the whole seriousness of address help in the control of the difficult personal material just as they support the severity of the analysis. Coleridge's work was seldom deficient in the throb of personal feeling. What it lacked was coherence of pattern and stamina in organisation, and the formal, distancing qualities of the ode, while they strengthen the arrangement of the poem, do not subdue the intense and feeling part of it. In fact they help towards a steadiness of honesty and a continuity and patience of attention all too rare in Coleridge.

The formal elements of the poem are used with so much assurance and tact that they impose no limitations of tone—no undue or over-sustained solemnity, no ripe gestures. The poem begins in a relaxed, almost off-hand way, as though the poet were fingering over a set of modest reflections. The simplicity of 'Well!', puncturing notions already in train, the reference to the 'grand old ballad'—and what could be more natural, more ordinary, than such a reference for a 'library cormorant?'—the reference to the ballad which is on the face of it altogether a homely thing (although there are different and deeper reverberations in it too, but kept in suspense for the moment), the speculations about the weather—it is all accustomed and unexceptional and yet rich enough as well to hint at latent complexities. The other, deeper note, which the epigraph has touched warningly, is taken up successively in a number of places in the first stanza: first in the world outside:

> Unroused by winds, that ply a busier trade

then given a personal twist in:

> ... the dull sobbing draft, that moans and rakes
> Upon the strings of this Æolian lute,

and returned to the natural world again in:

> ... the slant night-shower driving loud and fast!

so that by the time the reader gets to the desolate ending of the stanza, he finds it, though a total transformation of the beginning, completely acceptable and prepared for:

> Those sounds which oft have raised me, whilst they
>   awed,
> And sent my soul abroad,
> Might now perhaps their wonted impulse give,
> Might startle this dull pain, and make it move and live!

The effect of this magnificent stanza is one of unfogged actuality. It is contributed to by several influences: by a buoyant and responsive rhythm, that is by the relevant life of the poem's movement. And this is supported by a structure of syntax—directions of mental movement—*if* and *were* and *might*—which shows the present opening out not into certainties but contingencies and which, because of the feeling of flux and incompletion, paradoxically reinforces the validity of the actual event. It is taking place at this moment. The other movements characteristic of the active human sensibility—not simply the poetic one—confirm the actuality of the poem. First there is a constant passage back and forth from personal feeling to the physical scene. The self looks at

> The coming-on of rain and squally blast.

and the 'sounds' affect the 'soul'. Place and its life are an extension of the living ego. And then there is a constant transition from particular to general and from general to particular: reflection feeds on the concrete and the concrete holds within it the impulse of the general. An image of this activity is the moon, the moon which is swathed in vagueness and yet defined with a mathematical accuracy:

> (With swimming phantom light o'erspread
> But rimmed and circled by a silver thread)

Let me now quote the stanza in its entirety so that the reader may test the relevance of my comments and—and more importantly—feel himself its lucid and flowing life.

> Well! If the Bard was weather-wise, who made
> The grand old ballad of Sir Patrick Spence,
> This night, so tranquil now, will not go hence
> Unroused by winds, that ply a busier trade
> Than those which mould yon cloud in lazy flakes,
> Or the dull sobbing draft, that moans and rakes

Upon the strings of this Æolian lute,
    Which better far were mute.
For lo! the New-moon winter-bright!
And overspread with phantom light,
    (With swimming phantom light o'erspread
    But rimmed and circled by a silver thread)
I see the old Moon in her lap, foretelling
    The coming-on of rain and squally blast.
And oh! that even now the gust were swelling,
    And the slant night-shower driving loud and fast!
Those sounds which oft have raised me, whilst they awed,
    And sent my soul abroad,
Might now perhaps their wonted impulse give,
Might startle this dull pain, and make it move and live!

Coleridge at this point has come to the source of the poem, the experience of which he wrote in a letter I quoted before, 'Life and all its forms move in his diseased moments like shadows before him, cold, colourless and unsubstantial'.[1]

    A grief without a pang, void, dark, and drear,
    A stifled, drowsy, unimpassioned grief,
    Which finds no natural outlet, no relief,
        In word, or sigh, or tear—

It is a condition in which awareness is self-enclosed. There is a break in the direction of consciousness. It cannot flow freely into the extra-personal world. Not because the poet is not aware of the world outside, aware of it even with a poet's fineness of perception, but because he is unable to be fully aware of it, when the word 'aware' means more than knowing intellectually. Although he gazes on the western sky and notes exactly its 'peculiar tint of yellow green' and the 'thin clouds above, in flakes and bars / That give away their motion . . .', he sees them with a 'blank eye'. They are objects and events seen, as sight implies, in the distance but not felt, not intimate with and affected by the poet's emotion. The substance they have lost is a sympathetic capacity to be invested with the poet's feeling. There is, namely, not only an interruption in the continuity of consciousness—its movement from the inward impulse to the outward world—but also a division in its very nature, the separation of awareness and feeling.

[1] *Letters*, Vol. II, p. 928.

So that the poet, his consciousness caged, himself 'stifled, drowsy, unimpassioned . . .' seems himself to be becoming an object or as near an object as a human being can. It is as though the Lockean universe is taking its revenge, reducing him to a mere object among a pointless heap of other objects.

Being reduced to the status of an object is a devastating experience for Coleridge, for whom the contribution of the subject to the constitution of reality was not only an abstract concept but a profound and living conviction:

> . . . from the soul itself must issue forth
> A light, a glory, a fair luminous cloud
> Enveloping the Earth. . . .

But when it does not issue forth, when there is no 'sweet and potent voice', no 'strong music in the soul', the self does not lie empty and passive. It is invaded by non-reality. When we cannot give, we cannot receive. It is the listlessness and impotence of negation Coleridge is smothered by. And indeed this is a poem not simply about a particular pathological condition special to Coleridge himself but one in which this is the symbol of the other side of life, 'the stricken part of man'. The theme of the poem is the smothering weight which is the correlative—not just the opposite—of joy. 'Reality's dark dream' is the counterpart of the 'shaping spirit of Imagination'. Man is both creative and powerless.

The poem takes the form of a statement of an effect together with an indication of a cause (the core of the poem is preceded by the superb first stanza which sets out the context of the experience and is succeeded by a rather looser one which voices a plea that the lady, Sara, will be spared the cause and so the effect). It is of course a poetic statement, a recreation of the poet's condition, not a cool exercise in analysis. The poet reconstructs the whole experience, and the reference to the cause—the annihilation of joy, the slow death of imagination—is justified because insight can always find the cause present in the effect. The best of the poem is in the laying bare of Coleridge's condition. This is both controlled and spontaneous, sad but not self-pitying. Its tautness, however, loses some degree of tension when he turns towards the end to the world outside and finally to the lady. It never collapses completely, of course, and there may even be a certain propriety in a gradual lowering of the temperature as the poet returns to something more approaching placidity and routine.

Coleridge was a great poet: that is, his concerns were human and universal, his manner utterly his own. Language, imagery, rhythm, the tone and pitch of the voice, the whole poetic idiom— all are transparent to the unique self within. Such translucence in the medium gives immediate access to an essential humanity as it is exhibited in a man of genius. Here are some lines, *Phantom*, written in 1805 in one of the Malta Notebooks which seem to me beautifully appropriate to the character of Coleridge's poetry:

> All look and likeness caught from earth
> All accident of kin and birth,
> Had pass'd away. There was no trace
> Of aught on that illumined face,
> Uprais'd beneath the rifted stone
> But of one spirit all her own;—
> She, she herself, and only she,
> Shone through her body visibly.

Chapter IV

COLERIDGE AND THEORY

I GENERAL THEORY

COLERIDGE lived passionately the life of theory. He mourned in *Dejection* the ruin of poetic imagination which forced him

> By abstruse research to steal
> From my own nature all the natural man

But the abstruseness of the research implied no compulsion on, no glacial duty in, the one who undertook it; while the nature he was rifling was only an instance of that human nature which, Coleridge declared, 'At the annunciation of principles, of ideas, ... wakes and starts up, as an exile in a far distant land at the unexpected sounds of his native language ...'.[1] The enthusiasm and force with which Coleridge's powerful intellect confronted ideas confirmed a naturally Platonic habit of thought which he kept all his life, apart from a brief Hartley associationist or rationalist phase and in spite of occasional affectionate remarks like, 'Plato says it is *harmony*. He might as well have said a fiddlestick's end; but I love Plato, his dear, *gorgeous* nonsense. . . .'[2] Ideas were accessible to Coleridge in a way in which they very rarely are to a poet. The most intractable conceptions became luminous at his enquiry. They also stirred him to wonder at their limitless creative possibilities. He affirmed not only as a general proposition but almost as a fact of sensibility the association between 'epoch-making revolutions' and 'the rise and fall of metaphysical systems'. '. . . every principle is actualised by an idea; and every idea is living, productive, partaketh of infinity, and (as Bacon has sublimely observed) contains an endless power of semination.'[3]

It was sensibility, his reaction to the life of his times and the facts of his own existence, which made it impossible for him in the face of an epoch-forming revolution in feeling to accept an

---

[1] *The Statesman's Manual.*   [2] *Letters*, Vol. I, p. 295.
[3] *The Statesman's Manual.*

intellectual system presided over by the ghosts of Descartes, Newton and Locke. That was a world of cool intelligence, of analysis, of correct feeling, of decorous arrangement, of given patterns, of 'objects' and 'little things'. The role of the subject was understood to be that either of faithful recorder or of umpire among a limited scope of choices. A movement which began with the aim of freeing intelligence from prejudice and history had refined itself into a manner in which convention substituted for vitality and routine for decision. The 'epoch-forming revolution' in feeling which found all this intolerable required—in Coleridge's idiom— the fall of the metaphysical system on which it was based and the rise of another. At least—as we should say—the new quality of feeling demanded a different set of intellectual assumptions. The extraordinary position of Coleridge was to be the poet of the one and—if not the 'philosopher'—the theorist of the other. Even René Wellek who judged Coleridge to be utterly derivative from, perhaps no more than a flyblown version of, Kant allows him to be, on this basis perhaps a dubious honour, 'the intellectual centre of the English Romantic Movement'.[1]

We may, like Leslie Stephen, doubt the adequacy of Coleridge's philosophy, particularly in respect of its coherence and completeness although J. H. Muirhead, its most thorough and perceptive student, thought the degree to which it was *un*systematic much overstated. But no one after the researches of Muirhead and Kathleen Coburn has any warrant for taking Coleridge to be in philosophy itself either a frantic dabbler or a vulgar plagiariser. He was, as we now see, clearly justified in his belief that the elements of all his opinions existed before he had ever seen a book of German Metaphysics later than Wolf and Leibnitz. In any case we are not concerned here with some narrow view or specific discovery to which we can attach an absolute originality. As Sir Herbert Read argued eloquently in his fine essay,[2]

> Let us realize, . . . that we are not dealing with the scholarly lucubrations of an academic coterie, in which priorities and credits are of some importance. Coleridge was involved in something much wider and more fundamental—in a revolution of thought such as only occurs once or twice in a millenium. Such revolutions do not come

---

[1] Wellek, René, *Kant in England, 1793-1838*, Princeton, 1931, p. 139.
[2] *Coleridge as Critic*, London, 1949, p. 15.

about as a result of individual efforts: the individuals are swept along in a current which they, least of all men, can control.

The originality of Coleridge lay in his registering so acutely the sandy insufficiency of the current system of thought, in his realising so sensitively the direction in which it should be turned, and in his lighting on the stream of ideas which was most apt to correct the fundamental deficiency of the ruling system, its theory of the passivity of the mind. Or more directly, Coleridge's originality lay in his realising how essential it was to change the contemporary account of the relationship between subject and object. This conviction came to him not only out of a scrutiny of the intrinsic defects of contemporary thought—although it *did* come from this—but first out of the felt discrepancy between his own experience as a poet and both the contemporary general explanation of human experience as well as its specific account of poetic activity. A naturally reflective mind like Coleridge's looked for the categories in which to fit the undeniable truth of his own poetic experience; and there were none to be found in contemporary theory. An examination of the historical antecedents of this theory only confirmed in him his self-supplied certainty of its partiality and error. A Lockean theory of passive subject—active object could be changed on the one hand by absorbing everything into the subject, as with Hume, or on the other hand making the object evaporate altogether into the subject, as with Berkeley. In either case one was left with domination instead of mutuality, whereas 'all knowledge rests on the coincidence of an object with a subject ...'.[1]

It was not in human nature Coleridge believed to meditate on any mode of action without enquiring after the law that governed it. Whatever the application of this view to the nature of the rest of us, it was undoubtedly an accurate reading of his own. His general doctrine of humanity was a product of reflection on the humanity which was instanced in himself; and his theory of mental activity in particular was drawn out from what he, gifted as he was with the purest, most disinterested insight, saw within himself. 'I laboured at a solid foundation, in which permanently to ground my opinions, in the component faculties of the human mind itself, and their comparative dignity and importance.'[2] True: and if we

[1] *Biographia Literaria*, XII.   [2] Ibid., I.

add that the human mind itself was the Coleridgean mind itself, accurate also. I have spoken already of his lucid awareness even in his childhood of his mind's activity. Here it was, using and kneading sensations, constructing not just accepting experience. His characterisation of the mind as 'act', therefore, is an enlargement of a personal experience. 'What is a thought, but "I" thinking?'[1]

> It is at once the distinctive and constitutive basis of my philosophy that I place the ground and genesis of my system, not, as others, in a fact impressed, much less in a generalisation from facts collectively, least of all in an abstraction embodied in an hypothesis, in which the pretended solution is most often but a repetition of the problem in disguise. In contradiction to this, I place my principle in an *act*—in the language of grammarians I begin with the verb—but the act involves its reality.[2]

We are not to take the act described in these words as no more than the product of organisation or the effect of a certain high degree of complexity of structure. While it *is* this, to conceive it as *just* this, would be to mistake the conditions of a thing for its cause and essence. The idea is itself productive. It is general and inclusive. It stamps itself upon particulars. It works towards completion outside itself. It brings into the jumble of actuality a rational force which both brings about and guarantees the stable existence of any human construction. At the same time the idea strives towards individuality: it is a force making for particularity. The instinct on which humanity itself is grounded, Coleridge argues, namely that by which in every act of conscious perception we at once identify our being with that of the world outside us and yet place ourselves at a distance from and in contradiction to it, this instinct involves the sense that the productive power existing in nature is balanced by a productive power in intelligence. 'In other words', he continues, 'idea and law are the subjective and objective poles of the same magnet, that is of the same living and energising reason. What an idea is in the subject, that is, in the mind, is a law in the object, that is, in nature.'[3] The great model of the working of an

---

[1] *The Philosophical Lectures of S. T. Coleridge.* Edited by Kathleen Coburn, London, 1949, p. 52, footnote.

[2] MS. Note quoted in Muirhead, J. H., *Coleridge as Philosopher*, London, 1930, p. 105.

[3] *The Friend*, X, footnote.

idea is the operation of language. 'A man of genius using a rich and expressive language (the Greek, German or English) is an excellent instance and illustration of the ever individualising process and dynamic Being, of Ideas. What a magnificent History of acts of individual mind, sanctioned by the collective Mind of the Country, a Language is. . . .'[1] A still more brilliant example of the productive and individualising energy of ideas is to be found in Shakespeare, where we find ourselves everywhere in touch with the same human nature and everywhere aware of its utter individuality.

> Shakespeare shaped his characters out of the nature within; but we cannot so safely say, out of *his own* nature, as an *individual person*. No! this latter is itself but a *natura naturata*, an effect, a product, not a *power*. It was Shakespeare's prerogative to have the *universal* which is potentially in each *particular*, opened out to him in the *homo generalis*, not as an abstraction of observation from a variety of men, but as the substance capable of endless modifications, of which his own personal existence was but one, and to use *this one* as the eye that beheld the other, and as the tongue that could convey the discovery. . . . Shakespeare in composing had no *I* but the *I* representative.[2]

Beneath—the crudity of the physical image at least indicates Coleridge's order of importance—beneath the highest form of human consciousness, the principle-creating power, there existed a generalising activity of consciousness much more dominated by experience. This is the activity of understanding just as the other is that of reason, or of imagination in another context. The supreme form of intellectual action is projected from within. 'It carries knowledge within itself and is prospective . . . evolving *B* out of *A*, and *C* out of *B*, and so on just as a serpent moves, which makes a fulcrum out of its own body, and seems forever twisting and un-twisting its own strength.'[3] As he was a Platonist and a Kantian in his account of the constitutive function of ideas, or rather the holder of an idiosyncratic doctrine in which Plato modified Kant and Kant Plato and both felt the influence of the Cambridge Men, so he was if not a Hartleyan Associationist at least something rather closer to Locke in his account of the arranging, generalising activity of understanding. Kant may have left a blank at the top of his mental categories which Coleridge felt had to be filled by Plato.

[1] *Coleridge on Logic and Learning.* Edited by A. D. Snyder, p. 138.
[2] *Lectures on Shakespeare*, 1818, Lecture VII.   [3] *Table Talk.*

But Kant, starting with the activity of the mind rather than with the senses (with the mind itself, that is), Kant still offered so much to men who have the power of thinking that Coleridge could not conceive of anyone in whatever pursuit or profession who would not derive incalculable benefit from the study of his works. Coleridge rejected the stoic and passive principle in Kant, and his religious sensibilities were sometimes offended by him, 'but with these exceptions I reverence Immanuel Kant with my whole heart and soul'.[1] And although Coleridge turned the whole of his strength against Locke, there is more than a touch of Locke, or rather what Locke was pointing to—the element of passivity in human experience—in his treatment of the understanding, except that what is partial in Coleridge is total in Locke.

Coleridge's account of the understanding (and of fancy, its correlative in art) leaves the reader with the feeling that he consistently undervalues it. No doubt this impression is to be attributed to the fact that Coleridge usually treats reason and understanding on a comparative basis, and that he was concerned primarily to establish the existence and the rights of the former. But there is a passage in which he draws on Bacon to specify the activity of the understanding in a more positive way: 'some well rounded purpose, some distinct impression of the probable results, some self-consistent anticipation as the ground of the *prudens quaestio*, the forethoughtful query, which he confirms to the prior half of the knowledge sought, *dimidium scientiae*. . . . With him, therefore, as with me, an idea is an experiment proposed, the experiment is an idea realised.'[2] While the highest form of consciousness is essentially creative and vital, struggling to idealise and unify, this other has to do with 'fixities and densities . . . is indeed . . . a mode of memory emancipated from the order of time and space, while it is blended with, and modified by, that empirical phenomenon of the will, which we express by the word choice'.[3] Perhaps the most direct discrimination of reason and understanding comes in a letter to Thomas Clarkson written in 1806 in answer to a number of questions on his opinions:

What is the difference between the Reason, and the Understanding?
—I would reply, that the Faculty of the Soul which apprehends and retains the mere notices of Experience, as for instance that such an

[1] *Letters*, Vol. IV, p. 792.   [2] *The Friend*, Essay, IX.
[3] *Biographia Literaria*, XIII.

object has a triangular figure, that it is of such or such a magnitude, of such and such a color, and consistency, with the anticipation of meeting the same under the same circumstances, in other words, all the mere φαινόμενα of our nature, we may call the Understanding. But all such notices, as are characterized by UNIVERSALITY and NECESSITY, as that every Triangle *must* in all places and at all times have its two sides greater than its third—and which are evidently not the effect of any Experience, but the condition of all Experience, & that indeed without which Experience itself would be inconceivable, we may call Reason.[1]

Coleridge in his reaction against the arid rationalism of the eighteenth century never became a simple anti-rationalist intuitionist of the Jacobi kind. He was never so impressed by the immediacy of experience as to consider like Jacobi the discursive side of it a mockery. Coleridge's intention was to extend the efficacy of reason upward beyond the point where Kant wished to arrest it. He had a richer sense than Locke, a fuller sense than Kant, of the range of human awareness. Like the congenial Schelling (perhaps a better philosopher, certainly a worse poet—but at least *both*) he saw reason and understanding themselves evolving from a depth of organic response which stretched down below the level of consciousness. Just as Coleridge did not believe that the essence of identity lay in *recollective* consciousness—"'twere scarcely less ridiculous to affirm, that the 8 miles from Stowey to Bridgewater consist in the 8 mile stones',[2] so he did not believe that the range of human awareness was identical with the range of human consciousness. I have referred before to the 'implicit wisdom deeper than our consciousness' which he gave as one of the sources of Shakespeare's creativity, and he felt himself, as a great poet would be bound to, his own dependence on something unforceable and profounder than ordinary consciousness. But he believed this was true of all men, and it was his sense of what lay below the clarity of consciousness that made him suspicious of excessive or too early definiteness in language. In the case of the young a too early habit of rendering our ideas distinct and indicable was highly unfavourable to intellectual progression; and in the case of the artist too great definiteness in language could consume 'the idea-meeting force'. Like Keats, like Lawrence, he saw that there were depths at which one had to let life take its own time and course.

---

[1] *Letters*, Vol. II, p. 1198.   [2] Ibid., Vol. I, p. 479.

Coleridge like others preoccupied with the existence of the unconscious was much taken with the problems of bordering states. One of his innumerable unrealised ambitions was to write a whole work on the subject of dreams, visions, ghosts and witchcraft. Sleep and dreams were the gates of the unconscious which he often tried to nudge open. He wanted in particular to explain in a much more satisfactory way than anyone had yet done 'the mode in which our thoughts, in states of morbid slumber, become at times perfectly *dramatic* (for in certain sorts of dreams the dullest Wight becomes a Shakespeare) and by what law the *form* of the vision appears to talk to us its own thoughts in a voice as audible as the shape is visible . . .'.[1] Nor were his interests of this kind only theoretical. There are entries in the Notebooks, literary rather than philosophic or psychological, and as evocative as anything in *Ulysses*, in which we are aware of treading on the edge of consciousness and feel the sensation, so strange and so exact, of consciousness itself lapsing and falling away from an explicit articulation into some obscure underworld.

When in a state of pleasurable and balmy quietness I feel my Cheek and Temple on the nicely made up Pillow in Cælibe Toro meo, the fire-gleam on my dear Books, that fill up one whole side from ceiling to floor of my Tall Study—and winds, perhaps are driving the rain, or whistling in frost, at my blessed Window, whence I see Borrodale, the Lake, Newlands—wood, water, mountains, omniform Beauty— O then as I first sink on the pillow, as if Sleep had indeed a material *realm*, as if when I sank on my pillow, I was entering that region and realized Faery Land of Sleep—O then what visions have I had, what dreams—the Bark, the Sea, all the shapes and sounds and adventures made up of the Stuff of Sleep and Dreams, and yet my Reason at the Rudder/O what visions ($\mu\alpha\sigma\tau o\iota$) as if my Cheek and Temple were lying on me gale o' mast on—Seele meines Lebens!— and I sink down the waters, thro' Seas and Seas—yet warm, yet a Spirit—[2]

There was a daring sweep in Coleridge's theory which put into living connection Plato and Kant and, by anticipation Freud (and in another field of thought, as Sir Herbert Read[3] persuades us, Kierkegaard also). In the same way the 'streamy nature of association' in his own experience encouraged him to recognise a

[1] *The Friend*, I.   [2] *Notebooks*, 1718.
[3] *Coleridge as Critic*, Herbert Read, London, 1949, p. 30.

flowing movement towards unity among the three divisions of mind in a way which bridged and softened the sharp divisions of Kant. Coleridge like Kant arranged human experience under the categories of *sense* which comprised whatever was passive in our nature: sensations, impressions, the *vis receptiva* by which we perceive things under the forms of space and time; *understanding*, by which he meant the faculty of thinking and forming judgments on the notices furnished by the senses; and *reason*, the power by which we become possessed of principles and ideas. Platonic tradition and habits inherited from the Schoolmen and the eighteenth century led him to speak of these capacities as separate faculties and sometimes even to argue for their separation. But he also understood that different notions do not suppose different things. When he made a threefold distinction in human nature he was fully aware that it was a distinction not a division, 'and that in every act of mind the man unites the properties of sense, understanding and reason'.[1]

The essence of Coleridge's conception of human experience was that life was initiated from within. It was self-conceived, self-born. He was bound, therefore, to reject any 'scheme of pure mechanism . . . which began by manufacturing mind out of sense and sense out of sensation and which reduced all form to shape and all shape to impressions from without'.[2] If the mind's action was not provoked from without (or wholly from without, one must rapidly insert, since Coleridge was perfectly clear about the force of external circumstances: the oxygen on the lungs, as he put it) on what, then, within the mind did it depend? It depended on the will, on the intelligent self, not acting as a step in a series of causes and effects, but determining its own activity. Intellectual life was founded on the moral life—a point I take up again in considering Coleridge's writings on children—just as every form of advanced human activity began with a decision or with something believed or accepted. Science had its axioms, mathematics its postulates, religion its necessary preconditions, namely truths derived from the moral being and not from external evidence like traditions or miracles. The postulate of human experience itself was the will. Or to put it another way, one begins with an intention and progressively realises it. The will is not merely energy responding to

---

[1] *The Friend*, I.
[2] *Coleridge on Logic and Learning.* Edited by A. D. Snyder, p. 130.

motives conceived of as externally antecedent causes. It itself makes its motives. Its permanent dispositions allot to motives their measure of attractiveness.

If intellectual activity starts in the will, in what does it come to rest? Sense, in the flow of mental life, converts itself to understanding, understanding converts itself to reason—and reason to what? 'May there not be a yet higher or deeper Presence, the source of ideas, to which even Reason must convert itself?'[1] In Coleridge's judgment human consciousness at its highest, at its most sensitively alert, was religious. The higher or deeper Presence was divine. It was both a Platonic God, the source of ideas, and a Christian God, a Power and a Presence. The object of converted reason was God, the activity into which reason was transposed was faith. 'What is faith but the personal realisation of the reason by its union with will?'[2] Since reason draws on understanding, understanding on sense and faith on them all, we see why faith is the opposite of whatever is partial and fragmentary in man. 'But faith is a *total* act of the Soul; it is the *whole* state of the mind, or it is not at all, and in this consists its power, as well as its exclusive worth.'[3] Faith was the answer Coleridge gave to his own question, 'Is it not possible to find a practical Reason or light of life, a focal power from the union and harmonious composition of all the faculties?' The defect of reason, Coleridge points out in *The Statesman's Manual*,[4] is to be taken singly and exclusively, when its comprehensiveness, impartiality and farsightedness become mere visionariness in intellect and indolence or hard-heartedness in morals. Reason has to be penetrated by a power which makes for concreteness and individuality, 'by a contraction of universal truths into individual duties', which is the religious spirit. The defect of religion is to be exclusively devoted to the specific and individual and to neglect or ignore the universality of reason so that it becomes more and more earthly and servile, 'wandering at length with its pack of amulets, bead-rolls, periapts, fetisches, and the like pedlary'. And both reason and religion to exist or co-exist as reason and religion have to be actuated by the will which is the sustaining and ministerial power of our nature, just as reason is the legislature and religion the executive.

Coleridge's religious theory like all the rest of his theory was

---

[1] *Inquiring Spirit*. Edited by Kathleen Coburn, p. 126. [2] *The Friend*, III.
[3] Ibid., II. [4] Appendix B.

drawn from within his own nature and written out of his private experience. The truths of religion like the truths of poetry, of criticism, of philosophy, are evolved from within. They cannot be demonstrated by arguments appropriate to something else. The existence of God cannot be proved by philosophical analysis— Kant himself recognised that he had failed to do it. Spiritual truths do not depend on the degree to which they can be accommodated to science or to psychiatry, or on the degree to which they are supported by external events like miracles. 'What then can we think of a theological theory, which adopting a scheme of prudential legality, common to it with the sty of Epicurus, as far at least as the springs of moral action are concerned, makes its whole religion consist in the belief in miracles?'[1] Had Coleridge's views prevailed on this subject, or on the Bible—namely that its parts were to be read in the light of the whole, that its spirit not its detail was inspired—how much the nineteenth and twentieth centuries might have been spared futile controversy on miracles, inspiration, science, evolution and so on, not to speak of the apologetic posturing of clergymen determined to show they can be as contemporary and scientific as the next one. The character of religious life is to be initiated within man's nature and to call upon the totality of his experience. Its corruption lies in reliance upon the external and division of its source and its appeal. 'This was the true and first apostasy—when . . . the divine Humanities of the Gospel gave way to speculative systems . . . and became a Science of Shadows under the name of Theology.'[2] Religion became spectacles and shows for the many, notions and abstractions for the few. 'The Christian world was for centuries divided into the Many, that did not think at all, and the Few who did nothing but think. . . .'[3]

The habit of Coleridge as a theoretician was to discern the unique property of an activity and upon that to raise his explanatory generalisation. First he identified the difference and then he turned it into the strength of his solution. Here is a brief example from the context I have just been considering. In a discourse on the Moral law, he writes, 'Man must be *free*; or to what purpose was he made a spirit of reason, and not a machine of instinct? Man must *obey*; or wherefore has he a conscience? The powers, which create this difficulty, contain its solution likewise: for *their* service is perfect freedom.' It was a habit which made his recom-

---

[1] *The Friend*, III.   [2] *Aids to Reflection*.   [3] Ibid.

mendations idiosyncratic and strongly positive. At the same time Coleridge has such an extraordinary range of sympathy that hardly anything was shut off from it by bias, indifference, distrust or downright hostility. The negative side of his doctrine, what he was against, is seldom disfigured by that mixed incomprehension and jealousy we notice in other, sourer critics. And although he put limitations upon his tolerance, at least as far as opinions and not motives, principles and not men were concerned, (That which doth not *withstand*, hath *itself* no standing place) he still saw that there was no speculative error appealing to many men which had not a golden as well as a darker side. So that we never want to observe about Coleridge what he himself noted and what we surely feel about so many writers on morals, a repellent quality on the negative side. 'The error of all sects, whether in religion or philosophy, is commonly to be found, not in the positive of their characteristic tenets, but in the negative—*nil, nisi hoc*, not in the positions but in the imposition.'[1]

II POLITICAL THEORY

'I am far from arguing that Coleridge is a practical person', writes Kathleen Coburn in *Inquiring Spirit*, her brilliant and sensibility-shaping anthology of Coleridge's writings, slightly startled, one cannot help but feel, at the very thought of being supposed to be doing so. One has every sympathy with her; a 'practical' Coleridge is certainly an extraordinary notion. And yet when one notices no more than some of the things he did in the political and social sphere, it is very hard to see how one can justly call him 'impractical'. He interested himself in business, tanning and farming with Poole, in chemistry both pure and applied with Davy, and during the blockade of the West Indies in the problem, for example, of making sugar from beet, a process on which he had taken notes during his German days; he was a working political journalist for more than 20 years on the *Morning Post* and the *Courier*, he was political consultant as well to Daniel Stuart the editor of the *Courier*, he was even on occasion a political lobbyist and he wrote a pamphlet to help Sir Robert Peel to get his Bill to reduce the working hours of the children in the cotton factories through the House in 1818.

---

[1] *Inquiring Spirit*, Edited by Kathleen Coburn, p. 412.

Coleridge was not a particularly boastful or immodest man, and he believed himself that his political writings had a by no means unremarkable influence. He attributed a rapid and unusual increase in the circulation of the *Morning Post*, with every reason, I think, to his own contributions. He was convinced that this influence reached into Europe and that Napoleon sent out an order for his arrest during his stay in Italy because of his essays in the *Morning Post*, a fate he was rescued from by a helpful Benedictine and the connivance of a kindly Pope. He was particularly delighted at the success that his political essays had in the United States, where they appeared in many of the federal journals as well as in the Massachusetts State papers, and there is no doubt at all of his influence upon the Christian Socialists, on the Tory Chartists and in particular on Disraeli, and through him on the humanisation of the Conservative Party. Coleridge, then, was not an a-political innocent: he was neither an academic spinning impalpable webs in his study, nor a publicist tearing up paper tigers in a newspaper column. He had a keen sense of contemporary issues and a thorough, even a hard-headed, acquaintance with the facts of political life.

Nor was his private political experience too unlike that of the ordinary man. He could, for example, be as prejudiced as the next. His political attitudes like those of others had patches of silliness and motiveless hostility. He detested Pitt with that obsessive and personal loathing that most people have for some political figure or other. He made the not uncommon passage from young/left to old/right, although the line his journey describes was altogether starker than the mild curve from Great Turnstile to Gower Street. If he ended as a conservative Christian sage, he began at quite the other end of the political scale. There was the ludicrous episode, the crazy counterpart of Private Silas Comberbache and the King's Light Dragoons, when he was under surveillance by a certain G. Walsh, a government agent, as a member of a highly suspect group. Walsh, however, was won over by his charm and was able to report to Whitehall that Coleridge like Wordsworth at worst belonged to a 'sett of violent Democrats' and 'a group of disaffected English' but he was not a member of a cell of spying Frenchmen surveying the waterways for the benefit of the French military, an opinion Coleridge wryly refers to in *Biographia Literaria*:

Many circumstances, evil and good, intervened to prevent the completion of the poem, which was to have been entitled 'The Brook'. Had I finished the work, it was my purpose in the heart of the moment to have dedicated it to our then committee of public safety as containing the charts and maps with which I was to have supplied the French government in aid of their plans of invasion.[1]

Coleridge's political theory occupied a middle position between the extreme rationalism and individualism of Rousseau on the one side and an excessive State absolutism on the other.[2] The origin of political power was to be found not where Hobbes placed it in a fear of extreme power, which could never be the source of anything permanent or valuable in human life. If, as Hobbes declared, the laws without the sword are bits of parchment, then, Coleridge rejoined, the sword without the laws is only a bit of iron. Nor was it to be placed where Rousseau put it in the pure reason alone, which could never truly represent the truth of our mixed and sensitive nature. Abstract reason alone would provide a pure, universal system of politics; 'but a constitution equally suited to China and America, or to Russia and Great Britain, must surely be equally unfit for both, and deserves as much respect in politics as a quack's panacea in medical practice'.[3] If in the search for political principle we go to the nature of man we must not on the other hand draw from reason political principles abstracted from complex historical conditions. Reason may be the sole sovereign, the only rightful legislator, but reason to act on man must be, said Coleridge, 'impersonated'. We must apply not to abstract reason but to the actual man. And the actual man is neither the excessively single individual of Locke nor the corporate creature of Hegel, the one independent of, the other sucked into, the group. The identity of the individual is modified by the otherness of society, but it is not blotted out by it. And the same is true of a political community. 'A state is an idea intermediate between the two (an organic and an inorganic body)—the whole being a result from, and not a mere total of, the parts, and yet not so merging the constituent parts in the result, but that the individual exists integrally within it.'[4] Coleridge wished to see *all* become a whole

---

[1] *Biographia Literaria*, p. 92.

[2] Cf. Cobban, A., *Burke and the Revolt against the Eighteenth Century*, London, 1929, p. 185.

[3] *The Friend*, I, 3.   [4] *Table Talk.*

but he abhorred any theory or any system which blended men into a state by the dissolution of what made them worth while as individuals.

The principles of political life like those of every other human activity are to be decided by reflection on the actual composition of human nature, namely on the nature of a reasonable being involved in society whose intelligence is both in origin and aspiration connected with morality. Morality is not an accidental quality of humanity, not simply the attribute of maturity. It is the ground of thought, and it both supplies the energy and regulates the direction of action. So that conscience in the individual must be balanced by the spirit of law in society, and 'the principles of morality in general ought to be made to bear on our public suffrages, and to affect every great natural determination'.[1] Coleridge made the law of nations identical with the law of conscience.

> It were absurd to suppose that individuals should be under a law of moral obligation and yet that a million of the same individuals acting collectively or through representatives should be exempt from all law, for morality is no accident of human nature, but its essential characteristic... none but a madman will imagine that the essential qualities of anything can be altered by its becoming part of an aggregate; that a grain of corn, for instance, shall cease to contain flour, as soon as it is part of a peck or bushel.[2]

The originality, as well as the permanent relevance, of Coleridge's political theory comes from the clarity with which he saw politics as a form of moral activity. It was also his consistency. This was the theme which joined the radical disciple of Godwin to the conservative admirer of Burke, and which related the Bristol Address of 1795 to the Lay Sermons of 1816 and 1817. 'Thus he became a Tory, and yet his essential faith was unchanged. For he demanded of Toryism what he had previously demanded of Radicalism—government according to ethical principles, the conduct of secular affairs *sub specie aeternitatis*.'[3] Even the theory of the Idea of an institution is in part a moral inspiration. With it Coleridge intended to release an historical institution from complete servitude to its past. The conception of *Idea* was meant to

---

[1] *The Friend*, X.   [2] Ibid., XIII.
[3] Beeley, H., *The Political Thought of Coleridge*, in *Coleridge, Studies by several Hands on the Hundredth Anniversary of His Death*, edited by Edmund Blunden and Earl Leslie Griggs, London, 1934, p. 161.

introduce a degree of freedom into historical process. Coleridge wished to change the current habit of thought from a reductive to a prospective one. He believed every institution, even the State itself, to be more than the product of antecedent causes. It was also an attempt to realise an indwelling conception which drew its vitality and character not simply from its historical conditions but from its final purposes. The future, that is to say, was to be as efficacious as the past. The paradox of this position was that while it gave Coleridge a critical freedom in judging institutions, the freedom analogous to the obligation on the institution to move in this direction rather than that, it sometimes landed him in the position of defending what seemed to be morally indefensible on the grounds that the idea of the institution meant so much more than the trivial accident of its immediate actuality. Thus he could defend the idea of the aristocratic dispensation of justice ('The unhired magistracy of England, taking in and linking together the duke to the country gentleman')[1]; he could justify inequalities of rank, and his opposition to the Reform Bill, he could uphold the idiocies of Bell's monitorial system of teaching—'an especial gift of providence to the human race . . . this incomparable machine . . . this vast moral steam engine'[2]—because it was the product of an Anglican; and he could argue sharply against Christ's Hospital taking in more boys than it used to. The personal prejudices of the feebler Coleridge tended to become metaphysical in the light of the mystical *Idea* of anything.

But this was Coleridge at his weakest. At his best, and Coleridge is more frequently at his best than not, his political criticism strikes one as sane and independent, welling up from a deep, central source of moral life. He had, for example, as little respect for 'the negative pull down- and clear away- principle' as anyone, but while he may have accepted the more delicate superstition of ancestry as against the grosser one of wealth, he detested its idolatry, as though 'by some pre-established harmony, some new refinement of predestination, a boorly soul was born a Boor— and all calm and lofty souls entered into the foetuses of future Serene Highnesses'.[3] He excoriated the inhumanity of those who cultivated sensibility while they accepted slavery. 'Provided the dunghill be not before their parlour window, they are well content

---

[1] *Table Talk.*   [2] *Lay Sermons.*

[3] *Inquiring Spirit.* Edited by Kathleen Coburn, p. 317.

to know that it exists. . . .'[1] His indignation was not for the childish
titles of aristocracy but for 'those institutions of society which could
condemn me to the necessity of 12 hours daily toil, would make my
soul a slave and sink the rational being in the mere animal'.[2] His
comments on social justice have that persuasive anger which
comes from provoked feeling rather than some vision of abstract
perfection. Commerce was certainly a blessing and pride of the
country. But commerce was only valuable as a means to an end
and ought not itself to become the end to which nobler and more
inherent blessings were forced into subserviency. What national
justice is there in a country where healthy labourers were commonly referred to as 'the labouring poor', or where people plumed
themselves on 'numerous soup-establishments, on charities kindly
and industriously set on foot throughout the Kingdom'?[3] What
was the moral situation in a nation in which the poor infant born
in an English or Irish hovel breathes the air and sees the light but
is disinherited of every other thing? To make him work as a brute
beast he is kept as ignorant as a brute beast. 'Over a recruiting
place in this city I have seen pieces of beef hung up to attract the
half-famished mechanic . . . fools! to commit robbery and get
hung when they might fight for their King and Country—yea, and
have 6d. a day into the bargain!'[4] And what can one think of the
law when one can read in a provincial newspaper of a man sent
to prison for twelve months for stealing a sack of coals or a young
woman sentenced to six months' imprisonment and to be whipped
for stealing six loaves? Coleridge may have had an outdated sense
of hierarchical difference; but he had a strong and relevant feeling
for the universal humanity in everyone—'every human being
bears in himself that indelible something which belongs equally
to the whole species'.[5] In his cogent pamphlets on Sir Robert Peel's
Bill he pounds his opponents with facts, with statistics, medical
arguments, economic instances, and historical precedents. But
the overwhelming conviction comes from the deep imaginative
sense of oneness with the maltreated children and a powerful and
humane morality. '. . . We offer no reply to the assertion hazarded
by the opponents of Sir R. Peel's Bill, that children from six to
sixteen years of age, who are kept at work, standing from thirteen
to fifteen hours in the twentyfour, in a heated and polluted atmos-

[1] Ibid., p. 319.
[2] *The Friend*, Essay 16.
[3] *Essays on his own Times.*
[4] Ibid.
[5] Ibid.

phere, are healthier and happier than those who are employed in
trades where the said grievances do not exist . . . either all the
opinions concerning all the laws of animal life, which have been
hitherto received by mankind as undoubted truths must be false:
or else there is a continued interference of a miraculous power
suspending and counteracting those laws, in mark of God's
especial favour toward the Cotton Factories.'[1] Conscience and
imagination are the sources of Coleridge's social criticism, sources
whose products are never stale. So that it is as fresh as it is
independent and as alive as it is relevant. It depends not on the
principles of abstract reason but on the lights of specific experience.
For all his reverence for the past, very little in his political
writing is antique or superannuated, and his conservative sense
of history goes with, or at least never stands in the way of, a
radical and cogent sense of what is humanly decent.

What is humanly decent includes not only the standard of living
in the economic sense but the standards by which we live in the
moral sense. That state is barbarian, Coleridge says firmly, when
the accumulation of knowledge and experience from age to age
is not put at the disposal of all, and when any class is in the same
grade of knowledge, morality and social comfort as it was in the
past: barbarian he adds, 'let it be as civilized as Taylors, Milliners,
Friseurs, Dancing-Masters, Drill-Sergeants, Cooks, Upholsterers
etc. can make it . . .'.[2] There are forms of barbarism now, as in
Coleridge's time, just as there are forms of cruelty and oppression
which make Coleridge's moral passion as necessary now as then,
even though it may have to be differently directed. In the same
way the details of his theory of government may no longer stand,
but there are principles in it as important now as then.

Of these the most important are a principle of proportion, a
principle of discrepancy, and a principle of balance. Coleridge
distinguished the mind of the Nation, its collective sagacity and
knowledge, from its defined legal powers. But between these two
distinct elements of national life, an imponderable wisdom on the
one side, and legal rights and structures on the other, there had to
be, as a precondition of political health, harmony and proportion.
Athens and Venice fell because of different degrees of disproportion:
Athens because of an overplus of intelligence which found no

[1] *Inquiring Spirit.* Edited by Kathleen Coburn, p. 351.
[2] Ibid., p. 315.

suitable channels of expression, Venice because its legal and administrative organisation was insufficiently informed by living intelligence: but one fell from a defect of organisation, the other from a stifling excess of it.

Secondly he distinguished between the active and passive powers of government. A Nation did not hand over to its rulers the whole of its powers. This would turn a government into a despotism, and deplete the identity of the nation of resources which could not be signed away. Freedom depended on preserving the discrepancy between the latent and the active power, and the strong tradition of liberty in England was the result of the nation's yielding its powers to its rulers only with measure and circumspection. The *Idea* of the nation kept back something; it preserved a kind of obscurity and never defined itself with absolute clarity. Coleridge scoffed at the omnipotence of Parliament, and at what he called the wild and the pernicious error of 'attributing to governments a talismanic influence over our virtues and our happiness, as if governments were not rather effects than causes. It is true, that all effects react and become causes, and so it must be in some degree with governments; but there are other agents which act more powerfully because by a higher and more continuous agency, and it remains true that governments are more the effect than the cause of that which we are.'[1]

The third principle was the principle of balance. 'All temporal government must rest on a compromise of interests and abstract rights.'[2] This is the general balance. The particular one in Coleridge's England was the equilibrium between permanence and progression, permanence represented by the landed, progress by the mercantile interest. The *Idea* of the State works itself out through this nicely maintained, constantly adjusting balance. It keeps its footing, as it were, through 'the play of antagonist muscles'. The balance is upset when one party is given a weight in the equation not justified by the facts of society—in his own day by the over-representation of the landed against the professional interest. It was because of his conviction of the necessity for an incessantly renovated balance in society that he wanted representative government rather than delegation. Organisation followed life and should be in keeping with it. The balance of powers was all the more necessary because Coleridge believed that

---

[1] *Letters*, Vol. I, p. 395.   [2] *Table Talk*.

Government was based on classes and interests and *unequal* property. The only other possible mode of unity in the State was 'by the absolute co-ordination of each to all, and all to each . . . and there was never an instance of the first, nor can there be without slavery as its condition and accompaniment, as in Athens'.[1] This was why Coleridge maintained that the great ends a statesman ought to propose to himself were security to possessors, facility to acquirers and hope to all, why he strongly opposed the concentration of capital into fewer and fewer hands, and why he supported every measure, even a property tax, which worked for the mobility of capital.

If Coleridge stressed inequality in property and the subordination of classes to a degree which would be found distasteful, even offensive, today, this was in part because of theoretical conviction, in part because of personal predilection, in part because of romantic nostalgia. But it was also because he believed that the State which is based on classes and property should exist side by side, or even within, a pure democracy, which is not concerned with classes or property or birth or rank. It disregards all external accidents and looks at men as individual persons. In this pure democracy, persons alone are considered and one person *a priori* is equal to another. There are focal points in it but no superiors except in wisdom or learning or goodness.

The purpose of this society or commonwealth of intelligence was to care for those qualities and faculties that are characteristically human rather than technical or economic. Coleridge called it rather bafflingly the National Church, although it was not identical with the Christian Church or any denomination of it. Such a society was no mere agency of the State. 'It is the State itself in its intensest federal union; yet at the same moment the guardian and representative of all personal individuality.'[2] Its soul is a learned class: 'a learned order, a national clerisy . . . is an essential element of a rightly constituted nation, without which it lacks the best security alike for its permanence and its progress'.[3] 'The clerisy of a nation, that is its learned men, whether poets, philosophers or scholars, are the points of relative rest: there could be no order or harmony of the whole without them.'[4] 'The objects and final intentions of the order are these—to preserve the stores

---

[1] *Table Talk.*   [2] *Aids to Reflection:* Aphorisms, XI.
[3] *Church and State.*   [4] *Table Talk.*

and guard the treasures of past culture, and thus to bind the present with the past; to perfect and add to the same, and thus to connect the present with the future.'[1]

If its soul is this, its support is those whose office is to diffuse through the community at large the practical results of science, and that kind and degree of knowledge and cultivation, which is requisite or useful for all. Coleridge, that is, saw co-existing with the political State an educational State, devoted to the quality of civilisation and to the enrichment and refinement of the general consciousness. Coleridge, perhaps before any other modern mind, saw the supreme value of education and the vital necessity for a system of education distributed throughout the whole of society. It sustains the spirit of a nation and it humanises the individuals who comprise it. The educational society, which fosters intelligence and individuality, and in which there is submission to standards but not to superiors, is all the more important since in Coleridge's view the quality of civilisation depended far more on individual than State action. He had no great faith in acts of parliamentary reform. 'All the great—the permanently great—things that have been achieved in the world, have been so achieved by individuals, working from the instinct of genius or of goodness. The rage nowadays is all the other way: the individual is supposed capable of nothing; there must be organisation, classification, machinery, etc., as if the capital of national morality could be increased by making a joint stock of it.'[2]

The ends of government, then, as Coleridge conceived them, included political, economic and educational purposes. Government, as he put it in the *Essay on Method*, had to support 'the two main directions of human activity, pervading in modern time the whole civilised world . . . trade and literature'. Negatively it was the business of government to ensure protection of life, of freedom, of property, of reputation, of religious belief. Positively it had the obligation to make the means of subsistence available to everyone, and in addition to see that from the union and division of labour every citizen obtained a share of the comfort and conveniences necessary to civilized life. Moreover, it was the business of government to help to develop those faculties which are essential to human nature, and to foster the increase of every man's intellectual power. '. . . instruction is one of the ends of government, for it is

---

[1] *Church and State.*   [2] *Table Talk.*

that only which makes the banishment of the savage state an absolute duty; and that constitution is the best under which the average sum of useful knowledge is the greatest and the causes which awaken and encourage talent and genius, the most powerful and various.'[1] These ends are not simply the readings from history, not even the practice of the most civilized of States. They are models or *ideas* towards which the most advanced countries must still struggle. They have that very special note of contemporaneous and living relevance which belongs to ideals still in process, in painful process, of realisation.

It is this quality of present life, an immediacy and modernity which I want to stress in concluding. It is evident not only in Coleridge's general theory on the state and its operation but in so many of his incidental judgments and observations on political life. They are quickened by his feeling for the actual situation and they are kept steadily relevant because their sources are permanently human and moral. How much sanity would be introduced into the political action of so many countries today if men could see that 'a system of fundamental reform will scarcely be effected by massacres mechanised into revolution'.[2] How pointed, in particular for our own government, his caustic comments on the contribution of the State to cultivation:

> The darkest despotisms on the Continent have done more for the growth and elevation of the fine arts than the English government. A great musical composer in Germany and Italy is a great man in society, and a real dignity and rank are universally conceded to him. So it is with a sculptor, or painter, or architect. Without this sort of encouragement and patronage such arts as music and painting will never come into great eminence. In this country there is no general reverence for the fine arts; and the sordid spirit of a money-amassing philosophy would meet any proposition for the fostering of art, in a genial and extended sense, with the commercial maxim,—*Laissez faire*. Paganini, indeed, will make a fortune, because he can actually sell the tones of his fiddle at so much a scrape; but Mozart himself might have languished in a garret for anything that would have been done for him here.[3]

How prophetic his vision of the United States of America:

---

[1] *The Friend*, IX.
[2] Address delivered at Bristol.   [3] *Table Talk*.

The possible destiny of the United States of America,—as a nation of a hundred millions of freemen,—stretching from the Atlantic to the Pacific, living under the laws of Alfred, and speaking the language of Shakespeare and Milton, is an august conception. Why should we not wish to see it realized? America would then be England viewed through a solar microscope; Great Britain in a state of glorious magnification.[1]

And how apt his warning on the relation between Britain and the United States. 'It is related by D. Unzer, an authority wholly to be relied on, that an *ohrwurm* (earwig) cut in half ate its own hinder part! Will it be the reverse with Great Britain and America?'[2] How perceptive his comment about capital, 'I think this country is now suffering grievously under an excessive accumulation of capital, which, having no field for profitable operation, is in a state of fierce civil war with itself'[3]; and how acute his characterisation of the British spirit. 'We are . . . a busy, enterprising, and commercial nation. The habits attached to this character must, if there exist no adequate counterpoise, inevitably lead us under the specious names of utility, practical knowledge and so forth, to look at all things through the medium of the market, and to estimate the worth of all pursuits and attainments by their marketable value.'[4] Every page of Coleridge's political writing is strewn with evidence of his miraculous insight and his uncanny foresight. He combined great theoretical and analytical power with the nicest judgment of shades of difference. All that he wrote was warm and human, and even when he was wrong he was appealing;

> I have heard but two arguments of any weight adduced in favour of passing this Reform Bill, and they are in substance these: 1. We will blow your brains out if you don't pass it; 2. We will drag you through a horse-pond if you don't pass it; and there is a good deal of force in both.[5]

III EDUCATIONAL THEORY

If Coleridge is a seminal mind—and Mill's term is peculiarly appropriate to him—he was seminal in a way very different from another kind of nineteenth century sage, say T. H. Huxley.

[1] *Table Talk.* [2] *Anima Poetae.*
[3] *Table Talk.* [4] *A Lay Sermon.* [5] *Table Talk.*

Coleridge established no movements—Pantisocracy was only a dream—founded no institutions, sat on no committees (the picture of Coleridge the committee-man is an alarming one), he altered no machinery, and negotiated no agreements. He had not a portion of that flood of intellectual and administrative energy which Huxley employed so devotedly and effectively for what we must recognise were good if limited ends. Coleridge produced nothing in the way of observable results; even his literary works were fragmentary and incomplete. And yet who can doubt that it is Huxley whose importance is largely local, Huxley whose reputation has a nineteenth century aura, and that it is Coleridge who is unconfined by time and Coleridge who is increasingly relevant to us in the twentieth century? We have assimilated Huxley, taken some nourishment from him, and finished with him; we haven't even caught up with Coleridge.

But it is a crude gauge of educational importance which attempts to correlate a man's significance with a number of specifiable results in which his hand can be seen. Coleridge's influence worked at a more profound level, at the roots of action, where the quality of practice is determined. Coleridge's influence was seminal in that it operated in depth among motives and purposes, assumptions and values. It made a difference not just to men's judgments but it altered the kind of mind, the structure of beliefs, they brought to bear in making these judgments. One of the places in which Coleridge's influence in this sense has been most moving and prominent is in education. He has not, it is true, any extended work on the nature of children or the idea of education. But in letters, in poems, in his writings on education, in a profusion of remarks incidental to other themes, in the strangest places, for example in his notes on Jeremy Taylor, he reveals a sense for the exact nuance of childhood, so fine and sure, that it is not surpassed even by Wordsworth, Dickens or Mark Twain.

What distinguishes Coleridge in so many fields of thought is the co-presence of powers usually divorced. He united, as few others have, a poetic power of reconstructing experience in its fullness and uniqueness with a philosophic power of creative speculation. And this, while always relevant to the perception from which it rises, is also a source of new light and an aid to an even more seeing perception. His perception is peculiarly sensitive, tremblingly responsive and able to discriminate between the most filament-like delicacies. But for Coleridge no experience, however vivid, was insulated; it struggled to connect. No experience was complete until it had fulfilled its aspiration towards coherence. Thus his work has the vigour and definition of the concrete, and the flow and movement of that which strives towards order. His concern to give for an experience both the precise shade of its being, and the most relevant and general law of its being, may be seen in his remarkable commentary on the self of the child.

> Two things we may learn from little children from three to six years old: 1. That it is a characteristic, an instinct of our human nature to pass out of self—i.e. the image or complex cycle of images . . . which is the perpetual representative of our Inviduum, and by all unreflecting minds confounded and identified with it. . . . 2. Not to suffer any form to pass into me and become a usurping self.[1]

In these words Coleridge describes what is, as he indicates, a general characteristic of mankind, but one seen most clearly in the child. It is on the one hand that restless search for release from the confinement of the single image of one self, and on the other a solicitude to keep inviolable the privacy of another self. To one in touch with children this will come home as a strikingly first-hand and penetrating observation. And by his distinction between the representative and the real self, between the image and the principle of individuality, Coleridge succeeds in easing the tension between the two terms of his paradox and conciliates them in one consistent judgment. It is worth notice that he introduces his account with the phrase 'Two things we may learn'. The point of the lesson could be taken with profit by every adult, and especially by every teacher. For too many, maturity means a narrowing into a dull or resigned acceptance of a limited representative self and a disavowal or oblivion of the real self. Similarly, too much teaching offers insufficient opportunity and too feeble a provocation to enrich the image of self by imaginative participation in many modes of being; just as, all too frequently, it is, in face of the helplessness of the child, an unjust invasion of the real self. But the mature adult—and this is what every teacher should be—is one who senses in others, because he has felt it in himself, beneath the image of the representative self the secret movements of a deeper self. For the image he has imaginative liberality, sympathy in

---

[1] *Inquiring Spirit.* Edited by Kathleen Coburn, p. 68.

feeling and tact in action; for the true self he has reverence. 'Reverence the individuality of your friend. It is the religion of the delicate soul,' said Coleridge.

In speaking of the child's resistance to the intrusion of an alien form, Coleridge invokes a concept which he, in common with most of the best minds of the nineteenth century, accepted as part of the structure of the meaning of childhood, but which has today fallen into disrepute. The concept is that of the innocence of childhood. It is asserted by Coleridge rarely in overt statement, but rather—and with all the more effect—by implication, image, overtone and language expressing a note of delighted awe. In the past this idea was ridiculed by those religious puritans for whom the child was a limb of Satan, and at a later date by those behaviourists for whom the child is an animal, properly to be described as innocent only if the term signifies an inhuman tranquility of attitude and contentment in action. Coleridge reminded the puritans of his own day that Christ blessed the children not in order to make them innocent but because they already were so. And he would have agreed with the comment of Suttie that the child's mind is less like that of the primitive animal than the adult's. 'It is less like the animal mind since it is adapted to a milieu and a mode of behaving vastly different from that of the free-living, self-supporting animal.'[1] Moreover, and in another idiom, it may be remarked that it is sad but true that many are never so truly human as when they were children, never again so little dominated by appetite or so imaginatively free.

The innocence of children declares itself unmistakably in their play. Children's play, as David Riesman said, 'is often filled with terror and morbidity, but at its best it is one of the unequivocally good things of this earth'. To its unequivocal goodness Coleridge gives the respect of the religious man, while he evoked with a poet's force the special quality of joy that informs it; a feeling rapt, utterly faithful to that out of which it arises, unsullied by regard for the extraneous and the conventional. He writes of his own children at play: 'Hartley is a spirit that dances on an aspen leaf—the air that yonder sallow-faced and yawning tourist is breathing is to my babe a perpetual nitrous oxide'.[2] 'I look at my doted-on Hartley—he moves, he lives, he finds impulse from within and without . . .

[1] Suttie, I. D., *The Origins of Love and Hate*, London, 1935, p. 15.
[2] To Davy, July 25th, 1800.

he looks at the clouds and mountains, the living beings of the earth, and vaults and jubilates.'[1] 'Hartley and little Derwent running in the green where the gusts blow most madly, both with their hair floating and tossing, a miniature of the agitated trees, below which they were playing, inebriate both with pleasure—Hartley whirling round for joy, Derwent eddying, half-willingly, half by force of the gust—driven backward, struggling forward, and shouting his little hymn of joy.'[2] The joy of the child is so complete, so self-delighting, because it is the accompaniment of those primary movements of the imagination by which he discovers and furthers his humanity, and finds and increases his freedom. 'To carry on the feelings of childhood into the powers of manhood . . . this is the character and privilege of genius.'[3] It was a character Coleridge himself possessed. And *Dejection: An Ode* witnesses in its desolation at the demise of the 'shaping spirit of imagination', in its anguished sterility at the absence of joy, to the depth and power with which he had felt its presence.

It is necessary, and perhaps prudent in the light of Coleridge's reputation, to insist that he took no unduly ecstatic view of the nature of childhood. He was not a disciple of Rousseau, and if he was a Wordsworthian it was only in a severely qualified way. The attitude which sees in childhood a deserving object of admiration for certain ineffable or mystical qualities was both incomprehensible and distasteful to him.

In what sense [he asks, criticising this ungrounded and delirious sort of thinking in the *Ode on the Intimations of Immortality*] is a child of that age a philosopher? In what sense does he read 'the eternal deep'? In what sense is he declared to be 'for ever haunted' by the Superior Being, or so inspired as to deserve the splendid title of a mighty prophet, a blessed seer? by reflection? by knowledge? by conscious intuition? or by any forms or modification of consciousness? Those would be tidings indeed; but such as would presuppose an immediate revelation to the inspired communicator, and require miracles to authenticate his inspiration. Children at this age give us no such information of themselves; and at what time were we dipped in the Lethe, which has produced such utter oblivion of a state so Godlike? There are many of us that still possess some remembrance more or less distinct, respecting ourselves at six years old; pity that the worth-

---

[1] To Godwin, September 22nd, 1800.
[2] To Sotheby, September 27th, 1802.   [3] *The Friend.*

less straws only should float while treasures, compared with which all the mines of Golconda and Mexico were but straws, should be absorbed by some unknown gulf into some unknown abyss.[1]

Coleridge not only recognised the intellectual and moral limitations of childhood, but he also indicated precisely where they lay.

> Reflect on the simple fact of the state of a child's mind while with great delight he hears or listens to the story of Jack and the Beanstalk. How could this be if in some sense he did not understand it? Yes, the child does understand each part of it—*A*, and *B*, and *C*; but not *ABC*=*X*. He understands it as we all understand our dreams while we are dreaming, each shape and incident or group of shapes and incidents by itself—unconscious of, and therefore unoffended at, the absence of the logical copula or the absurdity of the transitions.[2]

The realism of his observation gives added point to his recommendations on intellectual education. Since immaturity of thought in the child consists in the appreciation of but few and simple relations and the command of few and crude transitions in expression, the education of the intellect, he maintains, should aim at refining the sense of relation and making subtler the power of 'pertinent connectives'. And it should attempt to realise this aim slowly and tactfully, 'for the comparing power, the judgment, is not at that age active, and ought not to be forcibly excited, as is too frequently and mistakenly done in modern systems of education, which can only lead to selfish views, debtor and creditor principles of virtue, and an inflated sense of merit'.[3] As these words suggest, he was, for all his conviction of a child's innocence, equally clear about its moral limitations, something borne out by his account of himself when a child, in a letter to Poole in 1797 which I quoted at the beginning of Part I. He spoke there, it will be remembered, of how fretful and passionate he was, how the boys detested him and the old women flattered him. These imperfections were certainly personal to the child Coleridge, but they are as well those to which not only gifted but all children have a positive inclination. The child is self-centred, self-admiring and

---

[1] *Biographia Literaria*, XXII.
[2] *Inquiring Spirit*. Edited by Kathleen Coburn, p. 204.
[3] *Lectures on Shakespeare*, XI.

often arrogantly unjust. Nor should it be supposed that Coleridge is imposing on childhood adult standards quite alien to it. For children the moral categories to which reference is made by Coleridge in his letter lack the clarity and complexity they have for the developed person. But they are in principle the same. The child's is a moral world. His actions are to be described as conduct rather than behaviour. The moral world of childhood is, in Coleridge's terms, 'a form proceeding' not 'a shape superinduced'. Because moral categories cannot be applied to children by adults without delicacy and tact, and because adults are frequently arbitrary and incompetent, some modern educationists fall into the worse error of obliterating the moral order for the child and of regarding him as an amoral being. But before the child satisfies the definition of a child he satisfies that of a human being, and as Coleridge says, 'It is still the grand definition of humanity that we have a conscience which no mechanic compost, no chemical combination of mere appetency, memory and understanding can solve'.[1] 'Children', he insists, 'are much less removed from men and women than generally imagined: they have less power to express their meaning than man, but their opinion of justice is nearly the same: this we may prove by referring to our own experience.'[2] It is not extravagant to maintain that children suffer more from those who fail to treat them as human beings than from those who fail to treat them as children. 'Never let it be forgotten that every human being bears in himself that indelible something which belongs equally to the whole species as well as that particular modification of it which individualises him.'[3]

Coleridge's collocation of the terms moral and intellectual is to be attributed neither to custom nor to accident. It is deliberate and significant. For Coleridge one is the source of the other. And in contrast to the more received opinion, which assumes the moral to be the consequence of developed intelligence, Coleridge considered the moral to be the impulse of the intellectual. 'All speculative truths begin with a postulate, even the truths of geometry. They all suppose an act of the will; for in the moral being lies the source of the intellectual.'[4] To know is preceded by to choose, and the moral life consists in decision enlivened by faith. The life of the child exemplifies this truth.

---

[1] *The Friend.*   [2] VIIth Lecture: 'New System of Education'.
[3] *The Friend.*   [4] Ibid.

Have you children [asks Coleridge], or have you lived among children, and do you not know that in all things, in food, in medicine, in all their doings and abstainings, they must believe in order to acquire a reason for their belief? . . . To believe and to understand are not diverse things but the same thing in different periods of its growth.[1]

To the belief of the child corresponds the authority of the teacher. Authority is a word likely in current educational discourse, pragmatically resistant to the external and the given, to be met with suspicion and dismissed with contempt. But the word cannot be avoided, for authority enters deeply into the relation of learner to teacher. Educational authority is not, of course, coercive power, nor is it anything that can be conferred like a diploma or assumed like a gown. It is the quality of one who can be consulted with trust; and it is to be attained only by labour, patience and the abdication of self. The authority of the teacher is constituted in part by his pupil's recognition of his sincerity, in part by the worth of the standards he upholds. The first part of this proposition receives some attention today, but the second in a collective and irrelevantly egalitarian age attracts only the minimum of formal notice. The plight of modern civilisation is to be menaced more and more closely by the barbarism of literacy uninformed by value, by what Coleridge called 'the plebification of knowledge'. Upon the teacher at all times rests the obligation of speaking for intellectual sanity and spiritual health. In our time his obligation is all the more urgent for he is one of the very few with any power to be heard. If value has not the protection of the teacher's authority, civilisation is condemned. Few teachers entertain the amiably simple, progressive reasons of Thelwall, Coleridge's friend, for passivity in the defence of value, but many more, through uncertainty, indifference or scepticism, are equally ineffective, acting as he would have acted and producing results that he would have approved.

Thelwall thought it very unfair to influence a child's mind by in-culcating any opinions before it should have come to years of discretion and be able to choose for itself. I showed him my garden and told him it was my botanical garden.

'How so?' said he, 'it is covered with weeds.'

[1] *Aids to Reflection.*

'Oh!' I replied, 'that is only because it has not yet come to the age
of discretion and choice. The weeds, you see, have taken the liberty
to grow and I thought it unfair in me to prejudice the soil towards
roses and strawberries.[1]

In fostering that 'prejudice towards roses' upon which depends
the humanity of the individual and the quality of civilisation, the
strongest appeal should be to the imagination, the power by which
the child prises himself free from the present and loosens the clutch
of the immediate. In the imaginative act the child disengages
himself from the partial and the broken, 'from the universe as a
mass of little parts', and comes to conceive of a larger unity and a
more inclusive whole. The now is extended, the here complicated.
The pressure of the momentary is relaxed and the actual charged
with the possible. Alternative courses of action loom up and define
themselves for choice. The source separates from the outcome,
and the distance between act and consequence increases. Thus a
centre of attribution is established, and the concept of responsibility begins its long and difficult pregnancy. In the *Eleventh
Lecture* Coleridge outlines the rôle of the imagination.

> In the education of children, love is first to be instilled, and out of
> love obedience is to be educed. Then impulse and power should be
> given to the intellect, and the ends of a moral being be exhibited. For
> this object thus much is effected by works of imagination;—that they
> carry the mind out of self, and show the possible of the good and the
> great in the human character. . . . In the imagination of man exist
> the seeds of all moral and scientific improvement; chemistry was first
> alchemy, and out of astrology sprang astronomy. In the childhood
> of those sciences the imagination opened a way, and furnished
> materials, on which the ratiocinative powers in a maturer stage
> operated with success. The imagination is the distinguishing
> characteristic of man as a progressive being; and I repeat that it
> ought to be carefully guided and strengthened as the indispensable
> means and instrument of continued amelioration and refinement.[2]

Imagination, it will be seen, receives an importance as an educative agency greater than the attenuated respect given it by most
modern educators. For these to exercise the imagination is to
cultivate a sense of the aesthetic. And this, in a civilisation which
confounds the artist with the aesthete, and confuses the severity

[1] *Table Talk.*   [2] Lectures on Shakespeare, XI.

and the chastity of the one with the preciousness and frivolity of the other, means a trivial and decorative addition to more seriously important human powers. But imagination is not a garnish of the soul, a mere finish according to a fashionable specific. 'The rules of the imagination are themselves the very powers of growth and production.'[1] The life of the child before school is quick with the propulsive energies of imagination which 'carry the mind out of self'; the duty of the school is to bring before the learner works of imagination of such quality (and science is also a human achievement imaginatively initiated) that 'they show the possible of the good and great in the human character'. The bleakness of so much schooling and the dehumanising influence of most science teaching come from confining imagination to a cramped parish of aesthetic activity. But imagination is the air in which new knowledge breathes, as it is the salt preserving the savour of the old. 'Knowledge', it has been said, 'does not keep any better than fish'.

Coleridge was an unusually brilliant literary psychologist. Bringing to bear upon others a minutely precise observation and upon himself an unprejudiced and microscopic introspection, and without any of the formidable apparatus of modern psychological study, he yet succeeded in anticipating important conclusions of some of its most elaborate and penetrating enquiries. In these remarks on arithmetic, for example, he forestalls one of the significant findings of Piaget's treatise on the development of the concept of number. 'In the child's mind there is nothing fragmentary; its numeration table is truly Pythagorean. The numbers are, each and all, units and integers, and slowly and difficultly does it exchange this its first and awakened arithmetic for that of aggregation, apposition, in one word of *result*.'[2] Again in the *Philosophical Lectures* he has an utterance which is only one of the many where he is, as Kathleen Coburn pointed out, astonishingly prophetic of Freud. 'The first education which we receive, that from our mothers, is given to us by touch; the whole of its progress is nothing more than, to express myself boldly, an extended touch by promise. The sense itself, the sense of vision itself, is only acquired by a continued recollection of touch.'[3] A child's sensory

---

[1] *Biographia Literaria*, XVIII.

[2] *Coleridge on Logic and Learning*. Edited by A. D. Snyder, p. 127.

[3] *The Philosophical Lectures of S. T. Coleridge*. Edited by Kathleen Coburn, p. 115.

activity begins with a direct tactual acquaintance with objects (including himself); it becomes, as sight grows keener and more adept in recognition, more distanced and more detailed, a fuller and more governed kind of awareness. The vision of the forms of objects ousts the feeling for their textures as the dominant mode of experience. But there is in the knowledge derived from sight a deceptive clarity which beguiles the mind away from speculation, and an illusory completeness which betrays it into a rigid and static certainty. In Coleridge's view a main end of education is to rescue the child from 'the despotism of the eye', a result to be achieved by cultivating in the child a greater consciousness in the use of words. Coleridge writes of the child so trained, in a passage that could serve both as model and warning to the genetic psychologist:

> He will at least secure himself from the delusive notion, that what is not *imageable* is likewise not *conceivable*. To emancipate the mind from the despotism of the eye is the first step towards its emancipation from the influences and intrusions of the senses, sensations and passions generally. Thus most effectually is the power of abstraction to be called forth, strengthened and familiarised, and it is this power of abstraction that chiefly distinguishes the human understanding from that of the higher animals—and in the different degrees in which this power is developed, the superiority of man over man mainly consists.[1]

More important than the explicit sense of Coleridge's statements is the direction of his thought, which is significantly different from the ruling trend of contemporary opinion. Whereas this is retrogressive and concentrated on the circumstances of origin, Coleridge is prospective and attentive to the possibilities of attainment. It looks forward rather than backward, to final rather than to efficient causality. The contemporary bias, introduced into educational thought by the influence of the more traditional sciences, has been confirmed by the general assimilation of the study of education to the social sciences. But the notion of conscious purpose is an essential part of the concept of education. Education, as distinct from training, may be defined as the transformation of necessary, confused and volatile motives into free, deliberate and constant purposes. The assumption—that it is the motives that make the man—on which the social scientists and

---

[1] *Coleridge on Logic and Learning.* Edited by A. D. Snyder, pp. 126-7.

their educational disciples proceed, is the exact opposite of Coleridge's.

It is not [he writes] the motives that govern the man but the man that makes the motives; and these, indeed, are so various, mutable and chameleon-like that it is often as difficult, as fortunately it is a matter of comparative indifference to determine what a man's motive is for this or that particular action. A wise man will rather enquire what the person's general objects are—what does he habitually wish.[1]

It is the teacher's business to be at all times making this enquiry of his pupils in the form of an indirect question; it is his aim to provoke them to make it of themselves in the form of a direct question. Until they do, they can come to no adequate conception of their humanity which is to be both conscious and responsible, since the questioning of purpose according to a criterion of value is the condition of the exercise of responsibility.

A good education, according to Coleridge's view, persists not as a collection of information, an arrangement of intellectual bric-à-brac, but as a certain unity of self, more or less coherent, more or less rich, and a certain method of thinking and feeling, more or less complex, more or less sensitive. Unity and method are, in Coleridge's view, the qualities of the educated mind.

What is that [writes Coleridge] which first strikes us, and strikes us at once in a man of education, and which among educated men, so notably distinguishes the man of a superior mind? . . .Not the weight or novelty of his remarks, not any unusual interest of facts communicated by him. . . . It is the unpremeditated and evidently habitual arrangement of his words, grounded on the habit of foreseeing in each integral part, or (more plainly in each sentence) the whole that he intends to communicate. However irregular and desultory his talk, there is method in the fragments.[2]

He develops the point further in *Biographia Literaria*:

. . . the intercourse of uneducated men is distinguished from the diction of their superiors in knowledge and power by the greater *disjunction* and *separation* in the component parts of that, whatever it be, which they wish to communicate. There is a want of that prospectiveness of mind, that *surview*, which enables a man to foresee the whole

[1] *Coleridge on Logic and Learning.* Edited by A. D. Snyder, pp. 132-3.
[2] *The Friend*, II, 4.

of what he is to convey, appertaining to one point; and by this means so to subordinate and arrange the different parts according to their relative importance, as to convey it at once, and as an organised whole.[1]

Contemporary education is certainly calculated to be one in which a multitude of facts is amassed and conveyed, but hardly one which encourages this kind of unity of self or this kind of method in communication. We have been too much concerned with 'specific information that can be conveyed from without, storing the passive mind with the various sorts of knowledge most in request, using the human soul as a mere repository',[2] and we have been too little concerned with exciting 'the germinal power that craves no knowledge but what it can take up into itself, what it can appropriate and reproduce as fruit of its own'. At the end of a course of training, the mind of the student is too frequently 'an aggregate without unity', too rarely informed with a principle of 'vitality which grows and evolves itself from within'.[3] Thus the ordinary professional course prepares not a full but a 'pollarded man, with every faculty except reason'[4]: reason, that is, in Coleridge's meaning, as the source and organ of self-consciousness and 'the power by which we become possessed of principles'.[5]

The sense of 'fine and luminous distinction'[6] that Coleridge praised in Wordsworth he himself possessed in an eminent degree. His own work is, indeed, an extended commentary on an array of fundamental distinctions, a commentary informed with the three powers he specifies as 'wit, which discovers practical likeness hidden in general diversity; subtlety, which discovers the diversity concealed in general apparent sameness; and profundity, which discovers an essential unity under all the semblance of difference'.[7] His various distinctions between fancy and imagination, understanding and reason, the outer and the inner sense, civilisation and cultivation, arise and flow harmoniously from one profound 'realising intuition', the distinction between an aggregate of parts and a vital whole, between the discrete many and a living unity.[8] The error of education is to ignore or neglect

---

[1] *Biographia Literaria*, XVII.   [2] *The Friend*, II, 4.
[3] *Lit. Rem.*, I.   [4] *Table Talk.*
[5] *The Friend*, I, 3, footnote.   [6] *Biographia Literaria*, XXII.
[7] *Lectures upon Shakespeare*: notes on Othello.
[8] Cf. Willey, B., *Nineteenth Century Studies*, London, 1949, p. 30.

the latter in concentrated pursuit of the former. In the practice of education the error expresses itself in a determination 'to shape convictions and deduce knowledge from without by an exclusive observation of outward and sensible things as the only realities', as well as in an obstinate inattention 'to the simple truth that as the forms in all organised existence, so must all true and living knowledge proceed from within'.[1] Such an intellectual policy may produce Coleridge's 'civilisation' or technocracy (for which his symbol is 'trade'), the efficient management of practical affairs, but not 'cultivation' or wisdom (for which his symbol is 'literature') the reverent appreciation of excellence. Such an education may produce a competent technician; certainly it will not produce a good teacher.

If in accord with the spirit of Coleridge's distinctions we contrast as ends the man who has been taught and the man who has been educated, the knowledgeable man and the wise man, we may also oppose as means corresponding to them the two modes of learning he named observation and reflection. No inconsiderable part of Coleridge's criticism both in literature and education derives from his concern to discriminate between these two, to exhibit their proper relation and to stress how seriously in contemporary society this had been disturbed. For him, to observe is to attend to evidence furnished by 'the notices of the senses' with the aim of enlarging knowledge of the world outside the borders of self; to reflect is to turn the mind's regard inwards in order 'to refine consciousness of self'. Reflection is not, it must be remarked, to be confused with reverie, a lackadaisical, bemused sauntering in the company of a mere sequence of notions and images. It is difficult, an athletic and ascetic exercise calling on the full energy of thought. 'It requires', says Coleridge, 'no ordinary skill and address to fix the attention of men on the world within them, to induce them to study the processes and superintend the works which they are themselves carrying on in their own minds.'[2]

If education is to become what Coleridge thought it ought to be, 'that most weighty and concerning of all sciences',[3] it must do so by an utter conversion here at its centre. It must become an enquiry, active and intimately personal, devoted to the interroga-

[1] *The Friend*, II, 10.
[2] *Aids to Reflection*: Introductory Aphorisms, 8.　　[3] *The Friend*, II, 9.

tion of self, to all that is grounded in the self, and to that transformation of self hoped for in learning. In this enquiry only those
questions should be posed which are pointed, revealing and
important. And these will be found to be those which have excited
and been framed by the best minds in any age. In no other way can
Coleridge's hope be realised, 'that men may be made better, not
only in consequence, but by the mode and in the process of
instruction'.[1] To ask that education should aim at self-knowledge
by the method of reflection is to require it to be very different from
what it is at present, namely a mode of liberal education. For as
Coleridge wrote to James Gillman in 1827, 'all knowledge, not
merely mechanical and like a carpenter's rule, having its whole
value in the immediate outward use to which it is applied . . . all
knowledge . . . that enlightens and liberalises, is a form and means
of self-knowledge, whether it be grammar or geometry, logical or
classical'. Education collapses into an invertebrate huddle
precisely because it lacks the leading idea that Coleridge named
'the self-unravelling clue'.[2]

Throughout his writings Coleridge insists that an essential
means of reflective self-knowledge—and an unsurpassed educative agency—is an active analysis of language, and especially an
interrogation of the texts of great writers.

> Reflect on your thoughts, actions, circumstances and—which will
> be of especial aid to you in forming a *habit* of reflection—accustom
> yourself to reflect on the words you use, hear or read, their truth,
> derivation and history. For if words are not things, they are living
> powers, by which things of most importance to mankind are activated
> combined and humanised.[3]

Since 'the best part of human language properly so called is
derived from reflection on the acts of the mind itself', attention
to the combinations, relations and the mutual accommodations of
words gives us direct access to the intimate operations of the mind.
When these are the words of a great writer, we have the liberalising
experience of being made free, luminously free, of a mind infinitely
more subtle, complex and powerful than our own. And by mind,
of course, I mean not just intellect but the whole concourse of co-
operative mental powers, of thought, feeling, purpose and imag-

[1] *The Friend*, I, 14. [2] Ibid., II, 11.
[3] *Aids to Reflection*: Preface.

ination. I say made free of. But I do not wish to imply that it is easy. It is something we have to struggle towards with discipline and abnegation. Without severity of effort there is no quality of attainment. To mitigate the difficulty Coleridge gives us his own technique of interrogation.

'The first question', says Coleridge, 'we should put to ourselves when we have read a passage that perplexes us in a work of authority is: What does the writer *mean* by all this? And the second question should be, What does he intend by all this?'[1] That is to say, each part of the text must be interpreted in the light of the intention of the whole. The meaning of particular parts is always modified and often constituted by the general intention of the author. The separation of meaning and intention here is made, it is clear, for purposes of discussion; in action they are not divided as we see from Coleridge's explanation of meaning. 'I include in the meaning of a word not only its correspondent object, but likewise all the associations it recalls. For language is framed to convey not the object alone, but likewise the character, mood and intentions of the person who is representing it.'[2] Throughout an analysis we have to be alert to detect confusion and equivocation. 'To expose a sophism, and to detect the equivocal or double meaning of a word, is in the great majority of cases one and the same thing.'[3] We have also to learn to refine our sense of distinction. To appreciate and to make fine—but always relevant—distinctions is the mark of an educated mind. And the subtler the distinctions, the better the mind. 'For one useless subtlety in our elder divines and moralists, I will produce ten sophisms of equivocation in the writings of our modern preceptors; and for one error resulting from excess of distinguishing the indifferent, I could show ten mischievous delusions from the habit of confounding the diverse.'[4] But the distinctions must always be relevant, appropriate that is within the sphere of discourse established by the author's intention. The quality of just and delicate relevance is the hardest come by, the most easily lost, of all the qualities of the educated mind. A leading idea, a quirk of intolerance, some failure in patience or self-restraint, and our analysis ceases to be critical—and educative—

---

[1] *Aids to Reflection*: Aphorisms of Spiritual Religion, 10.
[2] *Biographia Literaria*, XXII.
[3] *Aids to Reflection*: Preface.
[4] Ibid.: Prudential Aphorisms, I.

and the words of a great writer are made an occasion for rambling meditations of our own.

If we sought an account of the learning hoped for in humane education, we could find nowhere an exposition more perceptive and convincing than Coleridge's. The act of learning was a main and persistent theme of Coleridge's thought, likely in any context to come to the front of his attention. Its characteristics, therefore, are not detailed in a set piece of analysis but, as one would expect, are scattered in a rich variety throughout his work and letters. Their unity is in their source, in one mastering and decisive conviction, that the mind is an active power. 'To know is in its very essence a verb active.'[1] He had himself a mind unusually gifted with awareness and energy, or rather with awareness of its own energy. (As for his notorious lethargy in action, that is, when his accomplishment is fairly considered, partly a legend of his own devising.) From his earliest years he was conscious of his mind shaping and patterning his experience. 'I regulated all my creeds', he wrote of his childhood, 'by my conceptions, not by my sight, even at that age.'[2]

In learning 'things take the signature of thought'.[3] Where the mind has the initiative, 'things the most remote and diverse in time, place and outward circumstances are brought into mental contiguity and succession, the more striking as the less expected'.[4] When the mind is passive, human experience, 'the confluence of innumerable impressions in each moment of time',[5] falls asunder into a delirium of inconsequence. The activity of the mind, 'combining many circumstances into one moment of consciousness, tends to produce that ultimate end of all human thought and feeling, unity'.[6] The activity of thought, as of imagination and passion, Coleridge would add, is an activity of unification. What thought, imagination and passion connect is not separated facts, 'not things only or for their sake alone, but likewise and chiefly the relations of things, either their relations to each other, or to the observer, or to the state of apprehension of the hearers. To enumerate and analyse these relations with the conditions under which alone they are discoverable is to teach the science of method'.[7] It is also to teach the art of learning.

[1] *Biographia Literaria*, I.
[2] To Poole, 1797.
[3] *Aids to Reflection*: Introductory Aphorisms, 24.
[4] *The Friend*, II, 4.
[5] Ibid.   [6] *Lit. Rem.*, II.
[7] *The Friend*, II, 4.

Coleridge's insight into learning is not coarsened by any pretension finally to solve what is ultimately insoluble. He is as free from the vulgarity which seeks—to use the idiom of Gabriel Marcel—to degrade a mystery into a problem, as he is from its twin vice, that ignorant lack of reverence for life which Lawrence bitterly and justly complained of in his contemporaries. All too many, indeed, of the problems of education are mysteries made shabby by the absence of reverence. Coleridge was quick to see and to judge this particularly uncouth kind of provinciality.

> I have known [he wrote to Poole in 1797] some who have been rationally educated as it is styled. They were marked by a microscopic acuteness but when they looked at great things, all became a blank and they saw nothing, and denied (very illogically) that anything could be seen, and uniformly put the negation of a power for the possession of a power and called the want of imagination judgment and the never being moved to rapture philosophy.

But in Coleridge himself a miraculous clarity of discernment is inseparable from the restraint and sanity of humility, and the subtlest analytic intelligence from a sense of modesty and wonder. Perhaps nothing illustrates better this mature hospitality of mind than a remark in another letter to Poole, in 1801. 'My opinion', he wrote, 'is this: That deep thinking is attainable only by a man of deep feeling, and that all truth is a species of revelation.'

Here Coleridge anticipates the modern educational psychologist in that which has come more and more to engross his interests, the non-intellectual aspects of learning, the depth and urgency of its impulses. But at the same time he recognises that there is always more than the psychological conditions in learning, that learning is always something revealed as well as something performed. Learning as revelation is an idea with Platonic and Christian vibrations which may for some be sufficient to make it unwelcome. But however much these grate upon him, it is important for the teacher to realise that it contains at least an unmistakable negative truth, attested by his daily experience. Learning cannot be guaranteed. To believe that it can, even with every circumstance and effort co-operating, is to regard man as an infallibly adjusting organism, teaching as the cunning manipulation of environment, and learning as producing the appropriate reaction in a specific situation. But human dignity requires us to admit the possibility of failure, and the vocation of teacher involves a sense of reverence in the presence of mystery.

Coleridge then, for all his insistence on the activity of the mind in learning, was alive to what in it is beyond activity and not to be commanded by effort. Similarly, in spite of his regard for the transcendent or the 'grace' in learning, he could without incongruity offer a test of humane learning arrived at by psychological analysis. It was in the course of an examination of the intricate mode of learning by which the listener develops acquaintance with the art of music that he formulated his criterion. 'I allude', he said, 'to that sense of recognition which accompanies a sense of novelty in the most original passages of a great composer. If we listen to a symphony of Cimarosa, the present strain still seems not only to recall but almost to revive some past movement, another and yet the same.'[1]

The sense by which we recognise in the new a fulfilment of our finest experience, if it is felt with remarkably telling force in music, is not confined to that art. As a measure of its worth it is presupposed by Keats's judgment that poetry 'should strike the reader as a wording of his own highest thought, and appear almost a remembrance'. It is implicit in the Socratic theory of reminiscence. It informs Eliot's conception of tradition, 'an awareness that the mind of Europe is a mind which changes, and that this change is a development which abandons nothing *en route*, which does not superannuate either Shakespeare or Homer, or the rock drawings of the Magdalenian draughtsmen'. And it is the unspoken standard used by scientists in their collaborative effort to take up partial truths into a larger conciliation. The common ground in each case is a belief in the seamlessness of experience of quality, in the unity of texture between the finest whether familiar or utterly new.

The belief that experiences dissimilar in character but alike in quality fit together to make a coherent whole is one with heartening implications for education. It means that there can be a 'progressive transition' between the humblest sorts of these experiences which are relevant for children and the mature discoveries of genius. It means that there is for all an entrance into the world of value, a route through it and no point of necessary and final arrest. And it denies the natural existence of inveterate hostility between

---

[1] *The Friend*, First Landing Place, I.

experiences of quality belonging to different categories, whether these be scientific, humane, technical or religious.

A mind active in elaborating and unifying more and subtler relations, recollected in a patient attendance on the revelation of learning, possessed of a standard of value with personal significance and a more than personal validity—such is the mind that has profited from the discipline of humane learning as Coleridge conceived it.

Chapter V

COLERIDGE AND OTHERS

COLERIDGE is a permanent fact of English literature and thought. He is one of those stones which alter the flow and rhythm of the water running into them. It may be an interruption in the current or a submerged influence or simply something blocking and opposing the ruling drift. But *there* it is, and everyone at some time has to make a settlement with it. I want, therefore, to recapitulate some of the more significant reactions to this insistent, positive presence, and my hope is that this will both be illuminating about Coleridge himself and about the critical tradition he helped to develop.

I should begin by indicating something of the mind and sensibility on which Coleridge made his first impression. It was a sensibility in which the urbane convictions of the Augustans had become a clutch of decidedly rougher certainties. What had been decorous had become more coarsely conventional, and what had been sanctioned by *civilization* and *nature* had become a doctrine held on to with a certain anxiety and even desperation against the sensed antagonism of the day. Let me use as the voices of it Thomas Love Peacock and *The Edinburgh Review*. In each of these, when faced with Coleridge, we find the outraged sense of rationality confronted by lunacy. Each is lacking in the categories of mind and feeling necessary to comprehend, let alone assimilate, this strange new object. But where Peacock finds Coleridge merely ridiculous, *The Edinburgh Review* finds him both ridiculous and dangerous. Here, needing no commentary, is Peacock's Mr Flosky in *Nightmare Abbey*. '. . . a very lachrymose and morbid gentleman, of some note in the literary world, but in his own estimation of much more merit than name.'

> The part of his character which recommended him to Mr Glowry, was his very fine sense of the grim and the tearful. No one could relate a dismal story with so many minutiae of supererogatory wretchedness. No one could call up a *raw-head and bloody bones* with so many adjuncts and circumstances of ghastliness. Mystery was his mental element. He lived in the midst of that visionary world in which

nothing is but what is not. He dreamed with his eyes open, and saw ghosts dancing round him at noontide. He had been in his youth an enthusiast for liberty, and had hailed the dawn of the French Revolution as the promise of a day that was to banish war and slavery and every form of vice and misery, from the face of the earth. Because all this was not done, he deduced that nothing was done; and from this deduction, according to his system of logic, he drew a conclusion that worse than nothing was done; that the overthrow of the feudal fortresses of tyranny and superstition was the greatest calamity that had ever befallen mankind; and that their only hope now was to rake the rubbish together, and rebuild it without any of those loopholes by which the light had originally crept in. To qualify himself for a coadjutor in this laudable task, he plunged into the central opacity of Kantian metaphysics, and lay *perdu* several years in transcendental darkness, till the common daylight of common sense became intolerable to his eyes. He called the sun an *ignis fatuus*; and exhorted all who could listen to his friendly voice, which were about as many as called 'God save King Richard', to shelter themselves from its delusive radiance in the obscure haunt of Old Philosophy. This word Old had great charms for him. The good old times were always on his lips; meaning the days when polemic theology was in its prime, and rival prelates beat the drum ecclesiastic with Herculean vigour, till the one wound up his series of syllogisms with the very orthodox conclusion of roasting the other.

Nightmare Abbey was published in 1819; and the main elements in Peacock's treatment of, or charge against, Coleridge, namely his treachery to the cause of freedom, his desertion of the decency and solidity of common sense, for the horror of the visionary and mysterious, his crazy fascination with Kantian metaphysics, and his coming to rest in a more than medieval absolutism, had all appeared two years before in *The Edinburgh Review* of August 1817 in a review of *Biographia Literaria*. *The Edinburgh Review* had, the year before that, in a review of *Christabel*, *Kubla Khan* and *The Pains of Sleep*, declared its attitude unmistakably. The emphasis is on the poetry as 'mere raving . . . a number of incoherent words, expressive of extravagance and incongruity'. The verse is wild and lawless, pretentious and wilful, probably the product of drink or drugs, if not both together. On the other hand one is bound to admit that *Christabel* lends itself to a strenuous dismemberment. One cannot help feeling a wry amusement at the application of robust common sense to undisciplined magic. The tone of energetic mockery is indicated by the following. 'We now meet our old friend, the mastiff bitch, who is much too important a person to be slightly passed by—

> Outside her kennel, the mastiff old
> Lay fast asleep, in moonshine cold.
> The mastiff old did not awake,
> Yet she an angry moan did make!—
> And what can ail the mastiff bitch?
> Never till now she uttered yell
> Beneath the eye of Christabel.
> Perhaps it is the owlet's scritch:
> For what can ail the mastiff bitch?

Whatever it may be that ails the bitch, the ladies pass forward, and take off their shoes, and tread softly all the way up stairs, as Christabel observes that her father is a bad sleeper. At last, however, they do arrive at the bedroom, and comfort themselves with a dram of some home-made liquor, which proves to be very old; for it was made by Lady C.'s mother; and when her new friend asks if she thinks the old lady will take her part, she answers, that this is out of the question, in as much as she happened to die in childbed of her'.

Coleridge's poetry struck the Edinburgh Reviewers as 'one of the most notable pieces of impertinence of which the press has lately been guilty; and one of the boldest experiments that has yet been made on the patience or understanding of the public'. The 1817 review is a much more inclusive condemnation and distinctly more revealing of the half-suppressed worry that perhaps Coleridge was not a mere freak but a sign of things to come. There is the same splendidly self-confident reduction of Coleridge to a figure of fun, but there is also the spurt of malice which comes from the fear for one's own position. The reviewer fastens on, as one would expect, the total lack of order and the intrinsic deficiencies of discipline in Coleridge's writing.

> But the disease, we fear, was in the mind itself; and the study of poetry, instead of counteracting, only gave force to the original propensity; and Mr Coleridge has ever since, from the combined forces of poetic levity and metaphysic bathos, been trying to fly, not in the air, but under ground—playing at hawk and buzzard between sense and nonsense,—floating or sinking in fine Kantean

categories, in a state of suspended animation 'twixt dreaming and awake,—quitting the plain ground of 'history and particular facts' for the first butterfly theory, fancy-bred from the maggots of his brain,—going up in an air-balloon filled with fetid gas from the writings of Jacob Behmen and the mystics, and coming down in a parachute made of the soiled and fashionable leaves of the Morning Post,—promising us an account of the Intellectual System of the Universe, and putting us off with a reference to a promised dissertation on the Logos, introductory to an intended commentary on the entire Gospel of St John.

The reviewer turns with peculiar satisfaction to the demolition of Southey, a target more easily dealt with since so much more comprehensible than Coleridge. And again one sees exactly the positive remains of eighteenth-century sensibility in the quite unanswerable comments on Coleridge and Southey.

> Some people say, that Mr Southey has deserted the cause of liberty: Mr Coleridge tells us, that he has not separated from his wife. They say, that he has changed his opinions: Mr Coleridge says, that he keeps his appointments; and has even invented a new word, *reliability*, to express his exemplariness in this particular. It is also objected, that the worthy Laureate was as extravagant in his early writings, as he is virulent in his present ones: Mr Coleridge answers, that he is an early riser and not a late sitter up. It is further alleged, that he is arrogant and shallow in political discussion, and clamours for vengeance in a cowardly and intemperate tone: Mr Coleridge assures us, that he eats, drinks, and sleeps moderately. It is said that he must either have been very hasty in taking up his first opinions, or very unjustifiable in abandoning them for their contraries; and Mr Coleridge observes, that Mr Southey exhibits, in his own person and family, all the regularity and praiseworthy punctuality of an eight-day clock.

The balanced contempt of Southey gives way to incoherent fury at the name of 'The great German oracle Kant'. '. . . his system appears to us the most wilful and monstrous absurdity that ever was invented . . . an enormous heap of dogmatical and hardened assertions, advanced in contradiction to all former systems, . . . an elaborate account of what he has undertaken to do, because no one else has been able to do it—and an assumption that he has done it, because he has undertaken it.'

It deals too with another Coleridgean idol, Burke, a man who

'In the American war constantly spoke of the rights of the people as inherent and inalienable but after the French Revolution began by treating them with the chicanery of a Sophist and ended by raving at them with the fury of a maniac'. Coleridge's remarks on Wordsworth are used as an occasion for a tough restatement of the eighteenth century theory of poetic diction. 'The beauty of poetic diction is, in short, borrowed and artificial, it is a glittering veil spread over the form of things and the feelings of the heart. . . .' But perhaps what *The Edinburgh Review* most objects to in Coleridge is that he expects to be taken seriously because poets ought to be taken seriously.

We may venture, however, on one observation, of a very plain and practical nature, which is forced upon us by the whole tenor of the extraordinary history before us.—Reason and imagination are both excellent things; but perhaps their provinces ought to be kept more distinct than they have lately been. 'Poets have such seething brains', that they are disposed to meddle with everything, and mar all. Mr C., with great talents, has, by an ambition to be everything, become nothing. His metaphysics have been a dead weight on the wings of his imagination—while his imagination has run away with his reason and common sense. He might, we seriously think, have been a very considerable poet—instead of which he has chosen to be a bad philosopher and a worse politician. There is something, we suspect, in these studies that does not easily amalgamate. We would not, with Plato, absolutely banish poets from the commonwealth; but we really think they should meddle as little with its practical administration as may be. They live in an ideal world of their own; and it would be, perhaps, as well if they were continued to it. Their flights and fancies are delightful to themselves and to every body else; but they make strange work with matter of fact; and, if they were allowed to act in public affairs, would soon turn the world upside down. They indulge only their own flattering dreams or superstitious prejudices, and make idols or bugbears of what they please, caring as little for 'history or particular facts', as for general reasoning. They are dangerous leaders and treacherous followers. Their inordinate vanity runs them into all sorts of extravagances; and their habitual effeminacy gets them out of them at any price. Always pampering their own appetite for exitement, and wishing to astonish others, their whole aim is to produce a dramatic effect, one way or other—to shock or delight their observers; and they are as perfectly indifferent to the consequences of what they write, as if the world were merely a stage for them to play their fantastic tricks on.

Wordsworth exhibited his usual self-centredness in his relationship with Coleridge. He took Coleridge's devoted service as a right and his respect, even his reverence, for granted. But he did note one characteristic feature of Coleridge's literary habits. 'There are obviously, even in criticism, two ways of affecting the minds of men: the one by treating the matter so as to carry it immediately to the sympathies of the many, and the other by aiming at a few selected and superior minds, that might each become a centre for illustrating it in a popular way. Coleridge ... acted upon the world to a great extent in the latter of these processes.'[1] Keats' comments are sparse but as usual understanding and sensitive. (I have already referred to the famous statement on *Negative Capability*[2] for which Coleridge provided the occasion.) Keats disliked Coleridge's long convoluted sentences which he said, acutely, were modelled on the prodigiously elongated sentences of the early Protestant Divines. Coleridge felt a strong, positive preference for his own elaborate sentence structure. He detested the modern taste for 'skipping, unconnected, short-winded, asthmatic sentences, as easy to be understood as impossible to be remembered';[3] they were 'wanting all the cement for thought as well as style, all the connexions, and ... all the hooks and eyes of the memory....'.[4]

But the real bridge between an eighteenth-century and the nineteenth-century opinion of Coleridge is provided not by Wordsworth and Keats but by Hazlitt. In his treatment of Coleridge we find that strange mixture of eighteenth-century definition and common sense, and the fuzziness of an anxious individualism. There is a good deal of eighteenth-century balance as well as a mass of fumbling, half-evocative metaphor. In Hazlitt plain common sense is almost self-consciously sturdy; it has a slightly forced masculine strut. Hazlitt was the first to put into currency the reader's irritable consciousness of the disproportion between Coleridge's gifts and his achievements; he also made much of the lack of sustained will in Coleridge. Amid the mannered masculinity Hazlitt manifests his usual considerable shrewdness.

All his notions are floating and unfixed, like what is feigned of the first forms of things flying about in search of bodies to attach them-

[1] To W. R. Hamilton, January 4th, 1838.
[2] To George and Thomas Keats, December 21st, 1817.
[3] *Essays on his own Times.*
[4] *The Friend*, I.

selves to; but *his* ideas seek to avoid all contact with solid substances. Innumerable evanescent thoughts dance before him, and dazzle his sight, like insects in the evening sun. Truth is to him a ceaseless round of contradictions: he lives in the belief of a perpetual lie, and in affecting to think what he pretends to say. His mind is in a constant estate of flux and reflex: he is like the Sea-horse in the Ocean; he is the Man in the Moon, the Wandering Jew.—The reason of all this is, that Mr Coleridge has great powers of thought and fancy, without will or sense. He is without a strong feeling of the existence of any thing out of himself; and he has neither purposes nor passions of his own to make him wish it to be. All that he does or thinks is involuntary; even his perversity and self-will are so. They are nothing but a necessity of yielding to the slightest motive. Everlasting inconsequentiality marks all that he attempts.[1]

Hazlitt put down much of Coleridge's feebleness in design to his having been the most impressive talker of his age. If he hadn't been that he would probably have been the finest writer, just as if he had not been an excellent logician he would have been a great poet. If Coleridge was always talking about himself this was quite without egotistical passion, 'for in him the individual is always merged in the abstract and general'. In *The Spirit of the Age* Hazlitt acknowledges, and even makes an attempt to specify, Coleridge's extraordinary powers. But as well as ruin by talk, by defect of will, by hopeless inability in design, there was also, Hazlitt thought, ruin by philosophy: in particular Coleridge's wanderings into German thought where he lost himself 'in the labyrinths of the Hartz Forest and of the Kantean philosophy, and among the cabalistic names of Fichte and Schelling and Lessing, and God knows who'.[2] The one Coleridgean production that Hazlitt had complete confidence in and which he would put into any reader's hands in order to impress a favourable idea of Coleridge's extraordinary powers was *The Ancient Mariner*, a work of genius—of 'wild, irregular, overwhelming imagination, [with] that rich, varied movement in the verse, which gives a distant idea of the lofty or changeful tones of Mr Coleridge's voice'[3]. Hazlitt judged Coleridge's poetry to be inferior to his conversation, and his prose to be worse than that. Even *The Friend*, which he considered his principal prose work, although it contains some noble passages

---

[1] *Hazlitt's Political Essays*, London, 1819, pp. 122-3.
[2] *The Spirit of the Age*, 1825.　　　　　　　　　　[3] Ibid.

and fine trains of thought, is much more characterised by pro-
lixity and obscurity. One of the most illuminating pairings ever
made was Mill's of Coleridge with Bentham. Perhaps, as a small
prologue to that, I could give here Hazlitt's pairing of him with
Godwin.

No two persons can be conceived more opposite in character or
genius than Mr Coleridge and Mr Godwin. The latter, with less
natural capacity, and with fewer acquired advantages, by concen-
trating his mind on some given subject, and doing what he had to do
with all his might, has accomplished much, and will leave more than
one monument of a powerful intellect behind him; Mr Coleridge, by
dissipating his, and dallying with every subject by turns, has done
little or nothing to justify to the world or to posterity the high opinion
which all who have ever heard him converse, or known him intimately, with one accord entertain of him. Mr Godwin's faculties have
kept house, and plied their task in the workshop of the brain, dili-
gently and effectually: Mr Coleridge's have gossiped away their
time and gadded about from house to house, as if life's business were
to melt the hours in listless talk. Mr Godwin is intent on a subject,
only as it concerns himself and his reputation; he works it out as a
matter of duty, and discards from his mind whatever does not forward his main object as impertinent and vain. Mr Coleridge, on the
other hand, delights in nothing but episodes and digressions, neglects
whatever he undertakes to perform and can act only on spontaneous
impulses, without object or method.[1]

Carlyle's critique of Coleridge is emphatically 'personal'. He
dismisses even more firmly than Hazlitt Coleridge's writings,
which he takes to be as of hardly any account. 'His express contributions to poetry, philosophy, or any specific province of human
literature or enlightenment, had been small and sadly intermittent.
. . . '[2] He pictures Coleridge sitting on the brow of Highgate Hill,
a figure derived from Grimm's Fairy Tales and the Old Testament
'looking down on London and its smoke-tumult, like a sage
escaped from the inanity of life's battle.' This magus, 'girt in
mystery and enigma', is clothed in the body of a good old man,
with a brow and head of massive weight, and a face that is flabby
and irresolute. And when he is not sitting on Highgate Hill, he
shuffles loosely about, mildly despairing, speaking in a plaintive
snuffle, and preaching hopelessly about the weightiest things.

[1] Op. cit.   [2] Carlyle, T., *Life of John Sterling*, London, 1851, VIII.

As far as Carlyle is concerned Coleridge's work appears to be of no significance at all. All his power came from his talk, which was itself without form or shape, spreading everywhither in inextricable currents and regurgitations like a lake or sea. It was a confused unintelligible flood of utterance. There is some irony, it must be admitted, in a smoky seer like Carlyle finding Coleridge reprehensible on the ground of a lack of intelligibility. Not only was his talk—the only thing that really mattered—unintelligible, but it was also like himself irresolute. He could not be bothered with conditions or abstinences or controls or definite fulfilments. It was a lawless, meandering discourse, 'the moaning singsong of that theosophico-metaphysical monotony. . . .' Carlyle hesitated at one point, worrying whether he has been unjust to this memorable man: a hesitation which does strike the reader as an unusual scruple. But in spite of this qualification, Carlyle is forced to admit that 'Coleridge's talk and speculation was the emblem of himself: in it as in him, a ray of heavenly inspiration struggled, in a tragically ineffectual degree, with the weakness of flesh and blood'. He had a subtle lynx-eyed intellect, a sensibility to all that was good and beautiful, but he was lacking in courage, in will; pain, danger, necessity, duty, harnessed toil, were all abhorrent to him. Carlyle's account of Coleridge, clotted and unsympathetic as it is, reducing him to a talker with an inexplicably magic and hypnotic effect, has, for all its wild improbability, much affected later critics. Coleridge has been made a kind of Kantian Johnson, whose talk is more important than his work. At the same time Coleridge exhibits that appalling and un-British quality of feebleness of will which shrinks from everything disagreeable and painful. He is an horrible example of spiritual idleness and the lack of moral fibre. It is not surprising, therefore, that all one gets from him is a 'thrice-refined pabulum of transcendental moonshine'.[1]

How limpid and sympathetic, in contrast, is De Quincey's view of Coleridge. While De Quincey also concerns himself more with Coleridge than his writing, he has an altogether juster sense of Coleridge's stature and a more adequate estimation of the value of his work, including his poetry, His attitude is relaxed and quite free of any mottling of the high-minded disapproval which Coleridge's defects seem fated to provoke in writers as different as Carlyle and Coleridge's biographer, Sir Edmund Chambers. De

[1] Carlyle, T., *Life of John Sterling*, London, 1851, IX, p. 54.

Quincey had behaved with notable generosity towards Coleridge when as a young man, lately come to his majority and with plenty of money, he arranged in 1807 that an anonymous gift of £500 should be conveyed to Coleridge through the Bristol bookseller Joseph Cottle, who incidentally insisted that it be cut to £300. The genuine affection which breathes in De Quincey's comments on Coleridge didn't at all dull his eye for Coleridge's oddities. He noticed, for example, Coleridge's curious habit of occasional plagiarism—of others that is, not simply his regular one of plagiarising himself—and his refusal to accept the most obvious suggestions that this was what he had done. He utterly disowned, for example, any suggestion that the idea for *The Ancient Mariner* came from Shelvocke, much to the horror of Wordsworth, 'a man of stern veracity, who took the fact as being notorious'. Even more extraordinary, according to De Quincey, is the passage in *Biographia Literaria*, the dissertation upon the relationships of *esse* and *cogitare*, which is a *verbatim* translation of Schelling. Other oddities of Coleridge which De Quincey noticed were his strange pets and hates. Examples in the pet class were Sir Alexander Ball, the Governor of Malta, of whom he always spoke in a lavish style for which ordinary people could see not the slightest grounds. Dr Andrew Bell, the Anglican inventor of the factory system of schooling, was another for whom Coleridge had a craze. Of him De Quincey remarks, 'First came Dr Andrew Bell. We knew him. Was he dull? Is a wooden spoon dull!'[1] John Woolman the Quaker was another. But the strangest was Bowyer, the Master of Christ's Hospital, whom De Quincey considered the greatest villain of the eighteenth century—'why, this man knouted his way through life, from bloody youth up to a truculent old age'.[2] Coleridge balanced these whimsical partialities for characters whom he used as mirrors in which to see himself reflected, with others towards whom he held an equally irrational antipathy. Pitt, for example, always moved him to fury, and Paley he detested with a weird personal intensity which had very little to do with any philosophic disagreement.

De Quincey knew Coleridge intimately during one part of his life and even saw him daily. He paid the usual tribute to Coleridge's

[1] *The Collected Writings of Thomas De Quincey.* Edited by David Masson, London, 1897, Vol. V, p. 196.
[2] Ibid., p. 197.

'splendid art of conversation'. But he would not agree with the common view on Coleridge's intelligibility.

> Coleridge, to many people, and often I have heard the complaint, seemed to wander; and he seemed then to wander the most when, in fact, his resistance to the wandering instinct was greatest—viz., when the compass and huge circuit by which his illustrations moved travelled farthest into remote regions before they began to revolve. Long before this coming round commenced most people had lost him, and naturally enough supposed that he had lost himself. They continued to admire the separate beauty of the thoughts, but did not see their relations to the dominant theme. Had the conversation been thrown upon paper, it might have been easy to trace the continuity of the links: However, I can assert, upon my long and intimate knowledge of Coleridge's mind, that logic the most severe was as inalienable from his modes of thinking as grammar from his language.[1]

Coleridge, indeed, De Quincey thought, was not very accurate in anything except the use of logic. He had a fluent but inaccurate command of German, and French he read with too little freedom to find much pleasure in French literature. His knowledge of Greek had to be related to the state and standard of classical studies at the time. But while Coleridge was not really a well-grounded scholar in languages 'he yet displayed sometimes a brilliancy of conjectural sagacity and a felicity of philosophic investigation, even in this path, such as better scholars do not often attain, and of a kind which cannot be learned from books'.[2] In philosophy and theology of course Coleridge was profoundly erudite. 'The philosophy of ancient Greece, through all its schools, the philosophy of the schoolmen technically so called, Church history &c., Coleridge had within his call . . . he knew the whole cycle of schisms and audacious speculations through which Biblical criticism or Christian philosophy had evolved in Modern Germany.'[3]

There were two other topics which De Quincey selected for remark, politics and, naturally enough, opium. Coleridge took a sincere and enthusiastic interest in politics, and in his own day he was known for his political writing as much as for anything else. De Quincey would not have it that Coleridge was in the deepest

---

[1] Op. cit., Vol. II, pp. 152-3.
[2] Ibid., Vol. V, p. 201   [3] Ibid., Vol. II, p. 201.

sense either a Reformer or a Conservative. He was in favour, De Quincey claimed, of reform in Parliament because of the necessity for new classes to be given a less indirect share of political influence. In fact, the only avowed objects of the contemporary reformers which, according to De Quincey, Coleridge would have strenuously opposed, were those which had to do with the Church of England and the Universities of Oxford and Cambridge. He was also more in favour than many of his contemporaries of an aristocratic influence as a balance to new-made commercial wealth. But there was very little else that the modern reformers wanted, which De Quincey thought Coleridge would have opposed. His party connections were principally with the Tories, and there was a natural affinity between Coleridge's sensibility and the Conservative mind. But the cardinal principle of Toryism during the years in which Coleridge became connected with it was that 'Circumstances of position had thrown upon the Tories the *onus* of a great national struggle.... The Whigs were then out of power: they were therefore in opposition; and that one fact, the simple fact, of holding an anti-ministerial position, they allowed, by a most fatal blunder, to determine the course of their foreign politics. Napoleon was to be cherished simply because he was a thorn in Mr Pitt's side.'[1] Coleridge's connection with the Tories was based upon no motives of selfish interest, but upon the changes in the spirit of the French Revolution which turned its defensive war into a war of aggression. 'To be a Whig, therefore, in those days, implied little more than a strenuous opposition to foreign war; to be a Tory pledged a man to little more than war with Napoleon Bonaparte.' Most readers, I think, would make Coleridge's connection with Toryism much more inward than this, but De Quincey is right in two things: that Coleridge judged political issues on more than political grounds, and as with everybody else his actual political decisions were taken in the political situation of his time.

As one would expect, De Quincey shows charity and perception towards Coleridge's drug addiction. '... *originally* his sufferings, and the death within him of all hope—the palsy, as it were, of that which is life of life and the heart within the heart—came from opium'. Coleridge spoke of his own opium excess, the excess of twenty-five years, as a thing which could be laid aside in a week; and yet on the other hand he describes it—with 'a frantic pathos'

[1] Op. cit., Vol. II, pp. 218-19.

as the curse and blight which had desolated his life. De Quincey believed that opium killed Coleridge as a poet, and he believed also that it 'stirred his metaphysic instincts into more spasmodic life'. But if it turned him from poetry to metaphysics, and perhaps to the cloudiest metaphysics, it also caused him habitually to leave unfinished what he had started. 'Whenever Coleridge (being highly charged, or saturated, with opium) had written with distempered vigour upon any question, there occurred soon after a recoil of intense disgust, not from his own paper only, but even from the entire subject.' Coleridge did make quite prodigious efforts to free himself from opium. He went so far, De Quincey reports, in Bristol once, to hire a man whose sole purpose was to stop him from entering any chemist's shop. Naturally the scheme wasn't effective, but it did show Coleridge's pathetic effort to provide for himself, in the delegated man, an external conscience. The man according to De Quincey, did in fact stop Coleridge occasionally. De Quincey insisted that Coleridge took to opium because of disease, but he insisted too that the taking of opium could itself produce secondary sorts of disease and irritation which were no longer dependent upon opium and which would not disappear even with its disuse, 'a more than mortal discouragement to accomplish this disuse, when the pains of self-sacrifice were balanced by no gleams of restorative feeling'.[1]

The relationship of Matthew Arnold to Coleridge is one of the curiosities of criticism. The queerness lies not in the estimation, grudging and cautious as it was, that Arnold put on Coleridge, but in the very slightness of the attention which he, the second critic of the nineteenth century, gave the first. Coleridge figures hardly at all in Arnold's *Notebooks* or in his voluminous Reading List. He had no doubt absorbed a great deal of Coleridge from the family atmosphere, Dr Arnold having been a warm admirer of 'old Sam' Coleridge, but it doesn't seem to have been a very conscious position. It was to Spinoza not to Coleridge that Matthew Arnold acknowledged a philosophic and theological debt. His references to Coleridge's writings, although they cover a range of texts, are not given with any sense of sharpness or immediacy; they are not even particularly accurate. And although it is possible to trace similarities and parallels between the literary, political, and social doctrines of Arnold and Coleridge, Arnold, always punctili-

[1] Op. cit., Vol. II, p. 211.

ous in attributing his ideas to their sources, rarely names Coleridge as one of these. Coleridge, 'poet and philosopher wrecked in a mist of opium', he took to be the author of a few brilliant poems and of a larger quantity of inferior ones, someone who wasn't at all on the level of Wordsworth or Keats or even Byron. No doubt Arnold thought of Coleridge in a routine way as a distinguished intellectual influence, but it was one which had little personal significance for him. 'His impression of Coleridge', writes Leon Gottfried, the most thorough student of this relationship, 'as an important but rambling, disorganised, eccentric, and even premature initiator of modern ideas, was probably formed early and he never saw need to return to chaos and old night for the sort of stimulation which lay nearer and more attractively to hand elsewhere.'[1]

But it was a difference of temperament that deeply separated the two men. The pragmatic and collected Arnold felt only distaste for a man like Coleridge with his metaphysical inclinations, his streamy consciousness, his spiritual untidiness, his vast never-completed designs, and his whole air of moral sloppiness. To Arnold's fundamental scepticism, Coleridge's rapturous faith looked suspiciously bizarre and even vulgar. In the same way Coleridge's philosophic generalisations and metaphysic laws seemed to the cooler Arnold repellently cloudy and undisciplined. (And yet, ironically enough, this is the one department of Arnold's thought in which he himself to a contemporary reader seems most apt to fall into boneless generalisations and vague pieties.) It was the difference in sensibility which caused Arnold to prophesy, 'How little of his poetry or of his criticism, or of his philosophy do we expect permanently to stand'.[2] And while he praised Coleridge for his extensive knowledge—so different from the other Romantics—for his independence and originality, and for his will 'to get at and lay bare the real truths of the matter in hand, whether this matter were literary, or philosophical, or political, or religious',[3] it was the exemplary rather than the intrinsic value of the undertaking that he praised.

To have read J. S. Mill's great essay on Bentham and Coleridge[4]

---

[1] Gottfried, Leon, *Matthew Arnold and the Romantics*, London, 1963, p. 169.
[2] *Essays in Criticism*.
[3] Ibid.
[4] Mill, John Stuart, *Dissertations and Discussions*, London, 1867, Vol. I (2nd) edition.

is to have brought home to one not only the quality of Mill's analytical and admirably impartial intelligence but also—and how refreshingly—the seriousness of Coleridge's *work*. Mill leaves the picking over of Coleridge's personality and character, and the moralising which is apparently inseparable from the exercise, to others. Apart from a rather formal tribute to Coleridge's standing as a poet and to the more intelligent canons of criticism which he was mainly instrumental in establishing, Mill concentrates on Coleridge's philosophic and social theory. His was the influence which awakened in this country the 'spirit of philosophy within the bounds of traditional opinions'. He stood over against, and balanced, the influence of Bentham, his great counterpart, who questioned and tested within the bounds of radical opinions. They divided the intellectual authority of the age and their names 'are likely to be oftener pronounced, and to become symbolical of more important things in proportion as the inward workings of the age manifest themselves more and more in outward facts'.[1] These two great contraries did more than any others in their time to enforce the necessity for theory and principles as the ground for intelligent practice. They agreed that the groundwork of other philosophy must be laid in the philosophy of the mind. They employed different methods and materials, but as 'the materials of both were real observations, the genuine product of experience' then the results will finally prove not simply hostile but supplementary. 'Whoever could master the premises and combine the methods of both, would possess the entire English philosophy of their age.'[2]

Mill's observation has a biting relevance to our own situation. The feebleness of so much contemporary social and political dialectic is the consequence of a routine acceptance of Benthamite ideas on the one side, and the utmost indigence of ideas at all on the other. If only the revolutionaries were like Bentham who 'judged a proposition true or false as it accorded or not with the result of his own enquiries', or better still like Mill himself who joined with Bentham's method a more scrupulously self-questioning, an altogether more civilised habit of mind; and if only the Conservatives were like Coleridge, a Tory who was more radical

---

[1] Mill, John Stuart, *Dissertations and Discussions*, London, 1867, Vol. I (2nd Edition).
[2] Op. cit., p. 397.

than the Liberals and one who upheld both what was organised in institutions *and* the free play of critical human intelligence. At least we should then have a better chance to appreciate 'the importance in the present imperfect state of mental and social science, of antagonist modes of thought: which, it will one day be felt, are as necessary to one another in speculation, as mutually checking powers are in a political constitution'.[1] It is impossible in our day to put against each other antagonist modes of thought when one side offers cliché and the other echo, one an imitation of the present, the other an imitation of the past.

The essential questioning of established experience and assumption, in any society, Mill believed should be done both by those like Bentham who question it because it is there and on the presumption that it has outlived its use, and by those like Coleridge who thought 'the long duration of a belief . . . at least proof of an adaptation in it to some portion or other of the human mind'.[2] The Coleridgean works in the belief that if digging down to the root he does not find, as he generally will, some truth, at least he will discover some natural want or requirement of human nature which the doctrine in question is fitted to satisfy. The Benthamite demanded the extinction of the institutions and creeds which had hitherto existed; the Coleridgean that they be made a reality; 'the one pressing the new doctrines to their utmost consequences; the other reasserting the best meaning and purposes of the old'.[3]

The great contribution of the Germano-Coleridgean school was to a philosophy of human culture, and it was made in Mill's view in the only way it could have been made at that time, in the form of a philosophy of history. They resurrected the past which the *philosophers* wished to wipe out. At the same time they recognised in the character of the national education in any political society 'at once the principal cause of its permanence as a society, and the chief source of its progressiveness'. The whole point, then, of a National Church, and of the Church of England in that character, was to promote not primarily the practice of religion and the worship of God but the advancement of knowledge and the civilisation of the whole of society. And the *clerisy* of the National Church was to be the learned of all denominations, 'a theory', Mill points out, 'under which the Royal Society might claim a part of the Church property with as good a right as the bench of

[1] Op. cit., p. 399.   [2] Ibid., p. 395.   [3] Ibid., p. 436.

bishops'. Coleridge should be honoured for his doctrine of the national church on two grounds, Mill declares: first because his setting in a clear light what a national church should be was condemning in the severest way what in fact the National Church was; and secondly because he vindicated 'against Bentham and Adam Smith, and the whole eighteenth century, the principle of an endowed class for the cultivation of learning and for diffusing its results among the community'.[1]

Coleridge's theory of government was as perceptive and humane as his theory of the Church; and 'how much better a Parliamentary Reformer, then, is Coleridge than Lord John Russell, or any Whig who stickles for maintaining this unconstitutional omnipotence of the landed interest'. Because in considering any constitution Coleridge investigated the Idea or principle of a thing, because he asked what an institution *meant*, what he came out with as conclusion was never simply a party doctrine or the findings of expediency but always a view based on principle.

> Reformers ought to hail the man as a brother Reformer who points out ... what it is which we have a right to expect from things established—which they are bound to do for us, as the justification of their being established: so that they may be recalled to it and compelled to do it, or the impossibility of their any longer doing it may be conclusively manifested. What is any case for reform good for, until it has passed this test? What mode is there of determining whether a thing is fit to exist, without first considering what purposes it exists for, and whether it be still capable of fulfilling them?[2]

Mill is as perceptive and as generous about other elements in Coleridge's theory of culture, about his theory of knowledge—it did what the eighteenth century had *not* done—about his ethical views—if only all our opponents were like Coleridge, we should hardly have to wait for reform—about his theological views—too liberal for the liberals—even about his faculty for insight into subjects like political economy where he was decidedly not at home. But all the time Mill is absorbed by Coleridge's *work*, by its significance and relevance. There is more than enough there to occupy even a mind as active as Mill's.

A very different aspect, however, is presented by Leslie Stephen's lecture delivered at the Royal Institution in 1888, and

---

[1] Ibid., p. 445. [2] Ibid., pp. 437-8.

later incorporated in *Hours in a Library*. The tone is different, the interest focused elsewhere. Once again Coleridge's peculiar set of deficiencies succeeds in exacerbating even someone so genuinely liberal as Leslie Stephen. The line of the lecture is a not unaccustomed one: 'the history of early promise blighted and vast powers all but running hopelessly to waste'.[1] Perhaps Coleridge did see the vital issues more clearly than any of his contemporaries, but Stephen still cannot think that 'Coleridge ever worked with his mind clear, or was, indeed, capable of the necessary concentration and steadiness of thought by which alone philosophic achievement was possible'.[2] Stephen speaks with cool, rational dislike of Coleridge's frantic personal life. 'If a man of genius condescends to marry a woman, and be the father of her children, he must incur responsibilities . . . Coleridge's position was no doubt difficult, but the mode in which he solved the difficulty is proof that opium-eating is inconsistent with certain homely duties.'[3] It spoiled his personal life and his intellectual career. Coleridge has a strange power of fascination—very strange Leslie Stephen seems to feel. There was always someone to help him, his failings excited more compassion than indignation, people of all kinds served him with no other motives but reverence and love.

There is one point in his essay in which Stephen's deepest judgment of Coleridge comes through, and it is not where he is highmindedly declaring, as he does more than once, that he has no wish to moralise about Coleridge, or where he announces in a rather God-like manner, 'I desiderate an accurate diagnosis, not a judicial sentence. Coleridge sinned and repented. I take note of sin and repentance as indications of character. I do not pretend to say whether in the eye of Heaven the repentance would be an adequate set-off for the sin.'[4] (Maybe he doesn't *say* it: but it is pretty clear how in his view the eye of Heaven would in fact see the situation.) The place in which he does show his most serious response to Coleridge is in a discussion of Pantisocracy, the new society of which Coleridge was to be the Plato. 'Dreamland was his reality.' This comment is the clue to what Stephen really felt about Coleridge. Coleridge was above all essentially and naturally a poet. His genius is best represented in the poems he wrote before he was twenty-six, and supremely in *The Ancient Mariner*, in which

---

[1] Stephen Leslie, *Hours in a Library* (2nd Edition), London, 1892, p. 343.
[2] Op. cit., p. 342.   [3] Ibid., p. 328.   [4] Ibid., p. 319.

Stephen maintains somewhat extravagantly the germ of all Coleridge's utterances by a little ingenuity may be found. It is the world of *The Ancient Mariner* which distils what Coleridge has to offer us.

It is a world in which both animated things, and stones, and brooks, and clouds, and plants are moved by spiritual agency; in which, as he would put it, the veil of the senses is nothing but a symbolism everywhere telling of unseen and supernatural forces. What we call the solid and the substantial becomes a dream; and the dream is the true underlying reality. The difference between such poetry, and the poetry of Pope, or even of Gray, or Goldsmith, or Cowper— poetry which is the direct utterance of a string of moral, political, or religious reflections—implies a literary revolution. Coleridge, even more distinctly than Wordsworth, represented a deliberate rejection of the canons of the preceding school; for, if Wordsworth's philosophy differed from that of Pope, he still taught by direct exposition instead of the presentation of sensuous symbolism.[1]

It is clear that Leslie Stephen regarded *The Ancient Mariner*, *Kubla Khan* and *Christabel* as the high point of Coleridge's poetic achievement—he refers to nothing else—although he recognises that it was in any case a vein that could hardly be worked much further. But this is also in keeping with his view that in some fundamental way Coleridge was not only the artist of, but also himself the inhabitant of, a dream world. In the harshest contrast with Mill, for whom Coleridge was a skilled investigator of reality, Leslie Stephen takes him to be a drugged cultivator of unreality, '... this strange mystic world in which he was at home was so remote from all ordinary experience that it failed even to provide an efficient symbolism for his deepest thoughts, and could only be accessible in the singular glow and fervour of youthful inspiration'.[2] The exception Leslie Stephen makes to what is essentially an account of Coleridge as a narcoticised dreamer was to allow him as a literary critic to show great point and crispness. 'Coleridge's peculiar service to English criticism consisted, indeed, in a great measure, in a clear appreciation of the true relation between the faculties ...' although he adds it was a relation which Coleridge never quite managed to express clearly. Coleridge opposed the concrete symbolism of poetry not to prose but to the analytic and abstract habit of science.

[1] Ibid., pp. 334-5. [2] Ibid., p. 335.

He was something almost unique in this as in his poetry, first because his criticism (so far as it was really excellent) was the criticism of love, the criticism of a man who combined the first single impulse of admiration with the power of explaining why he admired; and secondly, and as a result, because he placed himself at the right point of view; because, to put it briefly, he was the first great writer who criticized poetry as poetry, and not as science. The preceding generation had asked, as Mrs Barbauld asked: 'What is the moral?' Has 'Othello' a moral catastrophe? What does 'Paradise Lost' prove? Are the principles of Pope's 'Essay on Man' philosophical? or is Goldsmith's 'Deserted Village' a sound piece of political economy? The reply embodied in Coleridge's admirable criticisms, especially of Shakespeare, was that this implied a total misconception of the relations of poetry to philosophy. The 'moral' of a poem is not this or that proposition tagged to it or deducible from it, moral or otherwise; but the total effect of the stimulus to the imagination and affections, or what Coleridge would call its dynamic effect.[1]

Leslie Stephen stands away from Coleridge, looking at him coldly from a long way off. He brings to bear on Coleridge a set of severe moral categories, the effect of which is to diminish the object they are applied to; and he turns what today we should be inclined to call temperamental difficulty into moral unsatisfactoriness. (Although, really, to see Coleridge, in any important sense of 'moral', as *morally* inadequate is an impossible position.) The same diminished effect is seen in Walter Pater's essay in *Appreciations*, which first appeared in T. W. Ward's *English Poets*. But the method is different. Leslie Stephen diminishes Coleridge by distancing him, Walter Pater by assimilating him. He begins by characterising the literary life of Coleridge as a disinterested struggle against that 'relative' spirit which is the distinguishing mark of modern thought. Coleridge was always 'restlessly scheming to "apprehend the absolute" '. And he concludes his rather high-pitched metaphysical distinction by speaking, significantly, of Coleridge's effort as, 'surely an effort of sickly thought, that saddened his mind, and limited the operation of his unique poetic gift'. It is this enervated, sickly quality which is stressed throughout the essay. Pater speaks of 'that whole physiognomy of the dreamer, already touched with narcoticism', 'the faintness, the continuous dissolution . . . which soon supplanted the buoyancy of his first wonderful years', of 'the grievous agitation, the grievous

[1] Op. cit., p. 337.

listlessness, almost never entirely relieved . . .', of Coleridge's 'diseased and valetudinarian temperament', and of 'the faintness and obscure dejection which clings like some contagious damp to all his work'.

There is a morbid quality in Coleridge's sensibility and Pater is responding to it. But he is turning what I have referred to earlier as a profound malformation in Coleridge's nature into something more like a neurotic Victorian languor. Missing from Pater's account are several Coleridges: not only the homely humorous Englishman whose favourite dish was Bacon & Peas and Bacon & Broad Beans[1]; not only the tough athletic mountain-climber; not only the stricken Coleridge whose interest even in his own diseases had a seventeenth century vigour and relish; but also the writer and thinker whose extreme, if unorganised, vitality crackles on every page. Coleridge's nature, in spite of the morbidity for which there is considerable evidence, stubbornly recurred to a central norm of humanity. The distortion of Pater's account comes not from its not having some warrant in reality but from its pushing what is exotic into the centre of the portrait. Pater finds support for his idea—a leading idea—of Coleridge everywhere in his writings.

Like his verse [his prose writings] display him also in two other characters—as a student of words, and as a psychologist, that is, as a more minute observer or student than other men of the phenomena of mind. To note the recondite associations of words, old or new, to expound the logic, the reasonable soul, of their various uses; to recover the interest of older writers who had had a phraseology of their own—this was a vein of inquiry allied to his undoubted gift of tracking out and analysing curious modes of thought. . . . The latter gift, that power of the 'subtle-souled psychologist', as Shelley calls him, seems to have been connected with some tendency to disease in the physical temperament, something of a morbid want of balance in those parts where the physical and intellectual elements mix most closely together, with a kind of languid visionariness, deep-seated in the very constitution of the 'narcotist', who had quite a gift for 'plucking the poisons of self-harm' and which the actual habit of taking opium, accidentally acquired, did but reinforce. This morbid languor of nature, connected both with his fitfulness of purpose and his rich delicate dreaminess, qualifies Coleridge's poetic composition even more than his prose: his verse, with the exception of his avowedly

[1] Cf. *Notebooks*, No. 163.

political poems, being, unlike that of the "Lake School", to which in some respects he belongs, singularly unaffected by any moral, or professional, or personal effort or ambition.—'written', as he says, 'after the more violent emotions of sorrow, to give him pleasure, when perhaps nothing else could'; but coming thus, indeed, very close to his own most intimately personal characteristics, and having a certain languidly soothing grace or cadence, for its most fixed quality, from first to last.[1]

Although Pater's eye is shut to so many Coleridges, although his view is so partial, he is still more sensitively open to one thing in Coleridge than most of his predecessors and several of his successors, namely to the individuality of Coleridge's poetry. He is not particularly original in his view that all Coleridge's best poetry was the product of the *annus mirabilis* 1797-98, when he lived at Nether Stowey. Coleridge was a poet whose talent blossomed suddenly through one short season, and then deteriorated as suddenly. Moreover, he takes the traditional view about the place of *The Ancient Mariner*, in which he finds, alone among Coleridge's *œuvres* 'completeness, the perfectly rounded wholeness and unity . . . one of the characteristics of a really excellent work'.[2] But even of *The Ancient Mariner* his treatment is distinctly more specific than the usual general tribute. He finds, for example, that it is 'the delicacy, the dreamy grace, in his presentation of the marvellous, which makes Coleridge's work really remarkable. The too palpable intruders from a spiritual world in almost all ghost literature, in Scott and Shakespeare even, have a kind of crudity or coarseness. Coleridge's power is in the very fineness with which, as by some really ghostly finger, he brings home to our inmost sense his inventions, daring as they are—the skeleton ship, the polar spirit, the inspiriting of the dead corpses of the ship's crew. *The Rhyme of the Ancient Mariner* has the plausibility, the perfect adaptation to reason and the general aspect of life, which belongs to the marvellous, when actually presented as part of a credible experience in our dreams.'[3] He finds in Coleridge a family relationship with Blake 'His "spirits", at once more delicate, and so much more real, than any ghost—the burden, as they were the privilege, of his *temperament*—like it, were an integral element in his everyday

---

[1] Pater, Walter, *Appreciations*, London, 1931, pp. 82-3. [2] Op. cit., p. 100.
[3] Ibid., p. 98. [4] Ibid., p. 99.

life.'[4] Pater points to Coleridge's 'highly sensitive apprehension of the aspects of external nature. . . . That record of the

> green light
> Which lingers in the west,

and again, of

> the western sky,
> And its peculiar tint of yellow green,

which Byron found ludicrously untrue, but which surely needs no defence'.[1] He found this a characteristic example of Coleridge's 'singular watchfulness for the minute fact and expression of natural scenery . . . a closeness to the exact physiognomy of nature, having something to do with that idealistic philosophy which sees in the external world no mere concurrence of mechanical agencies, but an animated body, informed and made expressive, like the body of man, by an indwelling intelligence'.[2] Coleridge's idealism produces in him not indifference to colour, form and process but the most minute realism. He had a similar feeling for the silent and unseen processes of nature, 'its "ministries" of dew and frost' for example; and Pater shows how in *Fears in Solitude* Coleridge by delicate, insistent repetition of the character of one spot makes place assume a kind of soul and expression.

Pater, then, responded sensitively to Coleridge's mastery in his poetry of the art of delicately discriminating among shades of being. His general reading of Coleridge's life was that it was the deterioration 'of productive or creative power into one merely metaphysical or discursive'. Coleridge had devoted a whole lifetime to the endeavour 'to present the then recent metaphysics of Germany to English readers, as a legitimate expansion of the older, classical and native masters of what has been variously called the *a priori*, or absolute, or spiritual, or Platonic, view of things'.[3] His weakness was rather an excess of seriousness. 'There is a certain shade of unconcern, the perfect manner of the eighteenth century, which may be thought to make complete culture in the handling of abstract questions. The humanist, the possessor of that complete culture, does not "weep" over the failure of "a theory of the quantification of the predicate", nor "shriek" over

---

[1] Ibid., pp. 90-1.   [2] Ibid., p. 91.   [3] Ibid. p. 81.

the fall of a philosophical formula.'[1] The contemporary reader will not have anything like the reverence of Pater for the resigned urbanity which he judged Coleridge deficient in. It will seem to him a manner which is all patina and surface and lacking in life and content. Coleridge had a vision which he believed in with passion and which he raged to communicate. Pater is looking at a tiger through a lorgnette. But he does conclude his essay with a statement with which we can agree, 'Coleridge, with his passion for the absolute, for something fixed where all is moving, his faintness, his broken memory, his intellectual disquiet, may still be ranked among the interpreters of one of the constituent elements of our life'.[2]

I turn now to a critic whose classicism was of a different sort. Eliot's is much less reminiscent and nostalgic, altogether more trenchant, having at the back of it a much greater weight both of ideas and moral force, and above all fed by a pure creative gift. For Eliot, Wordsworth and Coleridge are the two most original poetic minds of their generation. Each of them was deeply affected in his poetic life by the same woman, Dorothy Wordsworth, and their influence upon one another was considerable, although, Eliot thinks, Wordsworth's influence upon Coleridge was greater during their brief period of intimate association, than Coleridge's influence upon Wordsworth. They were vastly different in mind, learning, temperament, character and in what they made of their own lives. While Wordsworth was a happy man, and a successful one, Coleridge was an unhappy man, and by the time he had written *Biographia Literaria*, already a ruined man. ('Sometimes, however,' Eliot adds, 'to be a "ruined" man is itself a vocation.')[3] Wordsworth had no pursuing fates at his back, his inspiration never having been of that 'sudden, fitful and terrifying kind' that visited Coleridge; nor was he ever, apparently, troubled by the consciousness of having lost it.

Eliot is undecided whether the bulk of Wordsworth's genuine poetic achievement is so much greater than Coleridge's. But whatever his indecision on this point, there is no doubt about which of the two appeals to him more as a critic. Wordsworth, he says, is a most orthodox critic with Aristotle and the eighteenth century behind him. His good sense, his pragmatic and equable sensibility,

[1] Op. cit., p. 68.   [2] Ibid., p. 105.
[3] Eliot, T. S., *The Use of Poetry and the Use of Criticism*, London, 1933, p. 69.

his social interest, his appeal to the living language (whatever the oddities his particular formulation of this appeal may have led him into) were things that Eliot appreciated and approved of. Wordsworth indeed was only fighting the battle Dryden had fought before him and the battle which Eliot and Ezra Pound fought on the question of poetic diction at the beginning of this century, when they were affirming forgotten standards and not setting up new idols. Moreover, Wordsworth had written his *Preface to Lyrical Ballads* while young and at the height of his poetic powers. Coleridge, on the other hand, had published *Biographia Literaria* only in 1817 'when the disastrous effects of long dissipation and stupefaction of his powers in transcendental metaphysics were bringing him to a state of lethargy'.[1] Coleridge had behind him Hegel and Fichte as well as Hartley and Schelling, and, says Eliot,

> I have read some of Hegel and Fitche, as well as Hartley (who turns up at any moment with Coleridge), and forgotten it; of Schelling I am entirely ignorant at first hand, and he is one of those numerous authors whom, the longer you leave them unread, the less desire you have to read. Hence it may be that I wholly fail to appreciate this passage. My mind is too heavy and concrete for any flight of abstruse reasoning.[2]

These remarks occur at a point where Eliot is discussing *Biographia Literaria* and in particular the famous distinction between Fancy and Imagination. I want to take the opportunity here to quote the distinction as Eliot gives it, as well as Eliot's further comment on it. The reader will have noticed, and wondered at, my not having reproduced this famous distinction before. The reason for the omission was that while I believe Coleridge's theory of imagination to have a profound and permanent truth in it, his formulation of it, and in particular his distinguishing of it into different faculties of Fancy and Imagination, seem to me to combine the worst aspects of a false British psychology and a portentous Germanic importation. The contemporary reader will, I feel, share Eliot's view that it is all rather solemn fuss amounting to not much more than distinguishing good from bad poetry. Here then is the distinction in Eliot's setting.

[1] Op. cit., p. 67.   [2] Ibid., p. 77.

With the foregoing observations in mind, let me turn to consider the great importance, in the *Biographia Literaria*, of the distinction between Fancy and Imagination already touched upon, and of the definition of Imagination given in a later passage. 'Repeated meditations led me first to suspect ... that Fancy and Imagination were two distinct and widely different faculties, instead of being, according to the general belief, either two names with one meaning, or, at furthest, the lower and higher degree of one and the same power'. In Chapter XIII he draws the following important distinctions:

'The Imagination then I consider either as primary, or secondary. The Primary Imagination I hold to be the living power and prime agent of all human perception, and as a repetition in the finite mind of the eternal act of creation in the infinite I AM. The Secondary Imagination I consider as an echo of the former, co-existing with the conscious will, yet still as identical with the primary in the *kind* of its agency, and differing only in *degree*, and in the *mode* of its operation. It dissolves, diffuses, dissipates, in order to recreate; or where this process is rendered impossible, yet still at all events it struggles to idealise and to unify. It is essentially *vital*, even as all objects (*as* objects) are essentially fixed and dead.'

FANCY, on the other hand, has no other counters to play with, but fixities and definites. The fancy is indeed no other than a mode of memory emancipated from the order of time and space; while it is blended with, and modified by, that empirical phenomenon of the will, which we express by the word Choice. But equally with the ordinary memory the Fancy must receive all its materials ready made from the law of association.'

... If, as I have already suggested, the difference between imagination and fancy amounts in practice to no more than the difference between good and bad poetry, have we done more than take a turn round Robin Hood's barn? It is only if fancy can be an ingredient in good poetry, and if you can show some good poetry which is the better for it; it is only if the distinction illuminates our immediate preference to one poet over another, that it can be of use to a practical mind like mine. Fancy may be 'no other than a mode of memory emancipated from the order of space and time'; but it seems unwise to talk of memory in connexion with fancy and omit it altogether from the account of imagination. ... Coleridge's taste, at one period of life, led him first to read voraciously in a certain type of book, and then to select and store up certain kinds of imagery from those books. And I should say that the mind of any poet would be magnetised in its own way, to select automatically, in his reading (from picture papers and cheap novels, indeed, as well as serious books, and least likely from works of an abstract nature, though even these are aliment for some poetic minds) the material—an image, a phrase, a word—which may be of use to him later. And this selection probably runs through the whole of his sensitive life. There might be the experience of a child of ten, a small boy peering through sea-water in a rock-pool, and finding a sea-anemone for the first time: the simple experience (not so simple, for an exceptional child, as it looks) might lie dormant in his mind for twenty years, and re-appear transformed in some verse-context charged with great imaginative pressure. There is so much memory in imagination that if you are to distinguish between imagination and fancy in Coleridge's way you must define the difference between memory in imagination and memory in fancy; and it is not enough to say that the one 'dissolves, diffuses and dissipates' the memories in order to re-create, whilst the other deals with 'fixities and definites'. This distinction, in itself, need not give you distinct imagination and fancy, but only degrees of imaginative success. . . .[1]

'A turn round Robin Hood's barn' may be a trifle lacking in respect but it certainly fixes the feeling of many modern readers about this famous distinction. Eliot, in spite of his preference for Wordsworth, acknowledges that as a critic Coleridge writes with a richness and depth and an awareness of complication far superior to anything in Dryden. He attributes this superiority not to Coleridge's being a better thinker than Dryden, which he was, nor to Coleridge's being so well read in German philosophy, which in any case Eliot thinks was given much too much importance by Coleridge himself as a source of his insight. And while Eliot is clear that Wordsworth's critical insight in the *Preface* and the *Supplement* gives him the higher place—a position which seems to me not only revolutionary but absurd—he makes the very cogent point that the best of Coleridge's criticism comes from his own delicacy and subtlety of insight as he reflects on his own experience of writing poetry.

Eliot, then, attributes to Wordsworth and Coleridge together the highest historic importance: '. . . the two men together need no third with them to illustrate the mind of an age of conscious change'.[2] They did for the nineteenth century what he himself helped to do for the twentieth. They renovated the life, they extended the range, they altered the idiom, they re-established

---

[1] Eliot, T. S., op. cit., pp. 76-9.   [2] Op. cit., p. 80.

the centre of authority for poetry in a new age. And though as between the two, Eliot favours Wordsworth, he speaks with no great enthusiasm of either, and with more than a touch of frostiness about Coleridge. What is clear is that neither, and especially not Coleridge, had made any deep personal difference to Eliot himself.

The reader takes a very different impression on this score from the writings of I. A. Richards. Perhaps Coleridge has been *the* influence on his intellectual life. Richards refers to Coleridge always, both when he is regretting his theology or relishing his literary criticism, with that special tone of intimacy and appreciation that we use towards someone who has a profound personal significance for us. He speaks, in words with a genuinely personal resonance, of 'those who are drawn to Coleridge by some affinity, by any one of those myriad elections by which his influence is spread, who sense in him a larger-than-life resemblance to themselves, even in the utterances they would least claim kinship with —his highest poetry or his most maudlin prose, his philosophic summits or his apologetic ditches . . .'.[1] And there is no doubt whatever that Richards feels himself to be one of 'those'. He was drawn to Coleridge both negatively and positively. Mill divides the thought of the nineteenth century into its Benthamite and its Coleridgean currents. Richards presents the fascinating spectacle of both these currents co-present in one individual. In the first part of his career the Benthamite side attempted to assimilate into its own categories the Coleridgean. The monument to this is *Coleridge on Imagination*. Here Richards thinks of Coleridge's doctrines as 'an elaborated, transformed *symbol* of some parts of the psychology'.[2] He speaks quite explicitly as a Benthamite who finds the transcendental parts of Coleridge repugnant, and as a materialist trying to interpret the utterances of an extreme idealist. Richards was on the one hand powerfully attracted to Coleridge and at the same time determined to make Coleridge intelligible in the terms of Richard's own psychology of words and meanings, a science to which he gave the inharmonious name of 'semasiology'. This science was to render comprehensible and relevant to a modern mind what was still living in Coleridge's antique theological and philosophical theories. It was assumed, inexplicably,

[1] Richards, I. A., *The Portable Coleridge*, New York, 1961, pp. 1-2.
[2] Richards, I. A., *Coleridge on Imagination*, London, 1934, p. 10.

that this psychology was exempt from the ageing process which had rendered Coleridge's own doctrines irrelevant.

In the latter part of his career Richards seems to recognise—and to do so with considerable grace—the impossibility of Benthamising Coleridge, and he seems as he has grown older to draw closer and closer to the Coleridgean spirit itself. The evidence of this is to be found in the brilliant and sympathetic essay which precedes his imaginative anthology of Coleridge, in which he goes so far—surely an immense distance for one holding the views in *Coleridge on Imagination*—as to hope that the reader will not be resentful of 'some reachings towards the unsayable in the last section'[1] of his essay.

He takes a cool and sceptical look at the legend of Coleridge 'the Great Disappointment; the man who might have but didn't, a waster of unparalleled talent; the type specimen of self-frustrating genius; the procrastinator, the alibi fabricator and the idler'. Nor is he convinced by the oral explanation of Coleridge's troubles first set in motion by his former disciple Charles Lloyd. 'He is one of those minds who, except in inspired moods, can do anything—and his inspirations are *oral* and not *scriptural*'. Richards points out that the scribblings in the margins of Coleridge's books show this theory to be wrong since these random jottings often surpass even the best of his recorded talks. He considers that Coleridge was successful in more modes than most poets attempted, and that the volume of his poetry is more impressive now than when it used to be measured against the production of Tennyson, Browning, and Swinburne. Moreover the poet was a critic who 'in the range of his reading, in the fertility of his comments upon writers of every degree of difference from himself, in the span of his admirations and their depth, as well as in the originative independence of his perceptions, surpasses all fore-runners, and with due respect to later and better equipped "library-cormorants" all successors'. He was a philosopher who sought all the time for authority both for his all-encompassing philosophic position and for his most local act of critical choice.

And he is finding it, where Plato found it, in the dependence of all observations and of observation itself, of all inductions and of induction itself, of all that is understood and of understanding itself,

---

[1] Richards, I. A., *The Portable Coleridge*, New York, 1961, p. 52.

upon that which makes and sustains them. He calls this, perhaps unfortunately, Reason, a name which delays and misleads many. By recourse to this dependence, Coleridge like Plato solves the paradox in every account of authority—that it derives from those who should be subject to it.[1]

He was also a political journalist who was accused of being a turncoat only because he kept to his principles, principles made practical by 'a searching knowledge of contemporary affairs . . . a down to earth sense of present dangers . . . and a rather hard-headed concern with expediency'. He was the theologian who was first responsible in this country for a doctrine of biblical inspiration which was neither absurd nor un-Christian. And he was a teacher of genius. Perhaps it is this last point that makes Richards so sensitive to Coleridge's merits, since Richards himself in his best work puts the extreme clarity of a formidable intellect at the service of his passion for teaching.

An astringent corrective to the generosity of Richards's appreciation is provided by the view of Coleridge given by F. R. Leavis, the most notable and influential of contemporary critics. Leavis admires and reveres Coleridge, who combined a creative gift with a rare critical intelligence at an important moment in poetic history. He appreciates that in the religious and intellectual history of the nineteenth century Coleridge exercised a very profound and searching influence. But Leavis's concern is strictly with the art of literary criticism. His *Scrutiny*[2] essay on Coleridge takes its stand on the integrity and autonomy of literary criticism, which is a discipline of the most delicate relevance, focusing intently on what is actually there in this particular place in the poem, moving out from that to the poem as a whole, and from the poem as a whole to the context of ideas and sensibility in which it is set. It follows, therefore, that to approach Coleridge through his philosophy of art or through his metaphysics, or through a discussion of his indebtedness to, or independence of, Kant, Schelling, the Schlegels, or Fichte, is in Leavis's view an unprofitable expenditure for the literary student. On the one hand, one would not go to Coleridge for initiation into the key problems of philosophy, and on the other hand 'the literary student who goes to Coleridge in the expectations of bringing away

[1] Op. cit., p. 53.　　　　[2] Vol. IX, No. 1, 1940.

an improved capacity and equipment for dealing critically
with works of literature will, if he spends much time on the "philosophy of art," have been sadly misled'.[1] Coleridge's prestige
depends to much on an awed vagueness about his transcendental
philosophy.

Leavis acknowledges that the 'subtle-souled psychologist' with
a particular interest in language who was so brilliant as a practical
critic might well not have been able to exist at all at that time in
history had it not been for his metaphysics. But Leavis is left with
the feeling that Coleridge's actual achievement is disappointingly
incommensurate with the rarely gifted mind. Like Eliot, he is
unimpressed by the Fancy-Imagination distinction, although he
sees it as one way of calling attention to the organic complexities
of verbal life. He feels that Coleridge, while he did not inaugurate
the Bradley 'character' approach to Shakespeare, certainly lent
his prestige to it. And he would never think of proposing even the
work on Shakespeare to the literary student as an exercise in
classical criticism calculated to make much difference to his powers
of understanding and appreciation.

While the discussions in the group of chapters on Wordsworth
in *Biographia Literaria* show that Coleridge perceived certain
essential truths about poetic rhythm, which are not even yet
commonplace, the treatment of Wordsworth's poetry, however
interesting, hardly amounts to a profound and very illuminating
critique. Coleridge at his best, Leavis believes, is seen in the chapter
on 'The specific symptoms of poetic power elucidated in a critical
analysis of Shakespeare's *Venus and Adonis* and *Lucrece*'. In this
analysis Coleridge shows evidence of his peculiar distinction as a
critic. Principle emerges from practice, and 'we are made to
realise that the master of theoretical criticism who matters is the
completion of a practical critic'. It is a mastery which comes
evidently 'from the English critic who has devoted his finest
powers of sensibility and intelligence to the poetry of his own
language'. In this chapter Coleridge deals with themes which
have only recently established themselves as key ones in current
critical activity, with the idea of impersonality for example,
with the organic nature of imagery, with the nature of wit in
poetry. But, Leavis concludes, it is all impressive evidence of what
he might have done; no more. This is the depressing conclusion:

[1] Op. cit.

Coleridge's prestige is very understandable, but his currency as an academic classic is something of a scandal. Where he is prescribed and recommended it should be with far more by the way of reservation and caveat (I have come tardily to realize) than most students can report to have received along with him. He was very much more brilliantly gifted than Arnold, but nothing of his deserves the classical status of Arnold's best work.[1]

With Leavis—sounding a note of caution and realism—I want to bring this summary of critical opinion to a conclusion. I think it wise to end here since it is possible, even easy, to be drawn uncritically in the wake of Coleridge's attraction: by the fascination of a mind of such range and depth, of a character of such complicated richness, of a poet of such utter individuality, of a life at once so tattered and so triumphant. There are of course those who make the opposite mistake and bury the rational Coleridge in the frantic one. (Not to speak of Stephen Potter who, in *Coleridge and S.T.C.*, brings the two traditions of Coleridge criticism together, and puts at the centre of his own interpretation of Coleridge a species of psychological warfare between the two identities which provoked the double tradition.) But if I end here for what may seem a negative reason, I do also because of a positive one. Immediately before the remark I have quoted, Leavis referring to Coleridge's opinion of Donne speaks of 'pages that incline one to comment that if Coleridge had had real influence the vogue of Donne would have started a century earlier than it did'.[1] There is a clue here to an essential quality of Coleridge's genius, his power of anticipating and adumbrating the future. Earlier, A. C. Bradley had noticed the originality of Coleridge's use of light and colour in his poetry and prose,[2] something which pointed forward to current studies in the psychology of perception and, as Edmund Wilson[3] argued, to the Symbolist movement at the start of this century. Herbert Read[4] has shown how many of the themes and preoccupations of contemporary European existentialists were first worked on by Coleridge. Kathleen Coburn[5] sees him as a forerunner both of Freud and the *Gestalt* psychologists. It would not be hard to

---

[1] *Scrutiny*, Vol. IX, No. 1, 1940, p. 86.
[2] Bradley, A. C., *A Miscellany*, London, 1929, pp. 177-88.
[3] Wilson, Edmund, *Axel's Castle*, New York, 1954, p. 121.
[4] Read, Herbert, *Coleridge as a Critic*, London, 1949, pp. 29-30.
[5] Coburn, Kathleen, *Inquiring Spirit*, London, 1959, p. 15.

multiply instances since there are innumerable places throughout Coleridge's writings where one is aware of the strange and unmistakeable taste of the future; and not just the future of fifty years after Coleridge's death, or even a hundred, but the future which is constituted by our own age and, one is sure, by generations after it.

Index

DATE DUE